THE COMMONWEALTH AND INTERNATIONAL LIBRARY

Joint Chairmen of the Honorary Editorial Advisory Board

SIR ROBERT ROBINSON, O.M., F.R.S., LONDON

DEAN ATHELSTAN SPILHAUS, MINNESOTA

Publisher: ROBERT MAXWELL, M.C., M.P.

READINGS IN SOCIOLOGY

General Editor: A. H. RICHMOND

Readings in Urban Sociology

Readings in Urban Sociology

Edited by

R. E. PAHL

1966
THE QUEEN'S AWARD
TO INDUSTRY 1966

PERGAMON PRESS

OXFORD · LONDON · EDINBURGH · NEW YORK
TORONTO · SYDNEY · PARIS · BRAUNSCHWEIG

Pergamon Press Ltd., Headington Hill Hall, Oxford
4 & 5 Fitzroy Square, London W.1
Pergamon Press (Scotland) Ltd., 2 & 3 Teviot Place, Edinburgh 1
Pergamon Press Inc., Maxwell House, Fairview Park, Elmsford,
New York 10523
Pergamon of Canada Ltd., 207 Queen's Quay West, Toronto 1
Pergamon Press (Aust.) Pty. Ltd., 19a Boundary Street,
Rushcutters Bay, N.S.W. 2011, Australia
Pergamon Press S.A.R.L., 24 rue des Écoles, Paris 5^e
Vieweg & Sohn GmbH, Burgplatz 1, Braunschweig

First edition 1968

Reprinted 1969

Library of Congress Catalog Card No. 68–18898

Printed in Great Britain by A. Wheaton & Co., Exeter

08 013293 6 (flexicover)
08 013303 7 (hard cover)

Contents

Preface

THIS is one of a series of volumes to be published by the Pergamon Press. Each will consist of a collection of articles on a specialized aspect of sociology, together with an introduction designed to relate the selected Readings to the state of sociological knowledge and research in the field in question. Each volume of Readings has been prepared by a distinguished scholar who has specialized in the area. The individual editors have worked closely with an editorial board of international repute.

A characteristic of the series is the inclusion in each volume of a number of articles translated into English from European and other sources. English-speaking scholars and students will have the opportunity of reading articles which would not otherwise be readily available to them. Many important contributions to sociology made by European and other writers will be given a wider circulation in this way. It is hoped that the series will contribute to an international cross-fertilization of sociological theory and research.

York University,
Toronto

ANTHONY H. RICHMOND
General Editor

Acknowledgements

I AM very grateful for the help I have received from Professor R. P. Dore, Ingrid Hurren, Magdalena Mroz and Hedwig Thimig, who provided me with summary translations of a great deal of material, which enabled me to make my final selections with greater confidence. I would also like to thank Stanley Fukawa and Dr. Jiří Musil, who translated the Japanese and Czech contributions respectively: this work came at a particularly busy time for both of them and their ready co-operation is greatly appreciated. I also received valuable assistance when reviewing the German material from Professor H. P. Bahrdt, Professor Helmut Klages, Dr. Rainer Mackensen and Professor Elisabeth Pfeil. Similarly M. Jean Lallement and his colleagues at the Institut d'Aménagement et d'Urbanisme de la Région Parisienne, M. Paul Rendu and his colleagues at the Centre d'Études des Groupes Sociaux and Mlle Monique Coornaert of the Centre de Sociologie Urbaine helped me to gain a rapid overview of some of the French material. Dr. Z. Pioŕo and Dr. A. Wallis kindly sent me material from Poland.

I owe a special debt to Professor R. P. Dore, who not only helped in the selection of material but has also given generously of his time in checking the translation of Nakamura's article and writing an introduction for it.

My introduction has gained from the critical comments made on an earlier draft by friends and colleagues, particularly Dr. Derek Allcorn, Professor Michael Banton, Dr. Donald Read and Richard Scase: clearly I alone remain responsible for it as it stands. My wife has provided me with great encouragement and has given a second and most valuable opinion on many of the

ix

papers which were considered for inclusion: I owe much to her editorial assistance in preparing those pieces which are included.

Finally thanks are due to J. R. Goy and other members of the staff of the library at the University of Kent at Canterbury for providing books and photocopied articles so promptly and efficiently under difficult conditions and to Miss Gwyneth Horton for her speedy and meticulous typing.

Acknowledgement is due to the publishers, editors and authors whose material has been reprinted in this volume. The article by Ruth Glass, "Urban Sociology in Great Britain", first published in *Current Sociology* IV (4), 1955, appears by permission of Unesco. The article by N. Dennis, "The Popularity of the Neighbourhood Community Idea", first appeared in *Sociological Review* VI (2), 1958, published by the University of Keele. "Community and Association in a London Housing Estate" by Ruth Durant is an extract from *Watling, A Social Survey*, published by P. S. King and Son Ltd. The Tokyo Institute for Municipal Research (Tokyo Shisei Chosakai) kindly gave permission to reproduce "Urban Ward Associations in Japan" by H. Nakamura, which was first published in *Toshi Mondai*, 56 (5), 1965. B. Berger's "Myths of American Suburbia" is an extract from *Working Class Suburb* published in 1960 by the University of California Press. The material by H. J. Gans, "Urbanism and Suburbanism as Ways of Life", was first published in *Human Behaviour and Social Processes* (ed. A. M. Rose) and appears by permission of Routledge & Kegan Paul Ltd., and Houghton Mifflin Co. J. A. Rex allowed us to use his material "The Sociology of a Zone of Transition". The article by Jiří Musil, "The Development of Prague's Ecological Structure", was first published in *Demografie*, 1960 by Státní Statistický Úřad and has been translated from the original Czechoslovakian. "Migrancy and the Study of Africans in Towns" by P. Mayer was first published in *American Anthropologist*, 1962, and is reproduced by permission of the University of Pennsylvania. "The Pattern of Neighbouring Relations in

Dortmund-Nordstadt" by E. Pfeil is an extract from *Dasein-formen der Grosstadt* edited by Gunther Ipsen and published by J. C. B. Mohr (Paul Siebeck), Tübingen. "The Rural-Urban Continuum" by R. E. Pahl appeared in *Sociologia Ruralis*, **VI** (3–4), 1966.

Introduction

A Perspective on Urban Sociology[1]

R. E. PAHL

WHAT is a city? Alcaeus of Lesbos, a Greek poet writing about 600 B.C., argued "not the house finely roofed or the stones of walls well builded, nay, nor canals and dockyards make the city, but men able to use their opportunity" (quoted by Lopez, 1963). In the earliest hieroglyphic script the ideogram meaning "city" is a cross enclosed in a circle. The cross represents the convergence of routes bringing in men, merchandise and ideas: the circle is the moat or wall which physically binds the citizens together, emphasizing their distinctiveness. The argument for the distinctive quality of urban life is often illustrated by the adage from medieval Germany, "City air makes one free" (*Stadt luft macht frei*): the citizen had distinct rights not shared by plain countrymen and the city was distinguished by its separate institutional arrangements.

Yet when cities had to struggle for centuries to achieve self-government and when within cities the social structure very often prevented men from using their opportunity, it is doubtful whether cities as such have much in common. Cities are the products of the society which creates them. There can be no single ideal-type of pre-industrial city existing through millennia of history. Whether modern industrialism carries with it a particular form of urbanism, which may be one of the themes in the notion that advanced industrial societies are "converging" in several important respects, must remain a matter open to investigation.

Cities are, to borrow Maitland's phrase, "a marvellous palimpsest", reflecting in their physical structures the institutions and

---

patterns of social stratification of the societies which created them. The very permanence of bricks and mortar may ensure that certain features of a previous social order are bequeathed to a subsequent social order. Such physical relics may be simply re-evaluated as tourist attractions or may serve as a new focus for the city's spirit and aspirations as expressed by its controlling elites. The cathedrals, guildhalls and palaces of medieval splendour are re-evaluated as tourist attractions from Pisa to Pekin; eighteenth- or nineteenth-century housing, built for a leisured and servant-owning society, may become converted to offices or provide a source of rented accommodation. When larger and better proportioned houses and rooms than those built today are inherited in socialist societies the historical city introduces a differential from a previous social order, which may not be consistent with the social aims of the new order. However, despite such tangible reminders of the pervading influence of history, a city is clearly not simply a physical artifact. Cities are social entities and their physical characteristics only gain meaning when men give it to them. Cities are what society lets them be.

The industrial city of Western Europe in the nineteenth century was the arena for new and dynamic forms of urbanism. Industrialization, defined simply in terms of concentration of population at the workplace, and urbanization, defined similarly in terms of the concentration of the population, should be seen as two mutually reinforcing processes functionally related to each other and the rest of society. Together they created characteristic urban physical forms—for example, the segregation of small and often insanitary workers' houses from the mansions and villas of the rich—but also stimulated new forms of class consciousness. Depending on the local industrial situation, the inequalities in power, wealth and prestige were more or less transparent and in this period there were marked variations in class-consciousness in the different industrial centres. Urbanization as concentration of population does not lead to any single pattern of class action and conflict, but clearly, without this, what is loosely called "industrial society" could not emerge. All the familiar concomitants of social change were, for a relatively short historical period, associated with the concentration of population in what were called towns or cities.

Just as there was no single form of pre-industrial city so there is no single form of industrial city. Certainly for analytical purposes it is possible to construct typologies: this is what Max Weber tried to do in his classic essay on the pre-modern city and Leonard Reissman attempts to do for the city in industrial society. Unhappily there has been too much emphasis on whether the city is an independent variable in social change and on the distinctions between the quantitative and qualitative aspects of urbanization. The city is not simply "the crossroads within the walls" or "the council" or "the middle-class" or "a state of mind" or "a way of life" or "a place with a population of 20,000 or 100,000 or whatever inhabitants" or "a central-place supplying certain goods and services to a surrounding area" or any other of the working definitions which have been used by distinguished contributors to the field. This, as so many other fields of study, has suffered from the attempt to explain a complex interrelated system in terms of a single reified concept: by definition a total system cannot be explained solely in terms of one of its parts. Recent essays by Glass (1962), Martindale (1958) and Reissman (1964) make further comment on these lines superfluous. The study of the city has suffered from oversimplification: "the city is what we choose to make it for the purposes of analysis" (Reissman, 1964, p. 153).

"Urban" and "rural" are too imprecise as concepts in sociological analysis and the rural–urban dimension will differ in pre-industrial, transitional and industrial societies (Sjoberg, 1964). There is so much evidence now of "urban" patterns of social relationships in "rural" areas, that the terms have lost much sociological significance. The rural–urban continuum is "real but relatively unimportant" (Dewey, 1960). Some people are in the country but not of it, others are of the country but not in it. "Any attempt to tie particular patterns of social relationships to specific geographical milieux is a singularly fruitless exercise"

(Pahl, 1966). Because the common-sense view of the city as a physical object appears so straightforward, urban sociology has suffered considerably from over-simplifications and naïve generalizations; yet the spatial ordering of society is not without sociological significance.

APPROACHES TO THE SUBJECT

Gans suggests in his article on p. 95 that a sociological definition of the city cannot be formulated. This may be so and certainly urban sociology is a field of study which appears to lack coherence (Sjoberg, 1959). Indeed this theme is implicit throughout this introduction. Nevertheless, although it may be too formless to have a unified body of theory, as a field of study it should be approached in a disciplined way: some distinctive techniques and concepts have emerged in the study of social phenomena in urban areas, even if these do not together form a separate discipline. It might be helpful to set out some of the approaches which sociologists interested in the field of urban studies have adopted.

1. The Statistical Description of Large Populations

There are many who are at the simple "natural history" stage of the subject, who explore the urban landscape and bring back beautiful butterflies. Information is collected without necessarily having any specific hypothesis to test and this basic documentation may be useful to both Government departments and social scientists. The tendency is for the State to take over this work but there are still many useful descriptive studies which State census offices show little sign of undertaking—the ambitious London Atlas project is a good current example (Jones, 1965). Some present-day explorers may view urban areas as a challenge similar to that provided by remote parts of the world to a previous generation.

Work at this level also continues for other reasons:

(a) Market Research and Problem Solving

"The survey" is a technical tool for providing data for a whole host of interests including those who want to sell products, provide better amenities and services, or document a political argument. Certain kinds of questions are asked that certain preconceptions may be confirmed and sometimes without any preconceptions whatsoever. Government departments interested in economic and social statistics of urban populations may carry out or commission limited pieces of work. Information is gathered systematically on the social composition of households and emphasis may be placed on social or spatial mobility, vital statistics of selected sub-groups and areas, the relationship between income and rent, or rooms and size of household, on the number and frequency of social contacts of old people and so on. The reports which emerge are not always easy to read, and at best provide painstaking refutations or confirmations of hunches and opinions. One recent study of a block of flats could, in effect, be summarized by saying that life there was nicer than you might think but that the rents were too high; another study of a new housing estate revealed that if people had to travel a long way to work then the bus fares were expensive and also that buying a lot of new furniture cost a lot of money; yet another survey showed that people living in a New Town had not memorized the Master Plan which divided the houses into "Neighbourhoods". Such market research work is often ephemeral, rather dull and of little fundamental sociological interest. There are, of course, some notable exceptions, which it would be invidious to mention here. For example, work on time budgets and activity patterns is essential for more sociological studies of styles of life.

(b) Testing Quantitative Indices

Data may be collected within population concentrations as a means of testing and refining various quantitative techniques. This work is not primarily concerned with social phenomena as such, but rather with refining the techniques by which they may be manipulated: the interest is statistical rather than sociological. A useful survey of this field has recently appeared (Timms, 1965), and work continues to get more mathematically complicated (see also Moser and Scott, 1961). A recent component analysis of sixty variables revealed that "persons per room" was the most significant indicator of variations between different areas in Hampshire and Merseyside (Gittus, 1965).

Some research workers are so concerned with measurement that they appear to have lost sight of any meaningful sociological problem. Administrative convenience rather than sociological relevance is often the basis of the data which is available and this data then has to be twisted into sociological significance. Notions of "segregation", for example, could encompass anything apart from a random scatter of the relevant phenomenon. Such rampant empiricists appear to be "alienated by their research tools".[2]

2. (a) *Sociographic Descriptions*

A more literary and polemical tradition of sociography stretching back to Henry Mayhew and other nineteenth-century commentators attempts to bring groups of people alive by vivid description and verbatim comments. The unashamedly subjective may have a bigger impact than the objective "hard" data; yet, as Dollard so rightly observed, "We should remark how the bizarre is likely to stand out in experience and how selective our perception is, how we tend to see what makes us comfortable or wards off painful feelings. Odd people and those under pressure do and say the conspicuous things and we must beware of judging the whole situation by them. Comfortable people talk less and come forward less readily to the newcomer" (Dollard, 1957, pp. 20–21). To some extent there is a conscious search for the bizarre: an obsession with urban pathology has made deviancy seem more interesting than normality. Indeed, it seems that only

---

[2] As my colleague Richard Scase has expressed in a personal communication.

when the situation is full of change and problems does *urban* sociology appear to be significant. This is partly because "normal" is often a tacit pseudonym for "rural" and partly because sociologists may be sensitive to the charge of "vicarious neighbouring" if they describe people too much like themselves. Some novelists, who gather their data conscientiously and systematically, may also be perceptive sociographers without the sociologist's way of disarming criticism with the magic word "sample".

(b) *The Sociology of Specific Milieux*

Until recently perhaps the most useful sociological research analysed social processes in communities. Ruth Durant's study of a housing estate, reprinted on p. 160, or William F. Whyte's study of *Street Corner Society* are good examples. However, a quarter of a century later it is pertinent to ask whether there is a limit to the usefulness of such studies. There may be a case for investigating a new milieu such as commuterland (Pahl, 1965a and b), where the close juxtaposition of different sub-groups of the population in a "village" situation forces an unaccustomed consciousness of distinctive life-styles on the groups concerned, thus creating a social situation which is not generally found in segregated urban areas. Similarly there is a good case for doing the kind of study described by Berger on p. 119, since the very rapid development of suburbia was a relatively recent and inadequately documented phenomenon. These examples suggest that there is a case for *some* carefully selected milieu studies, but that, at a time when about a fifth of all households in Britain move each year and when the social network (Bott, 1957) is replacing the community as a framework for the study of social relationships, a strong argument would have to be put up for each one. Pfeil's study reprinted on p. 137 interesting in the way it illustrates the importance of face-to-face relationships in a high density central city area.

Perhaps the most important task which confronts urban sociologists in the late 1960's and 1970's is the need for more thorough and systematic work on the styles of life of distinctive groups. We know very little indeed about sub-cultural values amongst the middle class. Groups selected according to social origin, educational achievement, age and occupation of both husbands and wives (where appropriate) need to be studied in the complex inter-relationships between home, community, workplace and social network. To some extent research on careers and household activity patterns would cover the problem in something of the manner I am suggesting. However, sub-cultural values do not emerge out of the surrounding atmosphere, but nor are they always primarily related to the work situation: they also emerge from the complex inter-relationships of the socio-ecological system.

If we lack studies of middle-class styles of life, it is indeed encouraging that recent years have seen a more determined effort to probe the culture of poverty. Styles of life of the segregated poor have been described and analysed by various research workers over the past decade—for example, work by the Institute of Community Studies in East London, Mays and his colleagues in Liverpool, Lewis in Mexico City and Gans in Boston. A summary of the literature on "slums" with a strong bias towards practical solutions has recently been provided by Clinard (1966). The complex relationships between slums and society not only illustrate the distinctive viewpoint of the urban sociologist but also the need for a socio-ecological model.

THE SOCIO-ECOLOGICAL SYSTEM

Following the natural history phase of almost random data collection, some sociologists sought to classify this material: even though they did not understand how social processes worked, they at least understood that in some cities distinctive patterns of population grouping emerged. The segregated pattern of population concentrations in capitalist cities was understood by early commentators such as Engels and Booth. However, the school of human ecology at the University of Chicago did much to make explicit a fundamentally sub-social explanatory framework based on biological analogy. The theory of human ecology is discussed by Reissman (1964) and Stein (1960). As R. E. Park put it, "the metropolis is, it seems, a great sorting and sifting mechanism, which, in ways that are not yet wholly understood, infallibly selects out of the population as a whole the individuals best suited to live in a particular region and a particular milieu" (1929, reprinted 1952, p. 79). Studies of specific milieux revealed distinctive ways of life and sub-cultural values. Investigations in these "natural areas" produced some of the classics of early urban sociology—for example, Zorbaugh's study of *The Gold Coast and the Slum* or Wirth's study of *The Ghetto*. The use of concepts developed by the Chicago school such as competition, invasion and succession, is passing away from sociologists to geographers and others more interested in the non-social aspects of population study. Following Rex's study on p. 213 there are signs that a more fundamentally sociological model may be formulated in terms of the housing market, whose workings are less mysterious than Park appeared to think. Choice of housing— as of job, income and way of life—is severely limited for most of the population: Gans argues that spatial patterns are largely the function of class and life-cycle characteristics in his article reprinted on p. 95. Gans perhaps overstates his case: I would argue that there is reciprocal feedback between the social and the spatial systems and I enlarge on this point below.

Since the early capitalist industrial city developed in Europe and America at a time when technology forced concentration rather than dispersal, rents could be higher at the centre than the periphery. The economic value of centrality created a pattern of urban development which has served to preserve in fossil form a previous social structure. However, both cities and their social structures change, as Musil's study of Prague (at p. 234) suggests. The dominant values of the élite—that is those who can choose the way they accommodate space in their life-styles—may vary widely, and gods other than Mammon may help to produce polynuclear or other patterns of land use.

Arising out of the human ecology tradition, a number of studies have described and analysed the growth and development of "metropolitan communities". Realizing that the city, bound by its political limits, cannot be divorced from its hinterland, sociologists such as R. D. McKenzie and D. J. Bogue have used a variety of indices to divide the United States into urban regional complexes. "The metropolis or modern large and complex city, exercises an organizing and integrative influence on the social and economic life of a broad expanse of territory, far beyond the civil boundaries and thereby dominates all other communities within this area" (Bogue, 1949; see also Pahl, 1965b).

Few sociologists seem to be aware of other developments in spatial theory since the work of Christaller and Lösch. There seems to be a much greater understanding of, say, industrial techniques and the non-sociological aspects of the theory of organizations than there is of the comparable theoretical aspects of location. Haggett has provided an authoritative summary of some of the main lines of research and demonstrates regularities between different societies. For example, in his discussion of the functional hierarchies of settlements he notes similar results from the United States, Ceylon and New Zealand (Haggett, 1965, p. 115). The evidence quoted from Ceylon is particularly important since the exponents of central place theory have been criticized for limiting their empirical studies to relatively flat farming areas in southern Germany, southern Sweden, East Anglia and the Middle West of the U.S.A. Comprehensive summaries of the spatial logic, which urban sociologists will find particularly useful, are provided in the chapters by Harvey and Garner in the Chorley-Haggett symposium (1967). The dangers of neglecting this spatial logic are shown in Hruska's discussion of the reorganization of the settlement structure of Czechoslovakia which attempted to ignore the logic: after a trial period planners were forced back to the classical Christaller model (Hruska, 1964).

There is, of course, a danger that models of the spatial ordering of cities will be relegated to the concentration (i.e. technologically primitive) phase of urbanism, and that in a period of urban diffusion spatial models will be neglected or ignored. It is an awkward but inescapable fact that the spatial constraint is a tax imposed by society on the poor, who cannot afford to overcome it, so that the physical "bricks and mortar" environment cannot be dismissed as irrelevant to an understanding of urban social structure. Segregation of the poor in slums is qualitatively different from spreading them more randomly throughout the urban area. As conflict over differential access to essential ingredients of socially-defined styles of life increase, space and housing, as important yet scarce resources, will need to be incorporated more effectively into sociological analysis. In the same way that industrial sociologists consider techniques, technology and a socio-technical system in their studies of industrialism and industrial man, so, too, must the urban sociologist consider the way this socio-technical system operates spatially in the study of urbanism and urban man. Indeed this could provide a distinctive basis for urban sociology but the full elaboration of this notion must await a later publication.

However, at least some of the implications of the line of argument I am hinting at need to be clarified: is there some inherent logic in the organization of urban space in advanced industrial societies, dependent on the level of technology, towards which all societies are inevitably drawn? Is it the case that no matter what the political system or pattern of economic activity there is an underlying urban-technological system which is functionally interrelated with the social system? There is an obvious difference between societies in the amount of publicly built housing—whether by the state or by any other public authority. Yet such a difference by itself is not very revealing: much depends on whether the public authority works within a capitalist system and has to purchase land for its own needs on the open market. In this case those who, by virtue of their relationship to the housing market, are dependent on public housing may be at a disadvantage compared with those in a society where public authorities are not so limited. Again, the government policy towards public housing may in some societies fluctuate considerably over a relatively short period, so that at one period some sections of society are favoured and at another time a different section is favoured. Such fluctuations will be reflected in the urban form, and certain sections of the population which may have been favoured in the past may retain their advantage even when policies and parties change.

Perhaps, following Runciman (1966), we may distinguish two forms of Utopia. In the first form of Utopia there is equality of economic reward but not of social evaluation: that is, although everyone is paid the same economic reward for his work, different occupations are allocated different prestige, so that it is still, for example, "better" to be a professional worker than a clerk or a skilled worker than an unskilled worker. Under such conditions, with the inevitable division of labour, and even with identical houses for all, marked segregation by occupation may appear with distinct and separate styles of life in these physically similar, but socially distinct, areas.

In the second type of Utopia there is equality of social evaluation but inequality of economic reward: that is, there is a wide discrepancy between the economic reward paid to, say, a university professor compared with a university cleaner, but they treat each other in a spirit of mutual respect and equality. Given the ready availability of building land in appropriate sites, there may be wide variety of house types of different sizes and quality of building, but these are not segregated by status criteria and may be distributed in an urban area according to other criteria, such as nearness to work (so that the university professor and university cleaner may live next door to one another). In such a society the ecological models and quantitative techniques which imply a non-random scatter of the population would have to be modified. Certainly these methods might still be used, possibly to demonstrate segregation by industrial (as opposed to occupational) structure.

From this argument it can be seen that any "logic" of industrialism making for uniformity in industrial societies and, in particular, "*a continuing* increase in the degree of integration of the stratification systems of advanced societies" (Goldthorpe, 1964, p. 106) should be reflected in the urban structure, as shown by the growth or decline of patterns of segregation. The link between social structure and spatial structure has been explored recently by Beshers in his stimulating essay on *Urban Social Structure* (1962). "Undoubtedly, location of residence is not the only consequence of stratification that tends to have the circular effect of reinforcing stratification itself. But the fact that the underlying social distance is not the sole aspect of the stratification system to be transmitted to future generations is worth noting. The situational factors reinforcing social distance are also transmitted" (Beshers, 1962, pp. 125–6).

Comparative research on social stratification is slender and there is as yet no work which examines in any systematic way the notion that all advanced industrial societies must follow a similar logic in their ordering of urban space. Urban sociologists could make a significant contribution to the current discussions concerning the "convergence" of different industrial systems (see Halmos (ed.), 1964) but such work has not yet appeared. Indeed, there is a danger that those concerned with urban social structures will devote more energy to historical rather than comparative studies. It is particularly important that recent research in human ecology in Eastern Europe is incorporated into comparative urban sociology. Fisher has claimed that most of the planners of Eastern Europe "have not as yet come to terms with the idealized dictates of Marxist-Leninism . . . the predictable pattern of the future city appears to be more in conformity with the individual city's past evolutionary trends than with the present theory of planning" (1962, p. 259). Fisher suggests that state enterprises constructed residential complexes for those selected social groups which had special abilities desired by the State. Thus professional people were favourably treated. Building co-operatives also furthered group segregation: the more affluent pooled their resources to provide suitable housing, leaving the State to supply housing to those economically less privileged. The importance of this emerging urban segregation on patterns of stratification in socialist societies has, of course, to be demonstrated. One study that goes some way towards this is Piořo's empirical work on the ecology of

Polish towns. He concludes his study with a discussion on applying social ecology to urban planning. Urban spatial structure does
not depend only on such factors as the physical configuration, the
nature of the economic base or the town planner's ideology. It is
also, he argues, "in great measure the result of *spontaneous social
forces* whose relation to spatial structure is recognised by social
ecologists" (Piořo, 1962, pp. 171–2—my italics). Piořo then
argues that the town planner must envisage new social structures
and forms to which he then adapts new spatial structures and
forms. The contortions of the argument are not always easy to
follow, but it does appear that the new Eastern European School
of social ecologists find themselves gripped by the logic of a socio-
ecological system. What are these "social forces" which help to
determine urban spatial structure and how do the two articulate
together?

Musil's cross-cultural study on the housing policies of Great
Britain and Czechoslovakia is interesting in this context. Postulating two ideal-types or models he suggests one extreme where
the housing market is completely dominated by private builders
and individual consumers; at the other extreme all housing is
entirely the responsibility of the state or other public, non-private
body or organization. Both countries are shown to be at points on
"a continuum in housing policies with different degrees of state
responsibilities and interventions on the one hand and private
responsibilities and initiative on the other" (Musil, 1966, p. 129).

Ruth Glass has argued that "it is in the evaluation of planning
principles and processes that the main contribution of sociology
to planning can and should be made" (1959, p. 51). Norman
Dennis, in the article on the concept of the neighbourhood reprinted on p. 74 provides a good example of this kind of contribution. The basic problem, which is posed by Ruth Glass,
still needs to be explored more fully by urban sociologists: "As
there are conflicting interests and aspirations in society, and in the
same individuals, and as the moods of different decades and centuries exist simultaneously, there are bound to be conflicting value
judgements and *a priori* policies" (Glass, 1959, p. 52). There are

now signs of an international interest in the social objectives of planning, and recent papers by Chombart de Lauwe (1963), Foley (1960, 1962), Klages (1966), Berger (1966), Petersen (1966) and Ziolkowski (1966) and the more extended study by Willhelm (1962) discuss the issue from different perspectives. The Centre for Urban Studies in London has produced a valuable bibliography on *Land Use Planning and the Social Sciences* (1964). Given that advanced industrial societies have the power to determine the physical pattern of the future and that "Planning will come to be recognized as the positive, creative and imaginative regulation of change in the social interest in that complex system which is the physical environment" (McLoughlin, 1965b, p. 399), the problem is to determine what the social interest is in a situation of social conflict and differing sub-cultural values. McLoughlin in his clear and succinct summary of the situation from the planner's point of view (1965a, 1965b and 1966) claims that "the naïve imposition of the planner's personal value system on the community, or the supposition that the simple aggregation of individual values will yield a true and sensible social value index" (1965b, p. 399) are now seen as obvious pitfalls. Simulation models, computer technology and cybernetics provide the tools, yet "quantified projections show more clearly the extent to which decisions have to be based on value judgements" (McLoughlin, 1965a, pp. 260–1). Such value judgements are even more difficult to make when planners are concerned with systemic change in a situation in which there are seen to be a variety of social objectives. The principal outcome of the revolution in planning thinking and methods over the past few years is the new emphasis by planners on human behaviour. "Peoples' attitudes and values are seen to act as motivating forces toward developmental, locational and behavioural decisions, the outcomes of which are altering the state of the system at all times, thus setting up further motivations to change" (McLoughlin, 1965b, p. 399). Instead of simple questions about what "people" want, urban sociologists are now being asked by planners with increasing urgency to predict a plurality of "good lives". Planning for diversity and choice in new cities and regional complexes demands knowledge of the range and proportions of diversity and choice. Many planners find it difficult to escape from tacit utopian thinking. They often react against the idealism of Ebenezer Howard's Garden Cities or the Goodmans' "Communitas", but in its place put a new utopia of a metropolitan or city region. Urban form clearly influences life-styles and life chances but these in turn help to create urban form. These relationships deserve to be discussed more thoroughly: too often limited case studies are taken as indicative of broad trends. One of the best examples of this at a micro-level is provided by two American studies which purported to demonstrate that the interaction and friendship pattern of a housing area is determined by site-plan characteristics. The exceptional circumstances of these studies largely invalidated their conclusion as Form (1951) demonstrated, but it has taken a long time for this to be accepted.

The response of urban sociologists to this situation has been guarded. This is partly because few sociologists feel that the adjective "urban" is necessary in urbanized societies such as Britain or the United States. Industrial sociologists may feel that factory gates shut out enough of the rest of society to justify a distinctive specialism, whereas "urban" is everywhere. However, the type of urban environment does seem to be an important variable and some industrial sociologists are now arguing that it is not possible to separate the work situation from the social and spatial environment in which it is encapsulated. Goldthorpe has argued in a recent article on car assembly workers that these workers define work "as an essentially instrumental activity—as a means to ends external to the work situation" (1966, p. 240). In order to understand the nature of the work orientation of these men the *non-work* aspects of their lives, such as their "experience of both social and geographical mobility, their position in the life-cycle and their present patterns of family and community living" (1966, p. 241) need to be investigated. The problem is to evolve a conceptual framework into which this kind of information can be fitted for distinctive sub-groups in society. The emergence of distinctive styles of life as ends in themselves, related to the work situation but not entirely determined by it, is a characteristic feature of urban society. The fundamental constraints and restrictions may now be more severely imposed by the socio-ecological system—housing, distribution of employment, journey to work and so on—than by the socio-technical system in the work situation.

The spatial logic of location theory may determine the size of settlement in which an individual finds himself. This in turn will provide him with a given range of employment, housing choice and so on. On the other hand, certain types of employment may only be found in certain types of settlements. Depending on the individual's position in the social structure so he will be more or less able to accommodate himself to these restraints. Capital or certain types of job may be necessary to get a house elsewhere, low income may make a long journey to work impossible, and so on. Some people are able to choose to live in a close-knit network —for example the general practitioner who returns to practice in the town in which he was brought up. Others are obliged to live in a loose-knit network, often against their will—for example, miners forced to migrate after pit closures or manual workers rehoused under inner-city redevelopment schemes. Planning introduces a further restraint by attempting to control the location of industry or to limit the size of settlements. The economic sub-structure creates authority/compliance relationships and differential rewards in terms of power, wealth and prestige. Much of the pattern thus created is related to the techniques and technology involved in a given work situation. Yet men do not move out of the socio-technical system when they leave the factory gates. It is the non-work aspects of the socio-technical system which I have called the socio-ecological system.

At a time when urban planners are discussing systemic change it is disturbing that so few sociologists are professionally concerned with the reciprocal relationships between spatial and social structure. There is a danger that some sociologists, tempted by the funds which planners control, will offer to fill some of the empty boxes in the latest simulation model. Certain "factors" will be drawn out of complex reality, particularly those that are quantifiable, and the social survey will be a fashionable adjunct to model construction.

TRENDS IN URBAN SOCIOLOGY

Inevitably this Reader must present a very partial view of the subject. Its intention is simply to draw attention to lines of thought and it may be useful both in teaching and as a stimulant to further research. Over the past twenty years a large and relatively easily accessible literature has appeared in English. It now may be useful to draw attention to this under two main headings: the sociology of the American city and the study of urbanization.

1. Recent Urban Sociology in the U.S.A.

Despite the criticisms of American urban sociologists by Sjoberg (1959), Manheim (1960) and Reissman (1964) the last decade has been very productive. A brief survey of work produced in this recent period will on the one hand give some indication of what American urban sociologists do and also provide a guide to a literature which this Reader does not seek to duplicate. The six important Readers are listed separately on page 40. These should be seen as essential companion volumes to this for serious students of the field. In order to keep this introduction to manageable proportions I will concentrate the main focus of my comments on these Readers.

In 1957 there appeared the Revised Reader in Urban Sociology —*Cities and Society*—edited by Hatt and Reiss, which included sixty-two selections. The editors considered that these papers should "deal largely with generic urban community variables, even though in many cases it is not possible to separate them empirically from closely related ones, such as the independent influence of technology and industrialization". The selection reflects a strong demographic bias, showing a concern with city

size, vital processes and social mobility. Apart from a general
essay by Sjoberg on the Pre-industrial City, a report on some
work on certain Latin American censuses of about 1940, Miner's
paper on "The Folk–Urban Continuum" and one or two others,
the selections are all on the American city. Many of the papers are
short and at a very high level of generality—for example, "The
Protestant Church in an Urban Environment", "Voluntary
Associations in the United States" or "The Moral Integration of
American Cities". When studies are based on particular cities
there appears to be a disproportionate number of studies on
middle west cities: out of the seven papers on stratification, for
example, four are on Middle West cities.

Very few indeed of the papers are concerned with primary
face-to-face relationships in cities: with the notable exception of
extracts from Whyte's *Street Corner Society* and Caroline Ware's
Greenwich Village, evidence of any concern among American sociologists to examine patterns of social relationships by empirical
fieldwork is slight. They appear to be content to work from
national census material in a tradition of a somewhat ahistorical
empiricism. For European students the volume, however impressive by its sheer size and weight, must have limited value.

An even larger and more weighty volume edited by Burgess
and Bogue, *Contributions to Urban Sociology*, appeared in 1964 as a
record of the work done by graduate students in the Department
of Sociology at the University of Chicago during the past forty
years. This geographical concentration is enough in itself to give
it coherence and form which more eclectic Readers lack: in this
context the charge of parochialism is without foundation. The
forty-one papers are divided into four sections: Urban Ecology
and Demography, Urban Social Organization and Mass Phenomena, Ethnic and Racial Groups in Urban Society and finally,
significantly, Urban Social Problems. There is a staggering wealth
of material; Chicago is a huge social laboratory, and, as the
editors point out, there is at the University perhaps the greatest
collection of basic social data of any city in the world. They
are conscious of the danger that super-computers will tempt

sociologists to substitute correlations for ideas, "there is a disturbing prospect that we are faced with another wave of naïve raw empiricism such as that which followed the advent of the I.B.M. counter-sorter. Only this time the insufficiency of fundamental thoughts and concepts may be more attractively camouflaged with higher mathematics" (p. vi). Elsewhere they acknowledge that the Chicago School, over a long period of time, came to realise that the urban community was a highly intricate social as well as ecological and economic organization. For example, the study of primary groups in urban areas was for long neglected. They look forward to much more concentrated and systematic study of formal and informal social organization in the city: a trend to be welcomed, but which could not be clearly discerned in the earlier volume edited by Hatt and Reiss.

An overwhelmingly large proportion of the papers in the Chicago volume, however excellent in themselves, are concerned with a geographically very limited area of the city of Chicago—the Central Business District and the Zone of Transition. Yet it is now the case that the characteristic form of urbanism in the United States is *dispersal* rather than concentration, the central city is losing population as the suburbs and extra-suburban areas expand. Indeed the Committee for Economic Development estimated that by 1975 in the United States the central city population will have dropped to 42 per cent of the metropolitan total, while the suburban and fringe areas outside will have grown to 57 per cent of the entire metropolitan complex. Suburbia will then have 41 per cent of the nation's population. Perhaps too great a concern with social problems and social disorganization in the central city has hindered sociologists from studying normality. Whatever the reason for the apparent neglect of suburbia, it is clear that W. M. Dobriner's Reader on *The Suburban Community* (1958) filled an important gap and has done much to stimulate interest and further research. Almost inevitably a number of arguments were overstated, particularly with regard to the distinctiveness of suburbia: its "way of life", its ability to structure patterns of social relationships and so on. Nevertheless the twenty-four papers, despite being of somewhat variable quality, together provide a valuable corrective to what, until recently, was an almost obsessive preoccupation with the zone of transition in urban sociology. In a more recent work Dobriner has underlined and made explicit some of the themes which were confused or implicit in the earlier volume. In particular he discusses the fundamental differences between middle-class and working-class housing areas following the lead provided by Berger's *Working Class Suburb* (from which an extract is included here). Dobriner argues that the physical patterning of suburbia does have a direct impact on life-styles, arising out of transportation characteristics, degree of home-centred activity and so on (1963, pp. 55–59). He nevertheless insists on "the primacy of class over place variables". Perhaps unwittingly Dobriner helped to create a strawman which he then had to help to burn.

A fourth collection of articles, which appeared in 1961—*Studies in Human Ecology*, edited by Theodorson, made a conscious attempt to break away from specifically American material and to present a variety of cross-cultural studies. Although two thirds of the sixty-six articles relate to the American situation this is a reasonable proportion, since human ecology is, through the work of R. E. Park, a peculiarly American contribution to the study of urban sociology. Unfortunately there are no ecological studies from socialist industrial societies: this material is, of course, only recently published.

Almost inevitably Readers are open to the criticism that they lack form and do little more than provide hard bindings for an arbitrary collection of tenuously linked articles. Theodorson's work is in quite a different category: he imposes a form and structure upon his material which in itself is an original contribution to the subject and his introductory sections are models of lucid and cogent synthesis. That human ecology provides a descriptive rather than an analytical tool and that its theoretical concepts appear to have little potential for further refinement, does not detract from the value of this volume, which provides an admirable summary of a short period in the history of ideas.

American urban sociology is characterized by its lack of any theoretical base but two important books appeared during the previous decade which, in different ways, have forced urban sociologists to reconsider their theoretical foundations. The reissue of Max Weber's essay on *The City* in 1958, thirty-seven years after it was first published, provided an occasion for Martindale to consider, in a lengthy introduction, whether the theory of the city need be as boring as the textbooks made it. Two years later Maurice Stein attempted to draw American community studies into some kind of general framework in his seminal study of *The Eclipse of Community*. Both Martindale and Stein ask "Where *is* the city in urban-industrial America?"

For the medieval city Pirenne had argued that a middle-class population and a communal organization were the two basic attributes necessary to constitute a city: for him the city was the community of merchants. Weber, too, emphasized the distinctive institutional basis of the urban community and argued for "the presence of a special stratum, a distinct new estate". Under these conditions, true cities in pre-industrial times could be found only in Western Europe, yet even here there was no uniform pattern "During the period of maximum autonomy the cities displayed an exceptional variety of forms and trends" (Weber, 1958, p. 181). However distinctive the city, in Weberian terms, may have been, it is clear that the processes of urbanization, industrialization and bureaucratization have eroded effective local autonomy and this is the theme that Maurice Stein's stimulating study explores. He uses American community studies as cases to test the more general formulations of Weber and of Durkheim in his essay on the *Division of Labour in Society*. Every good community study, he argues, is a study of transitional processes: the urban sociologist should, therefore, be fundamentally concerned with social change. Too often, of course, those who have been concerned with case studies have made little attempt to make their work comparative or consciously sought to fill important gaps in some typology. R. E. Park, in the Chicago of the 1920's, was perhaps over-conscious of the processes of change and disorganization and this coloured the research work he directed on Chicago. It is never-theless unfortunate that this side of his work did not stimulate research on a scale comparable with that produced on the eco-logical and demographic aspects of the process. Thomas and Znaniecki's monumental classic on social change, *The Polish Peasant in Europe and America*, made a curiously slight impact on American urban sociology compared with, for example, the impact of the relatively modest contribution by Burgess in his zonal hypothesis of city growth. By focusing the attention of American urban sociologists onto the fundamental processes of social change, mainly through the work of Weber, Martindale and Stein have served an important function. As Martindale cogently remarks: "Weber thought that the task of sociology was to explain human conduct in its meaningful dimensions and not merely externally. One can determine a person's loss of weight objectively by weighing him repeatedly but it makes a lot of difference if he is losing weight because he is dying of an illness or because he is engaging in ascetic practices in connection with his religion. The task of sociology is to explain inter-human actions in terms of the meanings they have to the parties involved as well as in terms of specific physical changes they entail" (p. 51).

One further trend might be mentioned. In recent years there has been a sharpened interest in community power structures, among political scientists as well as sociologists. Floyd Hunter's *Community Power Structure* and Vidich and Bensman's *Small Town in Mass Society* have been followed by a number of other studies (Bonjean and Olsen, 1964). Polsby (1963) has provided a power-ful critique of the work of sociologists on community power and more recently Rose (1967, pt. III) has provided a further summary and critique of the last decade's work.

Another welcome development is a return to fieldwork in urban areas. Of course, each census still produces its crop of ecological and demographic data and these help to provide starting points for exploring metropolitan social structures. However, more studies such as H. J. Gans' *The Urban Villagers* and *The Levittowners* are needed. Despite these developments, the most exciting trend of the last decade has been the increasing concern shown by urban sociologists in the process of urbanization: this is a theme that deserves particular attention in its own right.

2. The Study of Urbanization

(a) *The Demographic Approach*

Urban sociology appears to be most productive during periods of rapid immigration to urban areas. The booming growth of Chicago in the 1920's is paralleled today in the rapidly expanding cities of Latin America, Africa, India and the Far East: in the same way that the Chicago social laboratory helped to stimulate empirical research and theoretical advance, so also, for example, did the towns of the copperbelt in Central Africa in the 1950's and early 1960's.

The first phase of the work involved some quantification of the problem—particularly by Kingsley Davis and Hilda Hertz— which formed the basis for much of the data presented in the United Nations' summary: *Report on the World Social Situation* (1957). By "urbanization" Davis refers to "the proportion of the total population concentrated in urban settlements or else to a rise in this proportion" (1965, p. 41). Thus according to this view cities can grow without urbanization, provided that the rural population grows at an equal or greater rate. Hence, Davis argues, urbanization is "a finite process". This strictly limited, administrative, view of the process of urbanization underlies much of the work published under the auspices of the United Nations. For example, in the report on Latin America, vague recognition was given to urbanization as a social process but in practice "it was agreed to use as the criterion of "urban", places of 20,000 and over, because the internationally comparable data were readily available on this basis" (Hauser, 1961, p. 75).

Much of the work on international comparisons of "urbanization", often sponsored by the United Nations or one of its specialist agencies, was prompted by a concern with specific social and physical problems associated with the rapid expansion of built-up areas. Thus, although only between 9 and 11 per cent of Africa's population live in towns of 20,000 inhabitants these centres may have an acute concentration of such problems. Typically the urbanization "process" is described (often from extremely inaccurate census material) in terms of urban concentration. Further analysis in terms of age, sex, fertility, mortality, migration rates and so on usually precedes narrative accounts of health, housing, nutrition, water supply, education, "problems of family life" and so on, and the report is likely to conclude with traditional pleas for more research so that the social administrator may be better qualified to devise appropriate policies.

From the urban sociologist's point of view this is of only limited value. It is hard to see how an understanding of urbanism and urbanization can be advanced with such crude concepts. Farmers collected together in settlements of over 20,000 inhabitants in West Africa or villages surrounded by the physical expansion of an Indian city can hardly be termed urbanized in a sociological sense. Similarly, certain aspects of "social disorganization", which are said to follow rapid urbanization—that is rapid immigration to an urban area—are presumably also found in rural areas into which there is rapid immigration for harvests, tree-felling, short-term mining activity and so on. Clearly under these circumstances there will be an unbalanced age and sex structure producing a strong likelihood of the conventional symptoms of "disorganization" such as prostitution and drunkenness. On the other hand, specific studies of parts of the central areas of cities, such as Delhi, Cairo, East London, Lagos, Medan, and Mexico City, suggest that *urban villages* exist in which there is a high level of social cohesion, based on interwoven kinship networks, and a high level of primary contact with *familiar* people. Many rural migrants are able to be in the city but not of it, using their more traditional "rural" culture as a shock absorber, or perhaps devising new transitional forms which are neither typically "rural" or typically "urban". As Mayer notes in the article which follows, although the migrants to East London might have "urban" behaviour forced on them in their work situation, they are not obliged to behave in an "urban" manner outside working hours: "while some are born 'urban' and others achieve urbanization, none can be said to have urbanization thrust upon them". Mayer uses the word *incapsulation* to describe the situation where migrants live in the city but are not urbanized. Similarly, studies of villages in, for example, the Sudan and India, vividly document the commuters who are "urban" by day and "rural" at night (see the discussion of these problems in Pahl, 1966).

Undoubtedly two of the most useful books on urbanism and urbanization to have appeared in recent years are Reissman's brave attempt to construct an urban sociology of industrial cities, emphasizing comparative urban studies and a typology of urbanization, and the rather more eclectic symposium edited by Hauser and Schnore on *The Study of Urbanization*. In these studies there are signs that at last some American urban sociologists are discovering that there are other social systems than their own and that distinctive forms of urbanism, which emerge in other societies, cannot be understood with the rather simple conceptual tools which may have served in the analysis of the United States city for some decades. Instead of presenting fertility or migration rates based on dubious sources, Reissman stresses that urbanization means rapid social change. "We do not understand the social dynamics that move a society from one form to another, and we do not fully comprehend the impact of change, except in the most general terms. . . . There is a need for a sense of history if one wishes to consider social change and urbanization. . . . Urbanization in this context means not only the transformation of rural, agricultural or folk society, but also the continuous change within the industrial city itself. Urbanization does not stop but continues to change the city into ever different forms" (pp. 155–6). Here is a new humility and a new enthusiasm facing one of the most challenging issues of the last part of the twentieth century. The industrial city is the physical form of a type of society which most of the world is now committed to achieve. As such it is an arena in which new dynamic social processes operate. It is a direct reflection of the stage of development that the society has attained. Of course with technological advance many of the previous advantages of concentration no longer apply, but since developing societies lag behind in technological development it is unlikely they will move to a diffuse and dispersed form of urbanism without first passing through, possibly at a more rapid rate, earlier physical forms of urbanism. Similarly, the emergence of class-consciousness and class action is likely to reproduce patterns typical of an early period in the evolution of what are now the more advanced industrial societies.

Given the framework of a typology, into which detailed empirical analysis can be fitted, the next crucial question is—What is to be studied? The rapidly expanding urban areas cannot be effectively analysed with the use of published data, which either does not exist or is of doubtful scope and validity. It is little good for eminent research workers to call for more multidisciplinary research on a comparative basis if there is no data to work on: there is more than a slight element of unreality in the proposals of the Committee on Urbanization reported by Hauser (Hauser and Schnore, p. 41). Multidisciplinary work can very often lead to generalisations at a very high level of abstraction which are acceptable to each specialist but which do little to further our basic understanding of human behaviour and social processes. Hard empirical data on patterns of social relationships in particular places is much harder to find and is urgently needed. It is through fieldwork in urban areas that some of the most fundamental advances have been made in the last few years, but this is not yet widely known in the literature of related social sciences.

(b) *The Return to Sociological Reporting and Analysis*

A problem facing the investigator seeking to understand the nature of urbanism in one of the booming cities of the modernizing nations is to know where to begin. The crowded jumble of people may seem to resemble the Hobbesian anarchy of all against all and the confusion is understandably daunting. Town life may appear "as a kind of phantasmagoria, a succession of dim figures, caught up in a myriad of diverse activities with little to give meaning or pattern to it all" (Epstein, 1964, p. 83). However, the arrangement of human atoms is not random: there is a pattern, a social system, and individuals are participating in social life. The problem, then is how to penetrate and understand this social life. Recent work on African cities has taken the whole study of urbanism and urbanization a stage further. This impetus may be as stimulating and productive to research workers in the coming decade as the Chicago School was to an earlier generation of scholars. Since a separate volume of papers (Bruner and Southall: in press) in urban anthropology has been prepared, the following discussions will only attempt to touch one some of the literature and the issues involved.

In a recent survey of African urban studies Professor Clyde Mitchell remarks that "the apparent complexity of social phenomena frequently bespeaks a lack of theoretical concepts available for this analysis" (Mitchell, 1966, p. 41). He describes the hey-day of the social survey as the decade 1950–60, when quantitative data was gathered and some interesting correlations emerged. It is now time, he argues, to develop more rigorous and comprehensive theory. Analysis of urbanism in Africa must be based on an *urban* system of relationships; the tribal origins of the population are of secondary interest. The urban social system may be considered in its own right with no obligation to look back to tribal, subsistence society, or to base the analysis on some notion of social change. The external factors which create the social situation in which the individual actors conduct their relationships are listed by Mitchell (drawing heavily on Epstein, 1961), as the population density of the settlement, residential instability due to the transience of the migratory population, ethnic and tribal heterogeneity, an unbalanced age and sex structure, economic, and hence occupational differentiation and the embryonic system of social stratification this entails, and finally, the administrative and political restraints, particularly in the towns of Southern Africa. Despite the unique quality of each individual town, dependent on the particular assortment of their external factors, a typology related to the economic base may be devised, which distinguishes between types of towns with distinctive social structures.

Mitchell suggests that the urban system may be explored by analyzing three types of social relationships: "structural", "categorical" and "personal". *Structural* relationships are those where the norms are defined in terms of the role expectations of others, for example, the work situation. There are few studies of structural relationships, although there has been some work on voluntary associations in African towns, recently summarized for West Africa by Little (1965). These associations, Little argues, provide a new basis for social organization and build a cultural bridge for the urban migrant by providing him with information about life at home and about town institutions. They inculcate new standards of dress, social behaviour and personal hygiene and provide both moral and material support. They have also taken over traditional functions of social control and help to establish fresh norms for society in general. Mitchell contends that these associations should not be compared with their tribal counterpart but should be described in relation to aspects of the social system in which they are embedded. The *"categorical"* types of social relationships are those where contacts are of necessity superficial and perfunctory: people tend to be categorized by some visible characteristic and other people are seen as stereotypes. There has been interesting work on the relationships between "races" and ethnic groups, such as that by the Sofers in Jinja (1955) or by Mayer in East London (1961), as well as the important study by Mitchell himself on joking relationships between formerly antagonistic tribes (1957). By considering ethnicity as a categorical relationship in towns an understanding of the way it operates to simplify or codify behaviour in otherwise "unstructured" situations emerged (Mitchell, 1966, p. 53). However, the full implications of urban associations of "ethnicity" have still to be explored.

Finally we come to Mitchell's third type of social relationships —the *personal*. The study of personal social networks is perhaps one of the most rewarding and promising fields in urban studies. One of the most interesting papers on this subject, that by Mayer, is reprinted here; however, another paper by Epstein (1961) is also extremely interesting. He sees his paper as looking "towards the development of a methodology or systematic approach to the anthropological study of urban communities" (Epstein, 1961, p. 32). His method is to set out in considerable detail the network of relationships in which a single African was involved in the town of Ndola, during the course of a number of days. We follow his assistant Chanda, on his bicycle, as he goes shopping and meets his friends near his home or in other parts of the town. He visits his kinsfolk, goes to watch football, gets merry at the Beer Hall. We are given snatches of conversation in these various social situations. The African, argues Epstein, is never a full and free citizen as that term would be understood elsewhere: Africans in the location have certain definite environmental restraints put upon them. Of course, as Epstein notes "Environment is a relative concept: its bounds are never set, but what it shall include varies according to the social units isolated for purposes of analysis" (Epstein, 1961, p. 42). The various institutions and policies operative within the urban system constrain the African and he has no control over them. "They provide a basic institutional framework, moulding and at the same time circumscribing the pattern of social relations amongst Africans in the towns" (p. 43). Chanda's associations differ both in degree and kind: some relationships depend entirely upon the mere fact of spatial contiguity, whereas others may be with a wide variety of kin. In any one day he may move through a whole continuum of role relationships, from superficial and segmentary to complex and multi-stranded. Very high value is attached to kin ties: in the urban context Epstein claims that kinship and the fundamental values of "brotherhood" become synonymous. After kinsfolk, Chanda is most at ease amongst his "home fellows" or fellow tribesmen. He appeared to have no close friends outside a rather broadly defined tribal category. Yet tribalism is always situational and it does not operate with equal intensity over the whole range of social relationships.

Epstein has also some perceptive remarks to make on prestige and the emergence of class consciousness, and also on the increasing segmenting and specialization of social interest and the development of churches, trade unions and the like. (There appear to be fundamental empirical differences in the scope, numbers and role of voluntary associations in Ndola as compared with the situation Little describes in West Africa.)

However, it is Epstein's analysis of the personal network which is of particular importance. Chanda is seen as the centre of a loose-knit network of friends, neighbours and kin, few of whom know each other, so that the degree of connectedness is slight. Yet Chanda does not interact with everyone in his network with the same degree of intensity. Parts of his network are more closely knit than others: the part which is fairly closely connected Epstein calls the *effective* network and the other is termed the *extended* network. In the *effective* network interrelationships are more likely between status equals, whereas in the *extended* network there may be a greater disparity of status in the relationship. The *effective* network is itself made up of *clusters* of persons fairly closely knitted together. Epstein suggests that the analysis by Elizabeth Bott relating network to conjugal roles within the family (Bott, 1957) could also be useful in the African urban situation. The network serves as an important element in social control; it "may also be seen as a series of links in a chain of gossip" (Epstein, 1961, p. 58). Norms of behaviours are reaffirmed by those who participate in this chain.

"It is within the *effective* network that gossip is most intense and the marriages, affairs, and conjugal relations of those within the effective network are among its major themes. In this way continuous gossip leads not merely to the reaffirmation of established norms but also to the clarifications and formulations of new ones. ... I suggest that new norms and standards of behaviour will tend to arise more frequently within the *effective* network of those who rank high on the prestige continuum and that through the *extended* network they gradually filter down and percolate throughout the society. From this point of view the network would also appear to have importance as an instrument in examining the processes of social and cultural change" (Epstein, 1961, p. 59).

Epstein's paper provides a useful parallel with Mayer's study reprinted here. It is in the light of such detailed studies that the notion of an urban social system becomes understandable.

A further concept which has been used to elucidate patterns of social relationships in urban areas is that of *role*. In an interesting paper Banton (in press) uses the phrases "dense network of social relations" and "standardized role-relationships" to describe specific social ties. Yet Banton ties his high density of social relationships to specific milieux, separated by "opaque partitions". The standardized role-relationships link the milieux, as it were, across these partitions. In this he echoes Durkheim whom he quotes. "It is not enough that society take in a great many people, but they must be, in addition, intimately enough in contact to act and react on one another. If they are, on the contrary, separated by opaque milieux, they can only be bound by rare and weak relations, and it is as if they had small populations" (Durkheim, 1893, p. 262).

Banton is especially concerned with the relationship between "rural" and "urban" and, following Southall (1959), attempts to elucidate this relationship through the concept of role. In the technologically primitive society there is a small number of inter-related yet undifferentiated roles, whereas in urban society there is "a complex but loose structure of independent roles overlying a pattern of fairly diffuse basic roles". Not only are there more roles to play but they are also very much more differentiated. A further theme developed in Banton's paper concerns the continuity between the rual and the urban. Whether or not one accepts the notion of a distinct urban system, which is stressed in the work of those who have studied copperbelt towns, Banton argues that "the degree of continuity between the rural and the urban social systems is therefore a factor that should be subjected to empirical examination". Factors which promote a high degree of continuity include premigration ties of kinship, a balanced age and sex structure in the immigrant community, the ability for migrants to create an urban village in a section of the city (which in turn depends on the housing situation), and employment amongst and supervised by their own kind. These structural differences are of fundamental importance. Banton then concludes "to the extent that town life constitutes an independent set of social relations so these relations will constitute a tighter social network displaying a higher level of social density". He calls for more comparative studies of the organization of social relations in different towns to demonstrate both the relationship between the overall structure and patterns of role differentiation and also the different kinds of relationships which may help to produce a network typology. In similar vein Kuper has argued that each society has its own structural and ethical antecedents "which interact with the introduced physical and social attributes of cities associated with modern industry, and so create distinctive forms of urbanism. Industrialisation cannot be treated as a given change, which then produces uniform consequential changes. Such a 'before' and 'after' approach ignores the dynamics of simultaneous change, the complexity of uneven sequence and the nature of structural conflict" (Kuper, 1965, p. 16).

The debate between those who believe in an urban social system and those who adopt a more pluralistic view of distinctive forms of urbanism must continue.[3] One of the satisfying aspects of the recent work on African urbanism is that important and fundamental problems have been raised, the resolution of which will help to advance our understanding of some of the main issues in sociological theory. This is certainly the case with Southall's work on role (1959) and also with the paper by Mayer which follows and those discussed above. The choice of a paper to illustrate these developments was particularly difficult: I have had to assume that the availability of the Bruner and Southall symposium provides some compensation.

---

[3] It is interesting that Epstein presents an extended discussion of this issue in an important paper published after this introduction was written. See Epstein, A. L., 1967, Urbanization and Social Change in Africa, *Current Anthropology* 8 (4), 275–95.

HISTORICAL AND COMPARATIVE APPROACHES TO URBANISM

1. (a) *Historical*

In this final section I can do no more than hint at some of the material which has appeared in recent years. Some of this work, particularly that by historians, is likely to give an added depth to urban sociology and I am certain that if historians and sociologists work closely together there are likely to be important advances in the understanding of urbanism during the next decade, particularly now that historians are moving away from more parochial and particularistic studies to more general themes and problems (Briggs, 1963, Thernstrom, 1964).

The recent burst of interest in urban history in Britain particularly at the Universities of Glasgow and Leicester is likely to provide plenty of stimulation for urban sociologists. Dyos has provided a useful review of some recent historical writing (Dyos, 1966) and is editing an important forthcoming collection of papers on urban history. In America the work of Lampard (1954 and 1963) is most impressive and the volume on *The Historian and the City* (edited by Handlin and Burchard, 1963) provides a convenient introduction to an extensive literature. There are, of course, many studies of particular cities and many of these are of very great interest from a sociological point of view. For example, Powell has studied Buffalo during the period 1810–1910, concerning himself with industrial capitalism and the development of anomie. "The spatial order of the American City", he argues, "is rational only in serving the ends of profit for the property owners" (Powell, 1962, p. 166). It is not the city but capitalism which creates anomie. This theme is echoed in the work of historians, and Checkland has provided a concise statement in his study of Glasgow—"it is businesses that form and sustain the city, it is business men that governed the British city over a large part of its history, and business men and their dependents constitute one of the great social classes whose housing needs help to determine the city's shape" (Checkland, 1964, p. 36). He then discusses

Glasgow in terms of both an economic and a spatial model, accepting that analysis in terms of both a social and a policy model is also required. Checkland maintains that a knowledge of the economic and spatial elements must precede a study of the social and he sees himself as a partner with sociologists and others in attempting to understand the city. Emrys Jones's elegant study of the social geography of Belfast (1960) is also of historical and sociological interest and there are many such examples of convergence between disciplines. Work by Redfield and Singer (1954), Sjoberg (1960) and Strauss (1961) shows what some sociologists have produced when considering the historical material. There is, however, scope for considerable development of this area of study.

One historical study which is likely to be of great interest to urban sociologists is Foster's careful study of class formation in three nineteenth-century towns in England. Painstaking analysis of the various historical sources, including marriage certificates and detailed census material, together with a sympathy towards and knowledge of the aims and interests of sociology has thrown fresh light on emergent urbanism. By comparing Oldham, Northampton and South Shields, Foster is able to demonstrate differences in class-consciousness which relate to the *local* social and economic structure. Consciousness of relative deprivation is less acute if there is no "resident *bourgeoisie*" in a community; consciousness of a common "working-class" situation is less likely if sub-cultures based on a variety of different occupations appear; finally, the prospects for social mobility and inter-status group marriages will also affect the development of class-consciousness. This kind of study demonstrates that, although industrial-urbanism and the development of class-consciousness are directly related, there are nevertheless important differences between towns. Oldham saw the most violent outburst of class activity, yet manual workers in the other towns were, if anything, the worse off.

The way in which industrial towns grow may have a lasting impact on local class-consciousness. Some towns are towns from the start, others never move beyond a collection of urban villages.

Rosser and Harris describe twenty-three such "villages" in Swansea: "In popular usage, they are 'communities', though they vary strikingly from one to another in their degree of community consciousness and in the psychological response of individuals to the physical fact of common residence" (Rosser and Harris, 1965, p. 67). More historical studies of class-consciousness under different patterns of industrial-urbanism are now needed.

(b) *Comparative*

Urbanization and the responses to urbanism differ markedly not only historically but comparatively. I have already commented on the important structural differences between West and Central Africa and in nineteenth-century England. We must be wary of assuming that because there may be statistical similarities between the growth of towns in the nineteenth century (Weber 1899) and in the contemporary world, it is necessarily the same process. Advances in technology may enable certain societies to avoid some stages in the emergence of industrial-urbanism. Similarly, any assumption that there is a necessary link between industrialization and urbanization needs to be questioned and the historical experience of say, Sweden or the contemporary situation in certain Latin American countries[4] should be examined in this context. However, there are signs that urban sociologists have left an ethnocentrism which sees the American city as the norm, and there is a welcome growth of interest in comparative studies. A brief and somewhat arbitrary introduction to some of this literature might be helpful.

Starting with Europe, Westergaard (1965) has provided a useful introduction to Scandinavian urbanism, suggesting that there are hopes of a distinctive contribution to the comparative study of urbanism when more studies become available. The literature on

---

[4] Touraine, A. (1961) Industrialisation et conscience ouvrière à Sao Paulo, *Sociologie du Travail*, 3 (4), pp. 77–95 and Touraine, A. and Pécant, D. (1967) Conscience ouvrière et développement économique en Amérique Latin, *Sociologie du Travail*, 9 (3), pp. 229–54.

French and German cities is briefly reviewed in two chapters by Chombart de Lauwe in a recent UNESCO publication (Hauser (ed.), 1965) and there are also useful surveys of the literature by Pfeil and the Centre d'Études des Groupes Sociaux. Research on urbanism and urbanization in Mediterranean cities appears slight, although there are the interesting essays by Baroja (1964) and Benet (1963).

The most comprehensive bibliography of the literature on Asia, Africa and Latin America has been prepared by Rowe (1965). The Turner Symposium (1962) is an important contribution to the study of Indian urbanism and Dore's authoritative account of social life in a Tokyo ward (1958) is a valuable introduction to a distinctive form of urbanism. Indeed, our increasing knowledge of Japanese urbanism is one of the strongest points in the argument against a single urban system in industrial society. The symposium edited by T. C. Smith (1960) and the recent papers by R. J. Smith (1963, and in press) provide important new material. An example of recent work by a Japanese sociologist is given on page 190 and Professor Dore's introduction places this paper in its wider context.

Rowe's bibliography provides a useful indication of the degree of interest by urban sociologists in non-western cities. A total of 446 items are listed on Africa, Asia and Latin America. Africa, south of the Sahara, leads with 153 items followed by India, Pakistan and Ceylon with 117. Latin America has 81, South East Asia and the Pacific 48 and North Africa and the Middle East 47 items respectively. There would appear to be sufficient material for a series of Readers on each of these major areas of the world. With such a huge field to select from the present collection must appear somewhat restricted and arbitrary. However, this volume may serve a useful purpose if it stimulates the study of urbanism by extending the range of comparative study and it may encourage another Editor to do better. Scholars interested in particular aspects of the field or with only a partial view of urbanism have together produced a large literature. There is now an urgent need for an overall understanding of urbanism in all its diversity. We have perhaps suffered too long from the demographic approach alone, which may mask fundamental differences between, say, Japanese and American urbanism.

When the physical city of industrial society is baffling in its complexity, when planners are talking of creating new cities and when urbanization is creating enormous slums throughout the world, sociologists are unlikely to find themselves short of funds for research.[5] Under these circumstances there may be a temptation to use "the survey" to provide quantities of social information which may be presented to the sponsors in well-set-out publications bulging with appendices and tests of significance. Sociologists working in the field of urban studies must resist this temptation: the most useful contribution of such sociologists to urban problems will, in the long run, depend on the quality of their contribution to sociology.

NOTE

The six other Readers in various aspects of urban sociology are listed separately below. These should be seen as essential companion volumes.

1. BRUNER, E. M. and SOUTHALL, A. (eds.) (in press) *Urban Anthropology*.
2. BURGESS, E. W. and BOGUE, D. J. (eds.) (1964) *Contributions to Urban Sociology*. Chicago U.P.
3. DOBRINER, W. M. (ed.) (1958) *The Suburban Community*. New York: Putnams.
4. HATT, P. K. and REISS, A. J. (eds.) (1957) *Cities and Society*. The Revised Reader in Urban Sociology. Glencoe: The Free Press.
5. HAUSER, P. M. and SCHNORE, L. F. (eds.) (1965) *The Study of Urbanization*. New York: John Wiley.
6. THEODORSON, G. A. (ed.) (1961) *Studies in Human Ecology*. Evanston, Illinois: Row Peterson & Co.

OTHER REFERENCES

BANTON, M. (in press) Urbanization and Role Theory. In *Urban Anthropology*, edited by E. M. Bruner and A. Southall. Aldine Press.

---

[5] This was written in 1966. Since then "the urban problem" has prompted the release of large sums of money, especially in the United States. For example, Harvard University and the Massachusetts Institute of Technology have recently received $6 million from the Ford Foundation for research and teaching in urban affairs.

BAROJA, J. C. (1964) The City and the Country: Reflections on Some Ancient Commonplaces. In *Mediterranean Countrymen*, edited by Julian Pitt-Rivers. The Hague: Mouton & Co.

BENET, F. (1963) The Ideology of Islamic Urbanization. *International Journal of Comparative Sociology* 4 (2), 211–26.

BERGER, B. (1966) Suburbs, Subcultures and the Urban Future. In *Planning for a Nation of Cities*, edited by Sam Bass Warner Jr. MIT Press.

BESHERS, J. (1962) *Urban Social Structure*. Glencoe: The Free Press.

BOGUE, D. J. (1949) *The Structure of the Metropolitan Community*, Ann Arbor: University of Michigan.

BONJEAN, C. M. and OLSEN, D. M. (1964) Community Leadership: Directions of Research. *Administrative Science Quarterly* 9, 278–300.

BOTT, E. (1957) *Family and Social Network*. London: Tavistock Publications.

BRIGGS, A. (1963) *Victorian Cities*. London: Odhams Press.

CENTRE D'ÉTUDES DES GROUPES SOCIAUX (1962) *Notes Bibliographiques de Sociologie Urbaine*, 2 vols. Paris.

CENTRE FOR URBAN STUDIES (1964) *Land Use Planning and the Social Sciences, A Selected Bibliography*. University College, London.

CHECKLAND, S. G. (1964) The British Industrial City: Glasgow. *Urban Studies* 1 (1), 34–54.

CHOMBART DE LAUWE, P. H. (1963) The Social Sciences, Urbanism and Planning. *International Journal of Comparative Sociology* 4, 19–30.

CHORLEY, R. J. and HAGGETT, P. (eds.) (1967) *Models in Geography*. London: Methuen.

CLINARD, M. B. (1966) *Slums and Community Development*. Glencoe: The Free Press.

DAVIS, K. (1965) The Urbanization of the Human Population. *Scientific American* 213 (3), 41–63.

DEWEY, R. (1960) The Rural–Urban Continuum: Real But Relatively Unimportant. *American Journal of Sociology* 66 (1) 60–66.

DOLLARD, J. (1957) *Caste and Class in a Southern Town*. Garden City, New York: Anchor Books (first published 1937).

DORE, R. P. (1958) *City Life in Japan*. London: Routledge & Kegan Paul.

DURKHEIM, E. (1893) *On the Division of Labour in Society*, translated by G. Simpson (1964). Glencoe: The Free Press.

DYOS, H. J. (1966) The Growth of Cities in the Nineteenth Century: A Review of Some Recent Writing. *Victorian Studies*, pp. 225–37.

EPSTEIN, A. L. (1961) The Network and Urban Social Organization. *Journal of the Rhodes–Livingstone Institute* 29, 28–62.

EPSTEIN, A. L. (1964) Urban Communities in Africa. In *Closed Systems and Open Minds*, pp. 83–102 edited by M. Gluckman. Edinburgh: Oliver & Boyd.

FISHER, J. C. (1962) Planning the City of Socialist Man. *Journal of the American Institute of Planners* 28 (4), 251–65.

FOLEY, D. L. (1960) British Town Planning: One Ideology or Three. *British Journal of Sociology* 11 (3), 211–31.

FOLEY, D. L. (1962) Idea and Influence: The Town and Country Planning Association. *Journal of the American Institute of Planners* 28, 10–17.

FORM, W. H. (1951) Stratification in Low and Middle Income Housing Areas. *Journal of Social Issues*, pp. 109–31.

FOSTER, J. (in press) Nineteenth Century Towns—A Class Dimension. In a forthcoming Reader edited by H. J. Dyos. London: Edward Arnold.

GITTUS, E. (1965) An Experiment in the Identification of Urban Sub-areas. *Transactions of the Bartlett Society* **2,** 107–35.

GLASS, R. (1959) The Evaluation of Planning—Some Sociological Considerations. In *Regional Planning*, Housing, Building and Planning Nos. 12 and 13, pp. 51–57. New York: U.N. Dept. of Economic and Social Affairs.

GLASS, R. (1962) Urban Sociology. Chapter 26 in *Society: Problems and Methods of Study*, edited by A. T. Welford *et al.* London: Routledge & Kegan Paul.

GOLDTHORPE, J. H. (1964) Social Stratification in Industrial Society. In *The Development of Industrial Societies*, pp. 97–122, edited by P. Halmos.

GOLDTHORPE, J. H. (1966) Attitudes and Behaviour of Car Assembly Workers: A Deviant Case and a Theoretical Critique. *British Journal of Sociology* **17,** 227–44.

HAGGETT, P. (1965) *Locational Analysis in Human Geography*. London: Edward Arnold.

HALMOS, P. (ed.) (1964) *The Development of Industrial Societies*. Keele: Sociological Review Monograph No. 8.

HANDLIN, O. and BURCHARD, J. (1963) *The Historian and the City*. Cambridge, Mass.

HAUSER, P. M. (ed.) (1961) *Urbanization in Latin America*. Paris: UNESCO.

HAUSER, P. M. (ed.) (1965) *Handbook for Social Research in Urban Areas*. Paris: UNESCO.

HRUSKA, E. (1964) Bemühungen um eine neue Siedlungsstruktur in der Tschechoslowakei. *Archiv für Kommunalwissenschaften* **3** (1), 57–80.

HUNTER, F. (1953) *Community Power Structure*. University of North Carolina Press.

INTERNATIONAL AFRICA INSTITUTE (1956) *Social Implications of Industrialization and Urbanization in Africa South of the Sahara*. Paris: UNESCO.

JONES, E. (1960) *A Social Geography of Belfast*. O.U.P.

JONES, E. (1965) The London Atlas. *Geographical Journal* **131,** 330–43.

KLAGES, H. (1966) Soziologische Aspekte der Stadt- und Verkehrsplanung. In *Planung, Bau und Betrieb des Schnellverkehrs in Ballungsräumen*. Berlin: Bauverlag GmbH.

KUPER, H. (ed.) (1965) *Urbanization and Migration in West Africa*. Berkeley and Los Angeles: University of California Press.

LAMPARD, E. E. (1955) History of Cities in the Economically Advanced Areas. *Economic Development and Cultural Change* **3,** 86–102.

LAMPARD, E. E. (1963) Urbanization and Social Change: On Broadening the Scope and Relevance of Urban History. In *The Historian and the City*, pp. 225–47, by O. Handlin and J. Burchard.

LEWIS, O. (1962) *The Children of Sanchez*. London: Secker & Warburg.

LITTLE, K. (1965) *West African Urbanization*. Cambridge: The University Press.

LOPEZ, R. P. (1963). The Crossroads Within the Wall. In *The Historian and the City*, pp. 27–43.

LOWENSTEIN, S. F. (1965) Urban Images of Roman Authors. *Comparative Studies in Society and History* **8,** 110–23.

MANHEIM, E. (1960) Theoretical Prospects of Urban Sociology in an Urbanized Society. *American Journal of Sociology* **66** (3), 226–9.

MARTINDALE, D. (1958) Prefatory Remarks: The Theory of the City, translation, with G. Neuwirth, of *The City* by Max Weber. London: Heinemann.

MAYER, P. (1961) *Townsmen or Tribesmen.* Cape Town: Oxford University Press.

McKENZIE, R. D. (1933) *The Metropolitan Community.* New York: McGraw-Hill.

McLOUGHLIN, J. B. (1965a) The Planning Profession: New Directions. *Journal of the Towns Planning Institute* **51,** 258–61.

McLOUGHLIN, J. B. (1965b) Notes on the Nature of Physical Change. *Journal of the Town Planning Institute* **51,** 397–400.

McLOUGHLIN, J. B. (1966) The Future of Development Plans. *Journal of the Town Planning Institute* **52,** 257–61.

MITCHELL, J. C. (1957) *The Kalela Dance.* Rhodes–Livingstone Papers No. 27. Manchester University Press.

MITCHELL, J. C. (1966) Theoretical Orientations in African Urban Studies. In *The Social Anthropology of Complex Societies,* pp. 37–68, edited by M. Banton, London.

MOSER, C. A. and SCOTT, W. (1961) *British Towns.* Edinburgh and London: Oliver & Boyd.

MUKHERJEE, RAMKRISHNA (1963) Urbanization and Social Transformation in India. *International Journal of Comparative Sociology* **4,** 178–210.

PAHL, R. E. (1965a) Class and Community in English Commuter Villages. *Sociologia Ruralis* **V** (1), 5–23.

PAHL, R. E. (1965b) *Urbs in Rure. The Metropolitan Fringe in Hertfordshire.* London School of Economics and Political Science, Geographical Paper No. 2.

PAHL, R. E. (1966) The Rural–Urban Continuum. *Sociologia Ruralis* **VI** (3, 4), 299–329.

PARK, R. E. *et al.* (1925) *The City.* Chicago University Press. (Reprinted 1967.)

PARK, R. E. (1952) *Human Communities.* Glencoe: The Free Press.

PETERSEN, W. (1966) On some Meanings of Planning. *Journal of the American Institute of Planning* **32,** 130–42.

PFEIL, E. (in press) *Grosstadtforschung,* 2nd ed. Bremen: Horn W. Dorm.

PIOŘO, Z. (1962) *Ecologia Spoteczna w urbanistyce* (Warsaw, Arkady).

PIRENNE, H. (1925) *Medieval Cities.* Princeton U.P.

POLSBY, N. W. (1963) *Community Power and Political Theory.* Yale U.P.

POWELL, E. H. (1962) The Evolution of the American City and the Emergence of Anomie: A Culture Case Study of Buffalo, New York 1810–1910. *British Journal of Sociology* **13** (2), 156–68.

REDFIELD, R. and SINGER, M. B. (1954) The Cultural Role of Cities. *Economic Development and Cultural Change* **3,** 53–73.

REISSMAN, L. (1964) *The Urban Process.* Glencoe: The Free Press.

ROSE, A. M. (1967) *The Power Structure.* New York: Oxford University Press.

ROSSER, C. and HARRIS, C. (1965) *The Family and Social Change.* London: Routledge & Kegan Paul.

ROWE, W. L. (1965) *Selected Bibliography for Urban Anthropology.* Duke University. Mimeo.

RUNCIMAN, W. G. (1966) *Relative Deprivation and Social Justice.* London: Routledge & Kegan Paul.

SJOBERG, G. (1959) Comparative Urban Sociology. In *Sociology Today*, chapter 15, edited by R. K. Merton *et al*. Basic Books.

SJOBERG, G. (1960) *The Preindustrial City*. Glencoe: The Free Press.

SJOBERG, G. (1964) The Rural–Urban Dimensions in Preindustrial, Transitional and Industrial Societies. In *Handbook of Modern Sociology*, pp. 127–59, edited by R. E. L. Faris. Chicago: Rand McNally.

SMITH, R. J. (1963) Aspects of Mobility in Pre-Industrial Japanese Cities. *Comparative Studies in Society and History* **5** (4), 416–23.

SMITH, R. J. (in press) Town and City in Pre-Modern Japan: Small families, small households and residential instability. In *Urban Anthropology*, edited by E. M. Bruner and A. Southall.

SMITH, T. C. (ed.) (1960) City and Village in Japan. *Economic Development and Cultural Change* (special issue) **10** (1, 2).

SOFER, C. and R. (1955) *Jinja Transformed*. East African Studies No. 4. Kampala: East African Institute of Social Research.

SOUTHALL, A. W. (1959) An Operational Theory of Role. *Human Relations* **12,** 17–34.

STEIN, M. (1960) *The Eclipse of Community*. Princeton University Press.

STRAUSS, A. (1961) *Images of the American City*. Glencoe: The Free Press.

THERNSTROM, S. (1964) *Poverty and Progress: Social Mobility in a Nineteenth Century City*. Cambridge, Mass. Harvard U.P.

THOMAS, W. I. and ZNANIECKI, F. (1920) *The Polish Peasant in Europe and America*. Boston: R. C. Badger.

TIMMS, D. W. G. (1965) Quantitative Techniques in Urban Social Geography. In *Frontiers in Geographical Teaching*, chapter 12, edited by R. J. Chorley and P. Haggett. London: Methuen.

TURNER, R. (ed.) (1960) *India's Urban Future*. Berkeley: University of California Press.

UNITED NATIONS (1957) *Report on the World Social Situation*. New York: Bureau of Social Affairs.

VIDICH, A. J. and BENSMAN, J. (1958) *Small Town in Mass Society*. University of Princeton Press.

WEBER, A. F. (1899) *The Growth of Cities in the Nineteenth Century*. Reprinted Cornell U.P. 1963.

WEBER, M. (translated 1958) *The City*, edited, with an introduction by D. Martindale. London: Heinemann.

WESTERGAARD, J. H. (1965) Scandinavian Urbanism. A Survey of Trends and Themes in Urban Research in Sweden, Norway and Denmark. *Acta Sociologica* **8,** 304–23.

WHYTE, W. F. (1943) *Street Corner Society*. Chicago University Press.

WILLHELM, S. M. (1962) *Urban Zoning and Land Use Theory*. Glencoe: The Free Press.

WIRTH, L. (1928) *The Ghetto*. Chicago University Press.

ZIOLKOWSKI, J. (1966) Sociological Implications of Urban Planning in *City and Regional Planning in Poland*. Ch. 7, edited by J. C. Fisher. Cornell U.P.

ZORBAUGH, H. W. (1929) *The Gold Coast and the Slum*. Chicago University Press.

Part I

The Nature of Industrial Urbanism in Britain

Urban Sociology in Great Britain

RUTH GLASS

Editor's Note
   Mrs. Glass is dealing specifically with industrial-urbanism at a macro-sociological level. Her analysis of the various schools of British urban studies is a personal one and should be seen in the context in which it was written. Her polemic against the anthropologists and sociologists is perhaps over-sharp, but her strictures against the anti-urbanism of the élite have great force. Since the original article was written Mrs. Glass has done much to develop urban sociology in Britain through the work of the CENTRE FOR URBAN STUDIES, *of which she is Director.*

THE SCOPE OF URBAN SOCIOLOGY

Just as urbanism is many-sided, so is urban sociology. It is impossible to find any single definition of the "city"—or of urbanism —which would stand up to a variety of empirical tests, and which would be appropriate for all sorts of periods and societies. Therefore, "urban sociology", too, is not a subject with a distinct stable individuality.

It is difficult, moreover, to single out specific sociological aspects of urbanism from all the configurations of social structure, institutions and behaviour patterns caused by the other aspects— physical, economic, political and administrative. It is thus not surprising that in the attempts which have been made to find sociological definitions of the city, the negative, non-rural, rather than the positive "urban" characteristics have been

   Editor's Note: This article was originally published as an introduction to a bibliography. The author acknowledged the considerable assistance from her colleague John Westergaard and several suggestions by Mr. H. L. Beales. For reasons of space the bibliography has had to be omitted. Mrs. Glass intends to produce before long a revised and expanded edition of the whole Trend Report and bibliography.

47

stressed: social heterogeneity, "anomie", weakening of primary groups and of face-to-face relations. But social heterogeneity as such does not imply a specific pattern of social grouping, nor do the other features mentioned do justice to the positive characteristics of urbanism. Such definitions, in their several variations, are indeed negative: they bear traces, more or less explicit, of nostalgia for the rustic lost paradise, and of the tacit assumption that what is abstract and impersonal is not "real". (Nodding to your neighbour is regarded as a "real" social link, but not the fact that you and he vote for the same political party, or share, perhaps unknown to yourselves, a prejudice against Negroes.) If generalizations are in order, it could be said, however, that is is one of the outstanding features (perhaps the outstanding one) of the city in the contemporary Western world to appear as a mirror of abstract, impersonal forces—of history, class structure and culture. It is from this aspect that the sinister and the admirable, the perilous and the eventually progressive qualities of modern urbanism are derived: the city represents the reality of both conflict and unity resulting from such abstract, impersonal forces. This aspect of urbanism is there for all to see; and it was seen in the past, though it has recently been largely forgotten.

In a period of increasing urbanization, moreover, when it is said that we live in a predominantly "urban culture", it hardly suffices any longer to explain urbanism in terms of non-rural characteristics. Nor are definitions of the common denominator "urbanism" then meaningful unless they are used as terms of reference in identifying types of town and city, past and present. The growth of towns, both in number and size, does not occur without differentiation. While some old distinctions—national, regional and functional—become blurred, while in industrial towns the common traces of uncontrolled growth remain, and a common "planned" design is often superimposed, new distinctions emerge. It is, therefore, beside the point to criticize, for example, a particular diagrammatic representation of patterns of land-use and socio-geographical zones within cities for not being true to the image of universal urbanism. Concentric, wedge-like and irregular patterns (discovered by, and the objects of debate between, the Chicago school, Hoyt and Firey respectively)[1] are neither mutually exclusive, nor does any one of them look exactly alike to observers at different vantage points. The main fact is that there are such patterns, seen from the ground or from the air, in development or at a particular moment of time: the faces of cities have been lined by competitive economic interests, by social and ideological cleavages. But this can be taken for granted: it is the range of differences exhibited by and in cities that is of special interest. There are working-class towns and middle-class towns; some with predominantly young, others with predominantly old populations; homogeneous as well as heterogeneous urban settlements. Urbanism, perhaps more strikingly than other social phenomena, because it combines so many, is a baffling mixture of uniformity and diversity. Urbanism as a whole, like each large city, is an entity of which we are acutely aware, though we cannot unanimously trace its boundaries, nor transfix its individuality.

Therefore, the outstanding, professional and non-professional, sociological writers on urbanism have not usually outlined an urban sociology as such, that is, a specific, clearly limited field. Max Weber, Pirenne, Sombart and others have dealt with the history of urbanism in its varied aspects, with comparative urban institutions and their interactions, in the endeavour to outline a successive typology of cities. Similarly, though in a less encyclopaedic manner, the origin and symptoms of internal city growth, and the resulting intra-city differentiation, have been studied and classified by the Chicago school. They have drawn attention to urban ethnic and social groups, to their clusters, their institutions, relations and behaviour patterns—to the ghetto, the "gold coast and the slum". Other investigators have considered cities in

---

[1] E.g.: R. E. Park, E. W. Burgess and R. D. McKenzie, *The City*, Chicago, Univ. of Chicago Press, 1925; United States, Federal Housing Administration, H. Hoyt, *The Structure and Growth of Residential Neighbourhoods in American Cities*, Washington, D.C., United States Government Printing Office, 1939; W. Firey, *Land Use in Central Boston*, Cambridge, Mass., Harvard Univ. Press, 1947.

general or individually as instances of social phenomena, seen separately or in combination. While Vaughan, for example, unlike most other nineteenth-century writers, welcomed the *Zeitgeist* and regarded great cities as images of the potential social progress following from the industrial revolution, for Engels they were arenas of class structure and conflict; for Booth and his successors they were the universe for the collection of data demonstrating the need for social reform. Again, the town has been regarded—as in the pioneer work of the Lynds—as a laboratory for the study of a "total" community, as a microcosm of society and culture, or of special aspects of the contemporary social structure and superstructure. Another branch of the literature represents attempts, intuitive or empirical, to define particular characteristics of urbanism (in terms, for example, of vital statistics and age composition, of the services and spheres of influence of towns) or to trace the influence of urban environment on particular social phenomena. Simmel's famous essay on "the metropolis and mental life",[2] for instance, and other studies of urban personality types, or of primary group relations in an urban setting, are in this latter category. Finally, rather ambitious suggestions have been made—as by Louis Wirth—to go one step further: that is, to provide a contemporary, complex typology of towns and cities by studying a whole range of urban characteristics in their variations and consequent diverse interactions.

It thus seems, judging from the variety of modes of urban social study, that "urban sociology" is not a subject that fits into a tidy pigeon hole. It is true that all the writers mentioned have one approach in common—that which might be described as the specific sociological approach. None of these writers is a narrator; though their horizons differ, they are all "correlators" and interpreters of social phenomena, seen in their mutual influence in a

---

[2] First published in German under the title 'Die Grossstädte und das Geistesleben' in T. Petermann, ed., *Die Grossstadt*, Jahrbuch der Gehestiftung zu Dresden, Band IX, Dresden, von Zahn und Jaensch, 1903. Since then published in various anthologies, e.g. in: P. K. Hatt and A. J. Reiss, eds., *Reader in Urban Sociology*, Glencoe, Illinois, The Free Press, 1951.

historical, social and physical setting of varying range. But there the resemblance ends. Moreover, does Max Weber's essay on *Die Stadt*[3] belong to social history or to "urban sociology"? How should Engels' *The Condition of the Working-Class in England* be classified? Anthropologists might well claim that the Lynds' two *Middletown*[4] books belong to their field. Should studies of juvenile delinquency in urban areas be regarded as contributions to criminology or to urban sociology? Clearly they are both; indeed, the customary divisions between the social sciences are hardly applicable to the many-sided social studies pertaining to, or carried out in, towns and cities. And especially in a highly urbanized country like Great Britain, urban sociology is bound to be ubiquitous. But as it is pluralistic, perhaps it is not a genuine singular at all? It could therefore be argued—as was done by Sombart[5]—that in fact urban sociology as a subject with an identity of its own does not exist.

Be that as it may, such considerations explain the uncertainty in the selection of items for this bibliography.[6] Inevitably, it had to be rather eclectic, for so are the relevant topics and disciplines. In Britain, moreover, it is particularly difficult to draw lines of demarcation: just because here, and especially recently, the material directly devoted to a typology of urban history, of urban settlements, institutions and social structure is very scarce, it is the more necessary to survey a wide field, so as to indicate the reasons for this deficiency, as well as the sources for future studies.

The scope of the bibliography was thus in fact suggested by the gaps in British literature. The selection of items, though primarily

[3] M. Weber, Die Stadt, pp. 513–600 in *Grundriss der Sozialökonomik*, III. Abteilung, *Wirtschaft und Gesellschaft*, Tübingen, Mohr, 1922.

[4] R. S. and H. M. Lynd, *Middletown* (New York, Harcourt, 1929), London, Constable (new ed.); *Middletown in Transition: a study in cultural conflict* (New York, Harcourt, 1937), London, Constable, 1937.

[5] W. Sombart, Städtische Siedlung, Stadt, pp. 527–33 in A. Vierkandt, ed., *Handwörterbuch der Soziologie*, Stuttgart, Enke Verlag, 1931.

[6] As this essay was originally an introduction to an annotated bibliography on urban sociology in Britain, some references to the bibliography, which is not attached here, are still included in the text.

designed to provide a general review of the background and of recent development of British urban social studies, was also intended to be of direct use to two main themes of future research. The first, the characterization of patterns of urban growth and of contemporary British towns, in terms of the major and later also of the more subtle concomitant variables, has already been referred to. A systematic outline of recent and present urban Britain, of the variations in urban conditions—in environment, institutions and society—is badly needed. It could be the basis for further comparative and more detailed studies of urban typology in Europe and elsewhere, and also for intensive studies in Britain, since samples (or examples) of towns and districts for such research can only be chosen when the principal "clustered" features in the British universe urban are known. Nowadays, studies of this kind are inevitably haphazard and therefore wasteful: as we do not know in what respects a particular corner of Liverpool, Coventry or Oxford is representative of other settlements, the findings of inquiries carried out in such places—and especially of those on the subtle aspects of social relationships—do not lend themselves to legitimate generalizations.

Equally essential is the second main theme—an analysis, in the manner of *Wissenssoziologie*, of the genesis of British ideas about urbanism, and of the movements in which they have been, and are still, expressed. Such a study would help to explain the lack of interest in Britain in the first theme mentioned. Through it, the concepts of urbanism could be developed, and with them also British urban sociology.

Research for both these themes has to draw on historical studies of town development. Though there is no definite historical starting date, by and large the mid-nineteenth century had to be regarded as such for the present purpose.

The source materials for both these branches of studies—on the typology of, and ideology concerning, urbanism—are by no means provided solely by social statistics and systematic investigations. Indeed, the difficulty in distinguishing between formal and informal, explicit and implicit sociology is particularly striking in comparing the publications of the nineteenth and early twentieth centuries with the current literature. When Greenwood spent *A Night in a Workhouse*, and when many of his contemporaries joined in urban "low" life and street life and reported their experiences, were they less genuine participant-observers than those of our present social investigators who occasionally have tea with a working-class family or attend a tenants' meeting? Of course, there is a difference: Victorian and Edwardian social reportage was inspired by sympathy and anger; it was written in a virile, lucid prose. Now we have an "objective" scientific approach, that is, "hypotheses" (though not always) and a clumsy jargon. (Sam Smith has lost his name; now he is called "Ego".) Moreover, when case studies of a few odd families, not chosen within a sampling frame and not subjected to verifiable systematic investigation, are classified as sociology, what then are novels which tell us far more about the totality of "segmented" personalities, of their conditions and relationships? It will be said, of course, that sociology is distinguished from social reportage and fiction by having a coherent frame of reference: cumulative answers are sought to a chain of questions. But in terms of this distinction, is not, for example, Arthur Morrison's novel *A Child of the Jago* nearer to sociology than one of those modern community studies conducted by six research workers in search of a theme? Morrison certainly knew what he was looking for.

THE DEVELOPMENT OF BRITISH URBAN SOCIAL STUDIES

A commentary on the recent British literature of urban social studies, that of the last 20 years, has to be a commentary on its deficiencies. It is, therefore, the primary purpose of this paper to indicate the reasons for these deficiencies. They are clearly visible in contrast to, and are also partly explained by, the distinguished contributions of the previous hundred years—from the 1830's to the 1930's, from the period of the Reform Act to that of the great inter-war depression.

During those hundred years Britain experienced urban concentration and urban diffusion; towns and their suburbs grew up, expanded and later interlocked: conurbations emerged. In 1831, 34 per cent of the total population lived in local authority areas classified as urban; by 1931, as now, this was true of 80 per cent of the population. In the towns—certainly until the first world war—Britain's class structure was reduced to a frightening simplicity: here Disraeli's two nations met and then turned their backs upon one another; here wealth was manufactured and poverty accumulated. The cities were "the crowded nurseries of disease", "the devil's hotbeds of evil and crime". There was no means of escape from urban social problems: their solution, it seemed, was the key to universal social progress.

This key, moreover, was always looked for. The ambiguities in scientific, technological and cultural advances, which we almost take for granted nowadays, were not regarded as inevitable. On the contrary, perfection seemed to be attainable: there was too much confidence, gained by spectacular success in some fields, for failure in others to be suffered gladly. People still knew how to get angry about matters outside direct personal relationships. And although the Victorians and Edwardians were renowned for smugness and self-satisfaction, they also saw sharp contrasts in the social scene—black and white—and responded with strong emotions. Although their homes were cluttered with bric-à-brac, their observations and writings were often focused on essentials. Perhaps they did not need to be preoccupied with trivialities and could afford to see the clear outlines of an immediate picture, however harassing it might be, because they were still so confident of the long-term future.

Victorian Social Studies

A large pioneering literature of empirical sociology—in many respects still unsurpassed—thus grew up. It was inevitably concerned mainly with the towns as the theatre of social change. These publications fall roughly into three broad groups: the literature of social protest, that directed towards social reform, and that giving a wide view of society in time and space—a search for future trends amid current interactions.

The distinctions between these groups are, of course, not hard and fast. A direct interest in social change was common to all three: fact-finding, analyses and reports were intended to serve definite purposes; there was hardly ever a sign of *l'art pour l'art*. But while it was the purpose of the protest literature to reveal social maladies without necessarily suggesting remedies, to give literary expression, for instance, to *The Bitter Cry of Outcast London* (to quote the title of one of the most famous pamphlets belonging to this group), the authors of the nineteenth-century blue books, as well as Charles Booth and his followers, were concerned with the formulation of social policies. They were observing the manifestations of poverty in order to discover their causes, and thereby means for removing them. Accordingly, they had to be more systematic and painstaking in their inquiries than their predecessors from the protest school who wrote social reportage and pastiche studies. The Booth group spent their emotion far more in collecting facts and producing representative evidence than in dismay at the sight of the facts themselves. They were not agitators, but essentially social administrators, though as such rare in their insistence on systematic, as compared with *ad hoc*, empiricism. By contrast, the third group was thinking of long-term policy, rather than of specific social policies. Writers like Gaskell and Vaughan, Escott and Masterman provided what we would now call general intelligence reports—though there are no exact modern counterparts—on *The Age of Great Cities* and on *The Condition of England*. The width of their horizon is remarkable, though not a characteristic confined to this group. It was yet another trait which the three branches of this sociological literature had in common.

Concern with social policy, short-term or long-term, direct or indirect, did not lead to a narrowing of interests. On the contrary, there was endless curiosity; a great variety of subjects was explored. The social protest literature dealt with all sorts of working class and minority groups and their institutions, with housing and industrial conditions, with the "London street-folk", with the "worst paid and most murderous trades", with various social maladies—*The Seven Curses of London*. Again, the sub-titles of the three series of Booth's monumental London survey—*Poverty*, *Industry* and *Religious Influences*—give at least a bare indication of his wide coverage.

In this respect, such literature was truly "sociological" in intention, if not always in effect. It was usually concerned with the interrelation of social phenomena, with particular aspects within a wider, yet still verifiable universe. This was shown, for example, also by the combination of methods of inquiry. In Booth's survey, as in the New London survey and in others of the same vintage, case studies were used to illustrate and interpret general facts and statistics; they did not appear on their own. Various specialized fields did already exist, but as stages in the attempt to integrate data, not as a number of discrete pursuits. And as the authors of such inquiries wanted to learn so much, they had to take elementary observations for granted: unlike many of the present social scientists, they had neither time nor inclination to reinvestigate the ABC of social knowledge or the trivial trimmings of social institutions.[7] Above all, they wanted to accomplish so much: there was then no need to advocate a *rapprochement* between social research and social policy. These two were happily married, and there was no rumour yet of separation.

The group that represented this alliance most clearly, and that may well take its name from Booth, was also the one that had the widest and most persistent influence. It largely succeeded the social protest school, though some of the latter's publications were issued during the period of Booth's London survey. And it was still regarded as a model when the distinguished contributions of the

---

[7] They did not undertake research, for instance, as is done nowadays, in order to discover the difference between husband-wife-child relationships and those of non-family households, e.g., households consisting of three sisters; or in order to find out which member of the family, on behalf of the others, deals with the plumber.

"intelligence report" writers had already been almost forgotten. Their example has not been followed. Sociology has become divorced from policy and politics and segmented itself, having responded to the increasing complexity of society with increasing specialization. There has thus been no genuine sequel to Masterman's *The Condition of England*, published in 1909 (though Masterman himself after the First World War attempted, not successfully, to write a sequel—*England after War*).

The Booth Tradition

The Booth tradition, on the other hand, has been continued and adapted to changing needs. It remained alive until the nadir of the inter-war depression. There were two main periods in the literature of this school: the first at the beginning of this century; the second in the mid-thirties.

Life and Labour of the People in London was followed, to begin with, by comparative diagnoses of urban poverty and its causes: Rowntree's first survey of York (1901) and *Livelihood and Poverty* by Bowley and Burnett-Hurst (1915)—the model for the statistical methods of subsequent studies. During this period, the Booth approach was applied also to the investigation of other social problems, especially to those concerning children and young people. Paterson's *Across the Bridges* (1911) is the most famous example. Other investigators were inspired by Booth's catholic interest in diverse aspects of town life. The first of these, Lady Bell, published *At the Works*, her admirable portrait of Middlesbrough, a northern steel town, in 1901.

Such a portrait of the varied social problems of a town was no longer unusual, though rarely equally successful, during the late twenties and thirties, when—after a hiatus—the Booth tradition was revived. By that time, most of the social reforms advocated by Booth, the Webbs and their colleagues had in fact been introduced, but had been found wanting under the impact of the depression and in the light of new standards. There was thus a new motive for investigations into questions of social policy, and especially into the question whether progress had been made. During that period, changes were traced, more comparisons were made, the area of inquiry was widened, and the search for quantitative data intensified. The poverty survey, following Booth's example, became once again a part of a broader social survey of a town or region, as in the *The New Survey of London Life and Labour* (1930–5); in Rowntree's second social survey of York, carried out in 1936 and published in 1942; and in *The Social Survey of Merseyside* (1934). Simultaneously, there was also an increasing diversity of specialized, often complementary, studies of living conditions. Housing, health and nutrition became new foci of interest, and through the study of such subjects both the factual knowledge and the research techniques relevant to the assessment of poverty—its levels and effects—were advanced.

Unemployment, not low and irregular wages as 40 years earlier in Booth's days, was found to be mainly responsible for poverty in 1929, when the New London and Merseyside surveys were carried out. Soon afterwards, before these surveys had been published, unemployment became far more widespread and prolonged. The depression descended upon Britain; it was the dominant and pervasive cause of poverty at that time. It prompted several studies of special aspects of unemployment, such as Bakke's *The Unemployed Man*, and *Men without Work* by the Pilgrim Trust, as well as reports and a series of blue books on depressed areas.[8]

Nowadays there is full employment; the range of acute poverty and its most atrocious symptoms have diminished. But there is still poverty: indeed, there is still a line of division between the comparatively prosperous south and the poor, bleak north of Britain. Nevertheless, since the new era of the second world war, the continuity of social studies directly influenced by the Booth

---

[8] Hilda Jenning's account of *Brynmawr* belongs to this group, while Ellen Wilkinson's story of Jarrow, *The Town that was Murdered*, is of a different order: it has a political and a wider purpose. "The idea of this book is to take one town, which has been through the whole process—the rise of capitalist industry, its heyday, and the rationalization period after the first world war—and to give a picture of capitalism at work."

approach appears to have been broken. Only a few traces remain. In the early war years, the irrationality and inconsistency of social administration, as exposed by war conditions, and also the special problems of evacuation, were the subjects of various inquiries, bearing the stamp of purposeful empirical sociology. The same is true also of several recent and current surveys carried out in Scotland, where a good deal of interest in urban social studies is now being shown. Again, the developing field of social medicine follows on from the health and nutrition studies of the thirties, and thus also from the classic social investigations of the nineteenth and early twentieth centuries. But these are exceptions; in general, the line of succession appears to have come to an end.

Thus the preoccupation with the town as a panorama of society has also come to an end. During the post-war years, pragmatic urban sociology of the characteristic British brand has almost disappeared, and so far there have been no new developments, practical or theoretical, empirical or speculative, to take its place.

Recent Studies

The recent and current literature which has any relevance to the sociological study of urbanism belongs mainly to three fields: human geography, town planning and social anthropology.

Investigators in the first field are bound to have a highly specialized interest in urbanism. They have been, and are still, mainly concerned with the institutional equipment of towns—such as wholesale and retail trade, banks, cinemas and newspapers—with their service functions and the spheres of influence derived from these. Such studies, though useful, lead to a rather narrow, superficial characterization of urban settlements and their network: showing similarities in terms of functions and communications, they cannot, and do not expect to, do justice to the historic, economic and cultural diversity of urbanism.

By contrast the second field—town planning—is by its nature rather synthetic. Here, it is true, the tradition of direct concern with social policy seems to have been continued, though not the tradition of craftsmanship in social investigation. For despite its apparent practical bent, sociological or quasi-sociological thought on town planning in this country follows on mainly from Ebenezer Howard and Patrick Geddes, not from Booth and the Webbs. It follows on from that motley group of enthusiasts in semi-philosophical speculation and social reform who helped to establish the Sociological Society and the *Sociological Review* at the beginning of the century. They were influenced by Le Play, as well as by the native utopias and community experiments of the nineteenth century. Though their early writings were contemporary with the classic poverty surveys, they had little in common with these beyond a general desire to improve society and its institutions. Their benevolence was mixed up with equally traditional British eccentricity—often endearing and no doubt stimulating. Their thought processes were instinctive rather than systematic; their universe was so wide as to be no longer verifiable. Sociology was for them another word for eclecticism—synonymous, too, with "the third alternative" that is, with "civics" and town planning, their panacea for social conflict and social ills.[9] As their influence declined during the late twenties, sociology and town planning parted company. In sociology, Patrick Geddes, Victor Branford, and their partners from the planning field like Raymond Unwin, left hardly any traces. From the early thirties on, and throughout the decade, the *Sociological Review* was a learned journal: articles on social theory and on coherent specialized investigations took the place of the previous general pronouncements on urbanism, civics and social betterment. Indeed, with this new professionalization, the anxiety about towns, the interest in them, even the

---

[9] For example, see the introduction to a series of articles on "the third alternative": "As many people think, the alternatives are the suppression of Bolshevism and the reinstatement of the old order of things, or the victory of Bolshevism and the ending of our civilisation. But . . . there is a third alternative . . . the search for and discovery of . . . 'Eutopia' . . . the nearest equivalent . . . attained by secular science to the conception of the 'Kingdom of Heaven'." Sociological Society, Cities Committee, Towards the Third Alternative, *Sociol. Rev.* 11 (1), 62–79, Spring 1919.

references to them, also became scarce. For town planning, however, Geddes' "sociology", as interpreted by his most prominent and persuasive disciple—Lewis Mumford—remained *the* sociology. To this day, planners in this country have taken little notice of other traditions and developments in the social sciences.

Town planning has thus been mainly the field of the amateurs in sociology, apart from technicians and architects, of course, who are concerned with land-use and design in terms of their own specialization. And it has been, paradoxically, the field of the anti-urbanists, who try to shape the town in terms of idealized rustic images. Surveys of towns and regions, as well as investigations of particular social aspects relevant to town planning, have therefore by and large not been sufficiently systematic to have made a cumulative contribution to the knowledge of urban environment and society.

Recently, moreover, some studies in this field, as in others, have shown the new approach to social research, which has been directly influenced by relativistic anthropology, and more indirectly by its philosophical counterparts.[10] Such studies make it increasingly difficult to see the wood for the trees. They tend to be devoid of general context and so microscopic that they get lost in the individuality of social phenomena: starting from a *tabula rasa*, sceptical of the objective validity of common social experience, the investigator, without knowing what to look for, can hardly see the social framework at all. Alternatively, he may laboriously reach the conclusion that two and two make four. (For example, he discovers that the home is important as the place for the internal activities of the family; or that wage earners' wives who go out to work have more acquaintances than those who stay at home.) Thus the institutions and relationships which are investigated—these are characteristically small-scale, mainly primary

---

[10] Sympathy for, and the prominence of, such studies in the British social sciences are far greater than is so far evident in published work (in 1955). Though there are as yet not many studies of this kind, they are a high proportion of the total, rather small, number of recent and current sociological research projects in Britain.

groups such as family, kinship, neighbourhood—may well have an urban background, but it is hardly visible. There is usually no theoretical background either: the striving for "scientific" purity has so far led to a plain piecemeal empiricism, barely disguised by some odd, *ad hoc* "hypotheses". The objects studied are so segmented that they can give no clue to social change, in terms of class and political alignments, for example. And they are observed in so intensive a fashion that the investigator himself needs to have no notion of social change, nor any commitments to value judgments and social theory: his families, for instance, are individuals, not representatives of social groups. As such, they are the most elusive of all objects of social study; as the research worker can never know enough about them, he cannot be expected to make generalizations. (A book about the Jones family is bound to be more inconclusive than one about the trade union to which Mr. Jones belongs.) Hence, though this approach to social research is apparently detached from politics and policy, it frequently serves as an apologia for the *status quo*, or results in nostalgia for an unhistoric past, despite the authors' insistence on the "dynamics" of social roles and situations.

It is not surprising, of course, that here, as in other branches of sociology, the British tradition of policy-oriented social investigation has weakened. As acute poverty has become less visible, the more subtle aspects of the social universe invite attention. In a period, moreover, in which both social conflicts and social consciousness have become increasingly acute, which is too sophisticated to share the previous confidence in the efficacy of administrative cures for social ills, and which sees the spectacular rise in the status and power of science and technology—to name only a few of the obvious reasons—sociology is in a dilemma. It can either become political or "scientific"; it can actively participate in social change or, remaining neutral, support conditions as they are and as they happen to develop. The second course is clearly the less harassing one—socially and intellectually. Thus the drift towards conformity exists in sociology as elsewhere in society. In sociology it has led to a distinction between technical assistance given to social policies as we find them, on the one hand, and "disinterested" research, on the other.

But this trend, together with the increasing, often legitimate specialization of the social sciences, does not wholly explain the current lack of interest in the broad canvas of urbanism. Nor is this lack of interest due to the fact that urbanism is now taken so much for granted that it is the study of particular aspects—in the fields of demography, criminology and social medicine, for example— which is appropriate, rather than research leading to a typology of urban settlements and "ways of life". On the contrary, Britain has not yet come to terms with her towns. And it is this fact which supplies the missing link in probing the reasons for the recent deficiency of urban social studies in this country. Two factors have been mainly responsible for it: the discontinuation of the Booth tradition of social inquiry, coupled with the continuation of the British tradition of anti-urbanism.

ANTI-URBANISM

British anti-urbanism has a long history. A large anthology could be devoted to writings on this subject, and an extensive treatise to comment and explanation. When we read the history of Roman Britain and that of Victorian England, we find that during the centuries the attitude of Britons towards the town has hardly changed. Collingwood, writing of the first to fourth centuries, describes the contrast between the Graeco-Roman and the British concept of the town. "Deep in the mind of every Roman, as in the mind of every Greek, was the unquestioned conviction which Aristotle put into words: that what raised man above the level of barbarism, in which he was a merely economic being, and enabled him to develop the higher faculties which in the barbarian are only latent, to live well instead of merely living, was his membership of an actual, physical city. Man's body and animal existence might be satisfied by the country; his spiritual needs could only be satisfied by the town." But "for the northern peoples, public life needs no town. Its elements already exist in every man's household; and its higher forms crystallize into shape round a tree or a stone where men meet together, and culminate in the court of a king who lives nomadically from manor to manor". Northern men were "conceiving the towns as a mere economic fact, a place where man only makes a livelihood and finding room for the development of his higher faculties only in the country".[11] Already by the third century it was evident that "the first attempt to romanize British life, by imposing upon it the civilization of the town, had failed. It was when its failure was most complete that the second attempt, based on the spontaneous development of the country house, began to display its most brilliant successes".[12]

During the new urban colonization of the nineteenth century, there was the same failure to accept the concept of urban civilization, as summed up brilliantly by G. M. Young. "In correspondence with its traditional structure, the traditional culture and morality of England were based on the patriarchal village family of all degrees: the father worked, the mother saw to the house, the food and the clothes; from the parents the children learnt the crafts and industries necessary for their livelihood, and on Sundays they went together, great and small, to worship in the village church. To this picture English sentiment clung. . . . It inspired our poetry; it controlled our art; for long it obstructed, perhaps it still obstructs, the formation of a true philosophy of urban life."[13]

Even now this anti-urbanism is unabated; indeed, it gained new impetus during the nineteenth century. The rising urban middle class fused with the landed gentry and aristocracy and emulated their modes of living. And for the maintenance of the balance of power in society this fusion was all to the good. For that reason it was welcomed by Escott, that shrewd observer of the

---

[11] R. G. Collingwood and J. N. L. Myres, *Roman Britain and the English Settlements*, Oxford, Clarendon Press, 1936, pp. 186–7.

[12] *Ibid.*, p. 207.

[13] G. M. Young, *Victorian England: Portrait of an Age*, Oxford, Oxford University Press, 1936, pp. 21–22.

Victorian scene. "The fact that the great country landlord is also, in many cases, the great proprietor of mines and factories, is at once a guarantee, and a sign of the fusion between the different elements of English life, and the diverse sources of our national power."[14] And again: "There are typical country gentlemen in the House of Commons and in society, but the country interest is no longer the sworn enemy of the urban interest. Our territorial nobles, our squires, our rural landlords great and small, have become commercial potentates; our merchant princes have become country gentlemen. The possession of land is the guarantee of respectability, and the love of respectability and land is inveterate in our race".[15]

Not all, of course, regarded the fact that the upper classes were mere parasites in the towns with approval and equanimity. Should they be allowed to abandon their own creations—these new "whirlpools" and "monster clots of humanity", where "the working man is pacing wearily the low, dim, swampy habitation good enough for the creation of all wealth"?[16] Should they not admit their responsibility for the sufferings of the urban poor who had made them rich, instead of letting children with "their grandfathers or grandmothers huddle and die in the same miserable dustbins"?[17] Several decades before Escott's hey-day, such views were frequently expressed with differing degrees of indignation, for instance, by Dr. Kay, in 1832, in reporting on his investigations in Manchester. "That the evils of poverty and pestilence among the working classes of the close alleys, the crowded courts, the overpeopled habitations of wretchedness, where pauperism and disease congregate round the source of social discontent and political disorder in the centre of our large towns" —"that these evils should have been overlooked by the aristocracy of the country, cannot excite surprise. Very few of their

---

[14] T. H. S. Escott, *England*, etc., 1885, p. 79.

[15] *Ibid.*, p. 315.

[16] Ernest Jones, De Brassier, a democratic romance, *Notes to the People*, vol. I, 1851, p. 242.

[17] Y. Hollingshead, *Ragged London in 1861*, pp. 72–73.

order reside in, or near our large provincial towns. . . . Their parks are not often traversed by those who are capable of being the exponents of the evils endured by the working classes of large towns, and the hoarse voice of popular discontent disturbs not the Arcadian stillness of the scene. . . ."[18] Again, a contributor to the *Quarterly Review*, in commenting on the social protest literature, made a rather moderate complaint. There were many, he said, who "withhold the co-operation which we might expect from their humanity, and which their wealth and intelligence would render highly important and efficient. Many of the wealthier classes treat their periodical visits to London as a mere episode in their existence, and regard their country homes as the allotted scene of their duties."[19]

The country house certainly remained the symbol of social success, "an important point of convergence between society and politics", the centre of the cultural life of a carefully assembled *élite*, though not of a closed clique. "It was said by Moore, the poet, that there was no receipt for taming a radical like an invitation to Bowood."[20] In most parts of Britain, the town was but a station on the journey to social status symbolized by the country seat.[21] It was not, as in other societies, the home of reason, intellect and a symbol of civic pride, but merely a place of new resources for the impoverished landed upper classes, and one where manufacturers and merchants could make money to buy their tickets of admission into the polite circle of the shires. And if the peerage and squirarchy were inaccessible, there were still their many imitations all down the social scale: those who could not reach the manor house could always retreat to the stronghold of a suburban villa, or at least to a semi-detached, jerry-built, mock-Tudor *Mon-repos*.

---

[18] J. P. Kay, *The Moral and Physical Condition of the Working Classes employed in the Cotton Manufacture in Manchester, 1832*, p. 8.

[19] Anon., The Charities of London, etc., *Quarterly Review*, September 1855.

[20] Escott, *op. cit.*, pp. 341–2.

[21] There are, of course, exceptions—in Scotland, for example—which it would be well worth while to study closely.

Retreat appeared certainly to be advisable. Those who left the towns went in search of safety as much as for the sake of social advancement, though their exodus brought to the towns themselves increasing misery and accelerated decay. Throughout the nineteenth century, the towns, the domain of the new industrial might, while growing in confusion, become more hideous and more unhealthy—physically and socially. Above all, they represented a formidable threat to the established social order: the more the towns were deserted by the upper and middle classes, the more plainly were they also the barracks of a vast working class whose lessons in the power of combination had already begun, and whose sporadic riots were portents of latent insurrection. The industrial town was thus identified with the working class: it was feared so strongly because the working class was so frightening. This was the persistent theme of Victorian literature as of Victorian movements for social reform. Superimposed upon a tradition according to which the individual home —humble or distinguished—is the castle, the country seat the symbol of social status, the countryside—idealized though occasionally real—the inspiration for emotion and the arts, and the town a mere place for earning money, the memory of this fear has continued to be a reason for British animosity against urbanism.

The Victorians expressed their anxiety in unmistakable terms. Cooke Taylor in his *Notes of a Tour in the Manufacturing Districts of Lancashire* in 1842 had this to say of Manchester: "As a stranger passes through the masses of human beings which have been accumulated round the mills and print-works in this and the neighbouring towns, he cannot contemplate those 'crowded hives' without feelings of anxiety and apprehension almost amounting to dismay. The population . . . is hourly increasing in breadth and strength. It is an aggregate of masses, our conceptions of which clothe themselves in terms that express something portentous and fearful. We speak of them . . . as of the slow rising and gradual swelling of an ocean which must, at some future and no distant time, bear all the elements of society aloft upon its bosom, and float them—Heaven knows whither. There are mighty energies slumbering in those masses."[22] Over sixty years later, Masterman, writing on the growth of cities, used similar expressions. "To some observers the change excites only a lament over a past that is for ever gone. They mourn the vanishing of a vigorous jolly life, the songs of the village alehouse, existence encompassed by natural things and the memories of the dead—the secure and confident life of 'Merrie England'. To others, again, the change is one charged with a menace to the future. They dread the fermenting, in the populous cities, of some new, all-powerful explosive, destined one day to shatter into ruin all their desirable social order. In these massed millions of an obscure life, but dimly understood and ever increasing in magnitude, they behold a danger to security and all pleasant things."[23]

Throughout the nineteenth century, this apparent danger was intensified not only by the flight from the cities, but also by the increasing separation of the social classes within cities. The middle and upper classes who did not leave the towns altogether, at least locked themselves up in separate quarters of their own. By doing so, they not only accentuated the actual social cleavages, but also their own fear of the other "nation": they were left with a distorted image of the poor. It was Cooke Taylor again who saw these implications of class segregation quite early and very clearly. "Another evil of fearful magnitude arises from this separation of Manchester into districts in which relative poverty and wealth form the demarcation of the frontiers. The rich lose sight of the poor, or only recognize them when attention is forced to their existence by their appearance as vagrants, mendicants, or delinquents."[24]

Though the fear of the working class persisted, it became less acute during the last two decades of the nineteenth century. By that time, in some quarters at least, imagination was already dulled: there had been so many false alarms. The heterogeneity

---

[22] W. Cooke Taylor, p. 6.

[23] C. F. Masterman, *The English City*, 1904, p. 61.

[24] Taylor, *op. cit.*, p. 14.

of the British working class was discovered and encouraged. "This diversity of thought, belief, and aim among the toilers of England is at once the consequence and the cause of exceptional national advantages." Thus Escott could say: "We have faith in the good sense, the good feeling, and the political docility of the English working man."[25]

The chain reaction of social imitation, moreover, had already started. The working classes themselves began to join the exodus from the cities, partly out of choice, and partly because they were compelled to do so as their homes crumbled around them and their standards rose. Suburbia tamed their radicalism. When Masterman in 1909 asked why London, unlike other European capitals, had not produced any revolutionary programmes, he saw a partial answer, at least, "hidden in these strings and congestions of little comfortable two-storeyed red and grey cottages . . . proclaiming with their cleanliness and tiny gardens and modest air of comfort a working population prosperous and content."[26] And while Masterman himself realized that his spectacles were perhaps too rosy and too much focused on London as compared with the industrial north—he also felt it still necessary to say that " 'poverty' is the foundation of the present industrial order"—he had nevertheless quite correctly recognized a new trend.

It is one which the utopians and community reformers of the nineteenth century would regard with mixed feelings. Though their dreams have not been realized, their ideas—modified and distorted in compromise—have gained belated importance. The actual flight from the cities was and is not as complete nor as radical as they would have wished, for on such a scale it is impracticable. Ideologically, however, the flight goes on all around us: all strata of society take an active part in it, and since the turn of the century none of them has spoken plainly against it.

Robert Owen, James Silk Buckingham, J. Minter Morgan, the Reverend Henry Solly, William Morris and Ebenezer Howard

---

[25] Escott, *op. cit.*, pp. 79–80 and 130.
[26] C. F. G. Masterman, *The Condition of England*, 1909, p. 100.

had all felt the menace of the towns. And so had the founders of model communities—of Saltaire, Bournville and Port Sunlight, to name only the most prominent ones, apart from the creations of the utopians themselves. They all thought, like Solly, that "the remedy, unquestionably, seems to be to turn back the tide from the town to the country by finding these folks [the working classes] employment, profitable to themselves and the community, where they can be decently housed and fairly well remunerated"[27]— and where they could, moreover, be under the close supervision of a paternalistic employer. Though these reformers believed that "certainly the reluctance of debased, or spirit-broken, hapless victims of an un-Christian civilization to exchange darkness for light, will have to be reckoned with",[28] they all had an indomitable confidence in the influence of environment on human character. Robert Owen, in writing on the New Lanaik Establishment, predicted that, if its principles were "generally adopted, the consequences will be, that not only our manufacturing but our entire population will gradually change its character".[29] And J. Minter Morgan, in advocating *The Christian Commonwealth*, expressed surprise because "no modern Government seems to have perceived that men are as clay in the potter's hand".[30] These schemes, the "New Institution", model towns, Christian colonies, industrial villages and garden cities, were all supposed to combine the best of both worlds—the past and the present, individualism and socialism, town and country. In fact, they were based on unhistorical fiction, and likely to combine the worst of both worlds, being neither. They were certainly regarded as the antidote to harsh social change, as "a peaceful path to real reform".

Another movement at the end of the century—that of the university settlements—had the object of combining "the latent power in the masses" with "the latent knowledge and the latent

---

[27] H. Solly, *Rehousing of the Industrial Classes*, etc., 1884, pp. 8–9.

[28] *Ibid.*, p. 7.

[29] Robert Owen, *A Statement regarding the New Lanark Establishment,* 1812, p. 22.

[30] J. Minter Morgan, *The Christian Commonwealth*, 1850, p. ix.

ability in the men and women of culture".[31] It was the dominant idea of the "Oxford settlers" in the East End "to give the poorest and most densely populated working-class districts the benefit of a resident gentry such as, in the clergyman or the squire, is generally commanded in rural parishes". While the authors of the utopias and community experiments had advocated the dispersal of working men to model villages under the aegis of their "masters" as a means of dispelling the danger of working class combination, the new "squires of the East End"—more realistically—were trying to meet the same danger by the dispersal of the "classes" among the masses in the cities. It was their ambition to become not only the social, but also the political leaders of the workers, and this was one which they have occasionally realized. They felt, as Canon Barnett said, in 1895, in his contribution to a symposium on the settlements in East London: "The two nations, that of the rich and that of the poor, are very evident. Each grows strong, and the danger of collision is the great danger of our time."[32] This danger, as Sir John Gorst explained in his introduction to the same book, could be averted. "If the people had wise counsellors whom they trusted, the trade unionists would gladly accept their co-operation, and take their views into consideration, and the selfish agitators would probably disappear. Such a position University men and women settled amongst the poor have every prospect of attaining . . . they have better chances than their poorer neighbours of arriving at a right judgment; and their advice, when the confidence of the people is gained, is likely to be sought and followed."[33]

In the settlement movement, too—both in Britain and America—there was the same tendency as in the other schemes for community reform to break up the large urban aggregates, not only by the infiltration of the upper classes among the lower, but also by the return to the comfort of the face-to-face group—the neighbourhood. Chalmers' "principle of locality", formulated in

---

[31] Y. M. Knapp, ed., *The Universities and the Social Problem*, etc., 1895, p. 15.
[32] *Ibid.*, p. 55.
[33] *Ibid.*, pp. 16, 17.

the 1820's, was once again accepted—his scheme for splitting up "the vast overgrown city" into separate parochial units so as to prevent the people "forming into a combined array of hostile feeling and prejudice".[34]

These ideas again, though perhaps not of great practical success in the settlements themselves, have become influential in other fields. In current town planning—as shown, for instance, by the emphasis on decentralization, low density development, new towns and neighbourhood units—the thought of the utopias and their relatives, such as model communities and university settlements, is still very much alive. Indeed, the mixture is as before; only the container—the language—is different. And as there has been no new genesis of ideas, this is hardly surprising. Twentieth-century Britain has not only inherited but also re-experienced the distaste for towns.

In sociology, the influence of anti-urban thought has been less direct than in town planning. Here, it has had mainly negative results ever since the close association between sociology and social policy, which inevitably drew the attention of investigators to urban social ecology and pathology, was dissolved. Since that time, just as British society has rejected the town as an object of affection, British sociology has rejected the town as an object of inquiry. Nowadays, British sociologists are concerned with odd corners, but hardly with the general contours, of urbanism.

It is unlikely to be a mere coincidence that the small-scale phenomena with which sociologists are now frequently concerned are precisely those which play so large a part in the make-up of British anti-urbanism, and also in its schemes and literature. Sociologists certainly share the nostalgia for the intimate, apparently discrete groups—the family, kinship and neighbourhood. They, too, find comfort in the collection of bric-à-brac.

Such interests, however, exist in other countries as well. The absence of any general British texts on urbanism, on the other

---

[34] T. Chalmers, *The Christian and Civic Economy of Large Towns*, 3 vols., 1821–6, vol. II, pp. 39–40.

hand, is undoubtedly in keeping with the native dislike of towns. It remains a characteristic feature of British sociological literature, even if allowance is made—as it should be made—for the general scarcity of resources for social research in this country, and also for the shortage of adequate source material.[35] As in Britain, especially, the stereotype images of urbanism—picturing the city as a soulless, frigid, menacing aggregate of people and buildings— have been retained, the diversity of habitat and society hidden behind these images has rarely been explored. Instead, social investigators, conditioned by such fixed ideas, have turned their attention increasingly to the trivial aspects of urbanism. And so the stereotypes persist.

Recently, this vicious circle has become very noticeable. The few, isolated attempts to view the urban social scene in wide perspective belong to the Victorian and Edwardian eras. Since the thirties, especially, there has been a total lack of comparative studies devoted to the characteristics of towns, to their diversity and changes. Neither their demographic and historical traits, nor their class relations, economy and culture have been systematically investigated; these aspects have not even been broadly mapped out. Indeed, in Britain, the most urbanized country in the world, we know so little about our contemporary towns— largely, it appears, because here they have not yet been accepted.

---

[35] The conclusions here reached were derived not only from a review of published studies, but also from information on current and projected research. However, in considering these conclusions, the lack of opportunities for social research in Britain—compared, for example, with the United States—should be kept in mind, and also the fact that basic data—historical, statistical and geographical—on urbanism in Britain are comparatively meagre and certainly rather scattered and patchy.

The Popularity of the
Neighbourhood Community Idea

N. Dennis

Editor's Note
   The notion of "community" is at the heart of many people's conception of the field of urban sociology. Norman Dennis probes the tacit assumptions and ideologies of practitioners in the field and points out what a sociological theory of the community is not. He could, perhaps, be criticized for neglecting the analysis of community power and for a lack of sympathy with, for example, religious institutions in the locality. However, his article remains an important contribution to the discussion.

IN THE vocabulary of the social scientist and the social worker there must be few words used with either the frequency or looseness of "the community". It is one of those terms which, as Le Bon said, are uttered with solemnity, and as soon as they are pronounced an expression of respect is visible on every countenance, and all heads are bowed. The following uses of the term can be distinguished, though they are not mutually exclusive.

"The community" may denote merely the houses and people located in a given area, even where there are few relationships of any kind, whether institutionalized or informal, manifest or latent.[1] The area referred to will usually be roughly comparable

---

[1] The distinction between "manifest" and "latent" relationships among the inhabitants of the same area is that drawn by Peter Mann in his article The Concept of Neighbourliness, *American Journal of Sociology*, vol. 60, no. 2 (September 1954), p. 164. "Manifest neighbourliness" is that which takes the form of overt behaviour—visiting each other, going out together for purposes of pleasure, and so on; "latent neighbourliness" refers to favourable attitudes which will result in manifest neighbourliness when the need arises, especially in times of crisis. Such a distinction is not, of course, new. It resembles, for instance, Hobhouse's "scale" and "efficiency" on the one hand, and "mutuality" and "freedom" on the other; it is almost identical with Homans's distinction between the "interaction and activity" and "sentiment" aspects of social relationships.

in size to a village. It will have people and dwellings in numbers which in the past have indeed entailed other social characteristics. People seem to find it extraordinarily difficult to realize that mere living together in the same locality can result in a conglomeration of very little sociological importance. The difficulty is immeasurably increased, apparently, when the people in the locality are sociologically homogeneous; and yet, clearly, more than mere aggregation is needed to make a group, however homogeneous the aggregate may be.

In text books the term often means "an area which contains all or most of the elements of a complete social system"—political, economic, religious, educational, scientific, artistic, ideological, hierarchical, and so on. MacIver, while he also emphasizes the idea of shared manners, traditions, and modes of speech, puts at the forefront of the concept of community as he uses it this idea of the total social system or a microcosm of it. "A community is a social unity whose members recognize as common a sufficiency of interests to allow of the interactivities of common life. . . . The completest type of community is the nation."[2] "Community is the greater common life out of which associations arise, into which associations bring order, but which associations never completely fulfil."[3] "Community life is the whole incalculable system of relations."[4] Ogburn and Nimkoff refer to the concept in similar terms: "the locality group or community . . . may be thought of as the total organisation of social life within a limited area. Human social life is characteristically carried on in such communities. They are the loci of group activity, of institutional organisation, and the development of human personality."[5] Writers not specifically sociological often speak of community in the same way. Amos Hawley, for instance, writes that he will use the term to refer to an "area the resident population of which is

---

[2] R. M. MacIver, *Community*, 3rd edition, 1924, pp. 109–10.

[3] *Ibid.*, p. 24.

[4] *Ibid.*, pp. 128–9.

[5] W. F. Ogburn and M. F. Nimkoff, *A Handbook of Sociology*, 3rd edition, 1953, p. 269.

interrelated and integrated with reference to its daily requirements whether contact is direct or indirect."[6] Elsewhere he writes
that "the community includes the area, the population of which,
however widely distributed, regularly turns to a common centre
for the satisfaction of all or part of its needs."[7] Hawley is thus going
even further than the sociologists quoted in stressing the idea of the
society in miniature, underplaying in doing so the idea of both
interpersonal contact and limitations on area.

Others reserve the term for situations in which there is present
a common opinion on topics of common interest. This is what
Thomas and Znaniecki call "the effectively organized community." It is the idea of community which is basic to "community development" in "disorganized areas". Community in
this sense involves a common culture; it also involves the idea of
autonomous social control—control which the inhabitants of the
same area exercise over one another.[8] Places differ widely in the
range of topics in which there is a shared interest, and even more
widely in the degree of consensus in relation to them; but the
broader the range of common topics in an area and the more
intense the degree of agreement (or at least of harmony), the more
community-like they would be designated by this definition.

There is finally the idea of community as involving interaction
of a certain degree and quality.[9] A place is thought to be the more

[6] A. Hawley, *Human Ecology*, 1950, pp. 257–8.

[7] *Ibid.*, p. 246.

[8] See, for example, C. R. Shaw and H. D. McKay, *Juvenile Delinquency and
Urban Areas*, 1942, p. 444. An urban locality is thought to merit the designation
"community" if there is solidarity and unity of sentiment. When this unity of
sentiment is not present, then the aim must be to generate it by work on common objectives.

[9] Tönnies himself emphasizes the quality of relationship in his concept of
Gemeinschaft. He does not, however, link it at all closely to the local area.
"Wherever human beings are related through their wills in an organic manner
and affirm each other, we find *Gemeinschaft* . . . only as long as these phenomena,
that is, mutual furtherance and affirmation, predominate, can a relation really
be considered *Gemeinschaft* . . ." *Community and Association*, first published 1887,
trans. Loomis, 1955, pp. 49–50. The three types of community he isolates are:
the community of blood (kinship); the community of place (neighbourhood);
and the community of mind (friendship). The two sets of ideas—that of the

community-like the more that people who live near one another mix with one another—"community is said to exist only when patterns of primary relationships exist within a residential context."[10] It is the decline of community in this sense which has been at the centre of interest in many of the studies of municipal housing estates in this country; it is certainly the idea of community which has received most popular attention.[11]

This paper will be concerned with the idea of community as it is applied to modern urban neighbourhoods—especially municipal housing estates. How far is it *desirable* that these areas should be made into "communities" in any of the above senses? Insofar as one or the other may be to some extent desirable how far is it *practicable* to foster it to that extent? The most interesting question, however, is: Why should the idea of the neighbourhood community be so much more popular than a realistic appraisal of the idea would lead one to expect?

Sociologists have already disagreed over the importance to be attached to research in urban localities. Some argue that the character of the residential locality is of little significance in the understanding of behaviour. From this point of view, studies of localities merely reveal an interest in finding "comfort in the collection of bric-à-brac". Instead of looking at "all the trivial aspects of 'living together', " sociologists ought to be studying "the community of ideas, and of broad social groups (like classes, political parties, trade unions, and other organizations based on common interests) . . ."[12] On the other hand there are two schools of thought which emphasize the importance of the neighbourhood.

---

locality, and that of community-type relationships—are of course linked in all sorts of ways. As Tönnies argues, locality plays a part in community in his sense of the term in two ways. It helps give rise to community—to an important degree in the case of neighbourhood, and to a lesser degree in the case of the other two types. Secondly, community seeks to reinforce and fulfil itself by means of common residence—this is the third of the three "great laws of *Gemeinschaft*", that those who love and understand one another remain and dwell together and organize their common life (*ibid.* p. 55).

[10] A. J. Reiss, Jnr., *A Review and Evaluation of Research on Community*, 1954.

[11] See, for example, Mann's approach in the article cited.

[12] R. Glass, *Current Sociology*, vol. iv, no. 4, 1955, pp. 19 and 64.

One points to particular areas in which markedly separate cultures do in fact exist, and which therefore exercise an influence over anyone coming within their orbit for a sufficiently long time.[13] The other points to the absence of culture altogether, and advocates the fostering of distinctive local communities;[14] the ideas of this school form the subject matter of the present discussion.

Interest in the idea of neighbourhood social cohesion has come from all sides. In religion the emphasis has ranged from the problem of *anomie* as a characteristic of our society as a whole, to the particular problem of the absence of neighbourhood solidarity.[15] In administration the interest has revolved round the conception of the Neighbourhood Unit and the New Town.[16] It is only since 1945 however, that social scientists in England have turned their attention in any large degree on the problem. An Institute of Community Studies has been founded, concerned mainly with primary-group contacts in particular localities. Other sociologists have carried out detailed studies of neighbourhoods at Coventry, Liverpool, Sheffield, and Oxford.[17] Psycho-

---

[13] J. B. Mays, *Growing up in the City*, 1954; N. Dennis, F. Henriques, C. Slaughter, *Coal is our Life*, 1956.

[14] As far as modern sociological thought is concerned the emphasis on the evils of *anomie* and isolation can be attributed mainly to Durkheim. He himself, however, insisted that the locality could not be regarded as the place in which a remedy for these evils could be applied. "The provincial spirit has disappeared never to return: the patriotism of the parish is an archaism that cannot be restored at will." *The Division of Labour in Society*, Glencoe, 1947, p. 27. See K. Popper's comment on Plato's thoughts on this subject, in *The Open Society and its Enemies*, 1945, vol. I, p. 150. For a representative modern statement of the same view, see E. Mayo, *The Human Problems of an Industrial Civilisation*, 1933.

[15] "The old signposts have gone and new and wider roads open in various directions. On all sides puzzled men and women hear the clamour of self-appointed guides who are really as baffled and ignorant as themselves. 'Whirl is king, having driven out Zeus.'" C. Garbett, *In an Age of Revolution*, Penguin, 1956, p. 75. See also e.g. William Booth, *In Darkest England and the Way Out*, 1890, pp. 233 ff.

[16] E.g. L. Wolfe, *The Reilly Plan: a new way of life*, 1945; C. B. Fawcett, *A Residential Unit for Town and Country Planning*, 1945.

[17] M. Young and P. Willmott, *Family and Kinship in East London*, 1957; L. Kuper and others, *Living in Towns*, 1953; G. D. Mitchell and others, *Neighbourhood and Community*, 1954; J. M. Mogey, *Family and Neighbourhood*, 1956.

logists have been taking into consideration "sociological facts" in their work, often heavily weighted with the idea of the "community", by which they mean the social character of the neighbourhood.[18] In addition, there have been studies which lay stress on neighbourhood factors in the aetiology of particular phenomena.[19]

Finally, there are the numerous philanthropic writings connected with this idea. There is the model-communities literature (which emphasizes physical at least as much as social and psychological advantages).[20] There are in addition those philanthropic suggestions which are concerned with existing urban neighbourhoods. The theme throughout is that it is necessary to make them into close-knit communities. The model of the close-knit community is either the rural village, or a certain idea of what working-class life in the centres of towns is like at present or was like at some (usually unspecified) time in the past. "Self-containedness . . . has encouraged much intermarrying, and there is a strong tradition of family parties. . . . Street parties to which everyone must contribute are also part of the tradition. These bring out a strong sense of *esprit de corps*—they are primitive orgies—with, very often, few repressions. . . . Such a wide family circle and neighbourhood acquaintance not only provide assistance and support . . . but also exert a powerful immediate pressure of public opinion in favour of traditional *mores*. . . . Has the time not

---

[18] L. J. Halliday, *Psycho-social Medicine: a study of a sick society*, 1948.

[19] D. H. Stott, for example, gives as two of his four reasons for unsettlement and delinquency the fact that: (i) ". . . there would appear to be something deleterious not in urban industralism itself, but in the breaking of the discipline and traditions of a settled community . . . among those with whom they have been brought up, people know where they stand; they are relieved of the strain of uncertainty about the reception and treatment they will meet from their neighbours. . . . From habit also, they respect the opinion of neighbours and relatives, whom they know are keeping an eye on their standards of conduct . . ."; (ii) delinquent neighbourhoods provide a social atmosphere of laxity, indifference, and suggestion, which renders a delinquent solution to anxiety and lack of fulfilment easier. *Unsettled Children and their Families*, 1956, pp. 175–6 and pp. 180–1. See also P. Sainsbury, Society and Suicide, *Howard Journal*, vol. 9, no. 3, 1956, and his *Suicide in London*.

[20] See R. Glass, *op. cit.*

come for a conscious reorientation of social policy at the highest
level, so that administration and legislation should become more
responsive to the claims of the family, including the desirability
of permanent neighbourhoods?"[21] How realistic and desirable are
such suggestions when made in relation to housing estates on the
outskirts of towns and cities? Is the fostering of "neighbourhood
communities" a sensible policy?

What of the "locality community" in the sense of a microcosmic social system? Though this has been a reality in towns in
the past, social-system local communities of even a rudimentary
sort are now the exception. Urban localities, and to a lesser extent
other types of settlement too, have been progressively deprived of
their social-system characteristics. Particular activities have been
transferred to special areas. The typical city presents a picture of
geographical specialization. The form and content of those activities which remain in the residential locality, generally speaking,
are progressively less locality-determined. Educational and industrial decision become increasingly centralized. Shops are managed
by people who administer policies decided elsewhere, with very
little reference to the locality as such. The same is true of the field
of local politics. Some activities remain in the locality. Education
is the prime example. Shops of a certain sort is another. Some
leisure facilities provide a third: leisure facilities for special groups,
who for one reason or another do not go further afield—old
people, youths, and home-tied wives. Some social services operate
in the locality: home visiting, some parts of the health service and
so on. But each of these remains attached to the bottom of its own
encapsulated hierarchy, and is neither individually autonomous,
nor linked in any organic way to other institutions at this level.
Furthermore, the persons who operate these institutions—shops,
schools, social services, leisure facilities—rarely themselves reside
in the district. What is true as a general tendency in the case of
all urban localities today, as "communities" in the "social-

---

[21] National Conference on Social Work, *Conference Papers: The Family*, 1953,
pp. 2–3.

system" sense, has always been true of housing estates. They were from the beginning archetypes of the "not-community", being areas in which only the activities of residence, internal family life, education, certain types of shopping, and limited kinds of leisure, typically take place.[22]

Is it possible to resurrect the locality community in this sense— to restore to it a comprehensive array of services and institutions? It has been argued by others that it would now be possible to have the advantages both of a "compacted" social environment *and* of the efficiency of specialized agencies. It is said that industry can now be located in residential areas without noxious consequences, and that large numbers of people can be congenially crowded together in a small living area, as a result of modern building techniques. It may be now technically possible for existing neighbourhoods to be revivified by industrial admixture without losses in industrial efficiency. But the limits of this movement would be in all cases very closely circumscribed; and it can be expected that it will be more closely circumscribed in housing estates than elsewhere, in view of the fact that housing estates have a very small catchment area, being as they are on the urban periphery.

Another example of the range of considerations which ought to enter into discussions of self-contained urban localities is provided by the problem of "locality government" on housing estates. There exists in some housing estates bodies called "Community Councils" or "Joint Councils". Their function is to foster the

---

[22] They were deliberately given this character, mainly as a reaction against the state of affairs they replaced—in particular as a reaction against the mixture of industry and housing. " 'Down in the Marsh' brings us to a gloomy vale enshrouded in almost perpetual smoke—this site of a vast rubbish heap to which for many years have been brought the litter and lumber scavenged from all parts of the city—the chosen home of manure manufactories, bone-crushing mills, knacker yards, horseflesh boiling factories and works in which the manufacture of chemical products throws off nauseous gases. Who can wonder that the pulse of social life beats feebly in many of the homes of the poor in such a place, where the smut-thickened air seems enough to 'snuff out the mirth of their existence', or that strangers should liken it to a noisesome sewer to which has been brought the 'dregs and feculence of every land'?" Special Commissioner to the Bristol Mercury, *Homes of the Bristol Poor*, 1884, p. 51.

affiliation of "leaders of the community" (doctors, teachers, shop-keepers, representatives of voluntary organizations, clergymen, social workers), and more generally to make the estate more community-like. They are thought by their members to be capable of participating in a wide range of locality affairs. They are thought of in the way their name invites them to be thought of—as "community" councils. But because such a "wide range of locality affairs" simply does not exist, the discussions revolve endlessly and impotently around such topics as children's playgrounds and amenity spaces. A fruitful approach to this problem would involve discerning clearly which internal matters could reasonably become the responsibility of such a body and therefore "returned to the community". There would be a few only. It would also involve seeing quite clearly what would be necessary if some of these tasks are to be successfully carried out. The crux of the matter in most cases is that the co-operation of much more powerful outside bodies is required if anything is to be done at all. At present it is very much a matter of *noblesse oblige* if these bodies take any notice of the representations of Community Councils, beyond polite acknowledgment. Such Councils have been most successful when they have acted like an efficient pressure group, with the circularization of city councillors and threats of public agitation.

What of the "neighbourhood community" in its second sense—as "locality social intercourse"? Assuming that a higher level of locality social intercourse is desirable, is it feasible? It is quite clear that the first and overwhelmingly most important condition is the carrying on of activities which require the persons concerned to interact frequently. These activities may be going to school, working together, shopping, or just passing to and fro. It is when many of these activities overlap that the social-interaction community is most frequently found. The prime condition of the existence of the social-interaction community is the existence of the social-system community, and the feasibility of the former depends upon the feasibility of the latter. The conclusions reached in the discussion of the notion of the self-contained locality community therefore apply here.

To say that this is the necessary first condition, is not to say that it is a sufficient condition. There will be no social-interaction community without the social-system community, but a social-interaction community is not the invariable concomitant of the social-system community. It is quite possible to have people co-operating in a social system context without them coming into actual face-to-face contact. This is generally speaking the actual state of affairs today. One of the additional necessary conditions is the absence of strong status feelings, with its corollary, the presence of feelings of being roughly on a par with one's fellows—sharing the same life-risks and life-chances. Social intercourse is inhibited by level-consciousness, and fostered by class-consciousness. There is a contrast between the former working-class value of "keeping down with the Atkins'," and the state of affairs in new working-class housing areas today. As Young and Willmott argue, this can be explained partly by the fact that people in the new housing areas do not know one another. They must therefore compete on the basis of externals, and this competition in turn leads to paucity of social contact.

Another condition favouring social intercourse is the sharing of common experiences, and the common memories these engender—to have been to school together, to have worked in the same factory, been in the same job, supported the same football team, participated in the same strike. There is a big difference between, say, a typical housing estate, where the occupational structure may be almost as diverse as that of the country as a whole, and, for example, "Ashton", a place of the same size, where nearly 70 per cent of the occupied population fall into the same occupational group—coal mining. A typical housing estate can be contrasted with even certain quite large towns where common trade experiences and common employment under the same few large employers facilitate locality interaction and solidarity on a wide scale. The possibility of the accretion of a fund of shared memories is further lowered in housing estates by the fact that each generation is dispersed. Houses are allocated on the basis of a wide consideration housing need—overcrowding, physical amenities of existing premises, health requirements, etc.; the need to foster or conserve neighbourhood solidarity is only one need among these, and one which is not considered a very weighty one. It is this which has lead to the remark that the private landlord (who allows houses to be passed down through the generations) is the guardian of the spirit of the community.[23] While this condition of a shared history ought not to be ignored, it ought not to be given more notice than it deserves. It must be emphasized that common experiences do not happen in a vacuum, as the invariable and inevitable result of the passage of time alone. Common experiences cluster round shared activities. They depend to a large extent upon the existence of the prime condition dealt with already—the existence of the social-system community. If an area begins to lose its character of a social-system community, it may survive for some time as an interaction community, but it will be living on the residue of a passing situation. Those who live in the pious hope that it is only a matter of time before housing estates settle down and take on the appearance of the Bethnal Green stereotype are therefore probably mistaken. It would be more realistic to predict that in so far as housing estates represent that exaggerated result of processes which are common to our society, it is only a matter of time before our Bethnal Greens become socially indistinguishable from housing estates.

What of the "community" considered as "locality social control?" Under which conditions, within which limits, for which types of person, is neighbourhood social control desirable, assuming that it is possible? It is necessary to distinguish between the individual's general need for some (indefinite) degree of normative structuring to his life, and the quite separate issue of his need to have that structure provided by *locality* rules, and supported by *locality* sanctions. With regard to the general problem, very many studies have drawn attention to the toxic consequences of *anomie*—a state of affairs characterized by indefiniteness of expec-

---

[23] Young and Willmott, *op. cit.*

tations, and the necessity for the individual to make his own choices.[24]

How can one assess the desirability of (i) neighbourhood norms, (ii) neighbourhood control? The particular locality would have to be examined with a view to judging whether there do seem to be problems springing from the fact that people "don't know where they stand", and from the fact that social pressure from neighbours is absent. Such a judgment, however, would have to consider more than the facts of the locality, and more theories than those which relate certain pathological phenomena to "lack of law" and the absence of control. It is not enough to demonstrate that some anti-social acts and some personal breakdown can be attributed to neighbourhood *anomie*. It is also necessary

---

[24] The most influential expression of this view is contained in Durkheim's *Suicide*. Mayo, to whose work reference has already been made, attributes a wide range of symptoms to absence of social regulation. See for example his comments on "the alleged 'new freedom'", and the "so-called freedom" of modern society, which "withdraws from the individual a measure of . . . support which he is unable to do without". *Op. cit.*, pp. 128–9. Margaret Mead has popularized this view (perhaps unintentionally) by her account of Samoan society. E. Fromm argues that large-scale manifestations of authoritarianism, destructiveness, and automaton conformity are pathological reactions to the fact that while the individual's "freedom" from all traditional bonds has become more pronounced, his possibility for individual achievement has narrowed down (*The Fear of Freedom*, London, 1942, p. 106). K. Horney's theory of neurosis has as its ". . . dynamic centre . . . a basic conflict between the attitude of 'moving towards', 'moving against', and 'moving away from' people". The basic conflict in Horney's view lies in the anomic state of modern society. "The kind, scope, and intensity of such conflicts are largely determined by the civilisation in which we live . . . if the civilisation is in a stage of rapid transition, where highly contradictory values and divergent ways of life exist side by side the choices an individual has to make are manifold and difficult" (*Our Inner Conflicts*, London, 1946, p. 18 and p. 24). In its restricted meaning of "lack of limitation on ends" it plays a central part in Merton's theory of deviance. *Anomie* in contemporary society is a central preoccupation of Parsons. Numerous field studies have been designed to test the hypothesis that there exists such a relation between social disorganization and personal demoralization. Among psychiatrists who take an interest in social factors, *anomie* in the sense of the lack of rules to live by appears to be popular now as a possible explanation of mental illness—see, for example, J. C. Carothers, *Journal of Mental Science*, vol. 97, 1951, esp. p. 13; for a discussion of the psychiatric literature on the subject see E. H. Hare, The Ecology of Mental Disease, *ibid.*, vol. 98, 1952, pp. 579–93.

to remember the price which has to be paid for the structured, controlled situation in which these problems do not arise—control by "the mass of mediocre minds". If techniques were available which would enable politicians, psychiatrists, etc., to make neighbourhoods more like communities in this respect, it would have to be demonstrated at each stage that the advantage of the increase in neighbourhood norms and neighbourhood control outweighed the disadvantages—and, what is more, outweighed the dangers. In order to minimize the disadvantages and dangers, such techniques would have to be such as to develop not just any culture, but "desirable" culture.

Are such techniques available? How far is it possible to alter neighbourhoods in this respect?[25] The extent to which a person cares about those sanctions neighbours do or can impose on him is a difficult matter to test. People can share the same values, and yet derive these values from sources outside the locality (for instance, from work, from the mass media, and by using another class or class-image as a reference group), and respond to outside controls (exerted, for example, by the police force, by superiors and colleagues at work, by housing officials, by fellow-sectarians, etc.). However, certain general comments can be made. In the absence of activities and interaction, the number of goals and means to attain them—and these are the substance of a "culture" —will be small. There is a second point related to this. The informal means of social control which keep the villager and the small-town dweller in line—"forcing him into the wholesome strait-jacket of provincial conformity"[26]—do not have the same force in the larger town. Social control, to be successful, requires the consequences of a deviant act to ramify in various ways which are unpleasant for the actor. It is the overlapping of various social relationships, economic and other, which are at the basis of locality social control; the basis, that is, is the existence of a

---

[25] See C. R. Shaw and H. D. McKay, *op. cit.*, and M. Ross, *Community Organization*, 1956.

[26] S. Riemer, Villagers in Metropolis, *British Journal of Sociology*, vol. 2, no. 1, 1951.

social-system community. Thirdly, and most importantly, there is the fact that the pressure of the social control exerted by neighbours can be escaped in the large town. This may take the form of spending leisure-time and work-time away from the ostracizing locality; there is, in addition, the greater ease in the large town of moving away from the locality altogether, without moving into an entirely strange environment.

The outcome of the argument is that the usefulness of the idea of the neighbourhood community is not commensurate with the kind of popularity the discussion on page 78 shows it to enjoy. Such a disjuncture is typically the interest of *Wissensociologie*: Why should such an idea succeed in pushing itself into prominence in a particular society at a particular time?

The first reason which would help to explain its popularity is what might be called its "reality component". The point of view that the restoration of the locality community would diminish the volume of social problems of various kinds can be supported by reference to various studies. It is interesting to see that the benefits of locality interaction and solidarity—the feeling of belonging, and mutual enrichment—are now increasingly sought by well-to-do Americans, and not just prescribed as a good thing for despised neighbourhoods. Indeed, it appears that the ideas of the Chicago Area Project have been more successful in the Chicago suburb of Park Forest than they were in the Chicago problem areas.[27]

But in view of the extreme difficulties in the way of resuscitating local communities, and of the fact that ordinarily other desirable goals can be attained only at their expense, this reality factor is

---

[27] The existence of a widespread belief in the desirability of locality cohesion can go some way to overcoming structural obstacles. But from the point of view of social policy, "community" is no more feasible as an objective, because the problem remains of how to inculcate the desire. The question is shifted to ground at least as tricky as before: what conditions are necessary for the "other-directed" or "social" man? The structural requirements are not, in any case, entirely absent from Park Forest. The young managers live in a society which is close enough to allow *economic* sanctions to be applied to nonconformist activity.

too narrow a base to support the weight of writing in their favour. What, then, explains the belief in the locality community; what gives it "that flavour of ideological beatification?" Although answers to this can be no more than conjectures, some suggestions will be offered.[28]

People apparently experience very great difficulty in breaking away from the idea that a collection of houses must form a meaningful social unit. This naïve view may be called "Usherism" —the belief that bricks and mortar themselves are of sociological significance. In the romanticizing of community life, there is secondly the element of nostalgia. "To some observers the change (the disappearance of local communities) excites a lament over a past that is for ever gone. They mourn the vanishing of a vigorous jolly life, the songs of the village alehouse, existence encompassed by natural things, the memories of the dead—the secure and confident life of 'Merrie England'. "[29] The question is, of course, who does the romanticizing, and why?

Some of the reasons have been brought forward by Mrs. Glass by reference to the nineteenth-century literature on the question. The quotations below are among those to which she refers.[30] The Settlement Movement hoped to ". . . give to the poorest and most densely populated working-class districts the benefit of a resident gentry such as, in the clergyman and squire, is generally commanded in rural parishes. . . . If the people had wise counsellors whom they trusted, the trade unionists would gladly accept their co-operation . . . and the selfish agitators would probably disappear. . . ." What of the opposite movement—the dispersal to the periphery of urban areas of large portions of the English working-class? It is suggested here that one of its latent functions has been to contribute in a small way to the relative mildness of

---

[28] The growth in the popularity of "community" and of the concepts closely related to "community" is dealt with briefly by C. Wright Mills in The Professional Ideology of Social Pathologists, *American Journal of Sociology*, vol. 49, no. 2 (September 1943), especially in pp. 172–6.

[29] C. F. G. Masterman, *The English City*, no. 4, 1904, p. 61.

[30] R. Glass, *op. cit.*

class conflict in England. The necessity of coping with the dangerous masses of working people accumulating in the centres of the
cities is a theme which is constantly repeated. T. Chalmers insists
on the principle of "locality" as an instrument of both religious
and civic administration in towns. Through the general application of the local system, he argued, the unmanageable mass which
would otherwise form into one impetuous and overwhelming
surge against the reigning authority could be split up into frag-
ments. In passing through Manchester in 1842, W. Cooke Taylor
observed that a stranger could not "contemplate those 'crowded
hives' without feelings of anxiety and apprehension almost
amounting to dismay. . . . It is an aggregate of masses, our conceptions of which clothe themselves in terms that express something portentous and fearful. We speak of them . . . as of the slow
rising and gradual swelling of an ocean which must, at some future
and no distant time, bear all the elements of society aloft upon its
bosom, and float them—Heaven knows whither." Masterman
said substantially the same thing: "To some observers the change
excites a lament over a past that is for ever gone. . . . To others
again," he continues, "the change is charged with a menace for
the future. They dread the fermenting, in the populous cities, of
some new all-powerful explosive, destined one day to shatter into
ruin all the desirable social order. In these massed millions of an
obscure life, but dimly understood and ever increasing in magnitude, they behold a danger to security and all pleasant things."
These writers are not quoted for the purpose of revealing the
existence of some all-embracing, diabolically clever, and hitherto
concealed purpose in housing policy. It is to show that the idea of
dispersing the perishing and dangerous classes was at one time on
the surface, and presumably as an argument did originally have
some influence. The second reason for quoting them is more important. It is to show that fears of "the unmanageable mass" of an
"all-powerful explosive", do not now exist in this country, and to
infer that dispersal has played at any rate some part in bringing
this about. When practices and the beliefs which surround
them act as stabilizers in this way, they will tend to have a high

survival value, whether in their manifest form they are valid or not.[31]

Once a large proportion of the working-class population has become suburban, then attempts to make the separate residential estates into inward-looking communities, would, if successful, still further reduce the evil of class conflict. A potential trade union leader, or a potential member of the Communist Party, is obviously less threatening if he is engaged in Community Association activities instead. The constitutions of Community Associations rigorously exclude politics from the range of their interests. Though Community Associations played little part in the ordinary lives of the residents, they do occupy a good deal of the time of a high proportion of potential trouble-makers—the "committee-likers".[32] This is not the purpose of Community Associations. But because their latent function does contribute to the stability of society, the ideology of neighbourhood community which gives rise to it is not closely questioned, though its actual manifest content is highly questionable. The ideology of the neighbourhood community remains popular for a much longer time than experience itself would warrant. But for those who try to practise the doctrine, the disparity between their beliefs and their experience cannot last for ever. Community Association officials expend

---

[31] In sociologically more sophisticated times the device of splitting up potentially dangerous populations is clearly recognized and used. See L. Kuper, Techniques of Social Control in South Africa, *Listener*, May 31st, 1956. "Critics of the South African Government often say that it has no plan for race relations. . . . Nothing could be further from the truth . . . its techniques are most carefully planned, according to basic sociological principles. . . . The danger is in the numerical preponderance of the non-whites. It is a threat, however, only if the non-whites are united. . . . The Group Areas Act (1950) gives the Governor-General the necessary power to sub-divide Coloureds and Natives, but not whites. . . . If my interpretation is rejected, then we must assume that it is sheer accident that the government has . . . discriminated against the whites by withholding from (them) the privilege of communal living."

[32] The Bantu Authorities Act (1951) is designed in part to give the "committee-likers" in the different native tribes the chance to exercise their talents on internal tribal affairs without allowing them to become concerned with more general matters. L. Kuper, *op. cit.*

their efforts to attain the objective of making their neighbour-hood a friendly place in which to live, not in order to stabilize society in general. Therefore, when the manifest function is not fulfilled the Community Association officials become more and more disillusioned, and either abandon the enterprise, or console themselves with a self-indulgent martyrdom. There is little doubt that the Community Association movement as a device for making housing estates into communities is moribund. It is the old sad story over again—the Murder of a Beautiful Theory by a Gang of Brutal Facts.

The fourth of the ideological elements (as distinct from the rational element) in the popularity of the neighbourhood community idea is very much the most important. The locality-community idea implies fixing one's eyes on the part locality factors play in the aetiology of social and personal problems, and it presumes that these problems can be dealt with efficaciously by adjusting locality institutional forms and applying psychothera-peutic measures to persons who work and live in the problem locality. This is obviously not a very threatening thing to do. On first sight it does not present a challenge to any fundamental insti-tutions or established social beliefs. It does not appear to involve the examination of the contribution of more general social-structural and cultural factors. Certainly, any serious study of problems which happen to be concentrated in a locality is bound to lead to a study of extra-local explanations. But such studies are comparatively rare. Generally, the presumption that neighbour-hood causes and cures are of very great importance effectively stultifies the study. No great good is achieved; but neither are any powerful interests affected, nor are any important established beliefs questioned. It therefore remains an ideology which can attract research funds, and catch the ear of established opinion. It is a minor example of a "myth" in Sorel's sense—a social belief which is not necessarily invalid (though it is likely to be so to some extent) but which is believed for reasons other than its objective validity.

Finally, there are many political ideas and theories of human behaviour which constantly sustain the belief in the desirability of the neighbourhood community. Those political ideas and theories of human behaviour are themselves believed in as a result of a mixture of rational and ideological motives—the amount of rational content varying from theory to theory, and the amount of rational motive for belief varying from exponent to exponent. They form a reservoir of more or less widely accepted doctrine which can be drawn on when the neighbourhood-community tank becomes a little parched in the hard sunlight of the actual world. The political doctrines which are associated with the neighbourhood ideology are those which talk particularly of the inherent wisdom, harmony, and integrity, of the community. In the science of human behaviour, the neighbourhood ideology is fed by those schools which equate "maturity" etc. with competence in inter-personal relationships. All these views tend to be highly acceptable, because the reality component in each is reinforced by the fact that they can easily be used to justify the existing order of things, and to minimize the value of nonconformity; that is, they are amenable to the view that difference, conflict, and the desire for change, are essentially unrealistic and pathological phenomena.

Part II

Responses to Urbanism

Urbanism and Suburbanism
as Ways of Life

H. J. Gans

Social scientists have noted that variations in residence—city, suburb, small town, open country—tend to be associated with different patterns of behavior. The late Louis Wirth described urbanism as a way of life in a classic article published in 1938. Professor Gans now reviews Wirth's theory in the light of subsequent research. He argues that residence is less a source of variation in behavior than an index (not always useful) to other sources, that no single urban—or suburban—way of life can be identified, and that differences in ways of life between the big city and the suburb can be explained more adequately by the class and life-cycle variations of their respective inhabitants.

THE contemporary sociological conception of cities and of urban life is based largely on the work of the Chicago School, and its summary statement in Louis Wirth's essay Urbanism as a Way of Life [40].† In that paper, Wirth developed a "minimum sociological definition of the city" as "a relatively large, dense and permanent settlement of socially heterogeneous individuals" [40, p. 50]. From these prerequisites, he then deduced the major outlines of the urban way of life. As he saw it, number, density, and heterogeneity created a social structure in which primary-group relationships were inevitably replaced by secondary contacts that were impersonal, segmental, superficial, transitory, and

---

† I am indebted to Richard Dewey, John Dyckman, David Riesman, Melvin Webber, and Harold Wilensky for helpful comments on earlier drafts of this essay.

often predatory in nature. As a result, the city dweller became anonymous, isolated, secular, relativistic, rational, and sophisticated. In order to function in the urban society, he was forced to combine with others to organize corporations, voluntary associations, representative forms of government, and the impersonal mass media of communications [40, pp. 54–60]. These replaced the primary groups and the integrated way of life found in rural and other pre-industrial settlements.

Wirth's paper has become a classic in urban sociology, and most texts have followed his definition and description faithfully [5]. In recent years, however, a considerable number of studies and essays have questioned his formulations [1, 5, 13, 15, 17, 19, 20, 23, 24, 27, 28, 30, 35, 38, 41].[1] In addition, a number of changes have taken place in cities since the article was published in 1938, notably the exodus of white residents to low- and medium-priced houses in the suburbs, and the decentralization of industry. The evidence from these studies and the changes in American cities suggest that Wirth's statement must be revised.

There is yet another, and more important reason for such a revision. Despite its title and intent, Wirth's paper deals with urban-industrial society, rather than with the city. This is evident from his approach. Like other urban sociologists, Wirth based his analysis on a comparison of settlement types, but unlike his colleagues, who pursued urban–rural comparisions, Wirth contrasted the city to the folk society. Thus, he compared settlement types of pre-industrial and industrial society. This allowed him to include in his theory of urbanism the entire range of modern institutions which are not found in the folk society, even though many such groups (e.g., voluntary associations) are by no means exclusively urban. Moreover, Wirth's conception of the city dweller as depersonalized, atomized, and susceptible to mass movements suggests that his paper is based on, and contributes to, the theory of the mass society.

---

[1] I shall not attempt to summarize these studies, for this task has already been performed by Dewey [5], Reiss [23], Wilensky [38], and others.

Many of Wirth's conclusions may be relevant to the understanding of ways of life in modern society. However, since the theory argues that all of society is now urban, *his analysis does not distinguish ways of life in the city from those in other settlements within modern society.* In Wirth's time, the comparison of urban and pre-urban settlement types was still fruitful, but today, the primary task for urban (or community) sociology seems to me to be the analysis of the similarities and differences between contemporary settlement types.

This paper is an attempt at such an analysis; it limits itself to distinguishing ways of life in the modern city and the modern suburb. A re-analysis of Wirth's conclusions from this perspective suggests that his characterization of the urban way of life applies only—and not too accurately—to the residents of the inner city. The remaining city dwellers, as well as most suburbanites, pursue a different way of life, which I shall call "quasi-primary". This proposition raises some doubt about the mutual exclusiveness of the concepts of city and suburb and leads to a yet broader question: whether settlement concepts and other ecological concepts are useful for explaining ways of life.

THE INNER CITY

Wirth argued that number, density, and heterogeneity had two social consequences which explain the major features of urban life. On the one hand, the crowding of diverse types of people into a small area led to the segregation of homogeneous types of people into separate neighborhoods [40, p. 56]. On the other hand, the lack of physical distance between city dwellers resulted in social contact between them, which broke down existing social and cultural patterns and encouraged assimilation as well as acculturation—the melting pot effect [40, p. 52]. Wirth implied that the melting pot effect was far more powerful than the tendency toward segregation and concluded that, sooner or later, the pressures engendered by the dominant social, economic, and political institutions of the city would destroy the remaining pockets of primary-group relationships [40, pp. 60–62]. Eventually, the social system of the city would resemble Tönnies' *Gesellschaft* —a way of life which Wirth considered undesirable.

Because Wirth had come to see the city as the prototype of mass society, and because he examined the city from the distant vantage point of the folk society—from the wrong end of the telescope, so to speak—his view of urban life is not surprising. In addition, Wirth found support for his theory in the empirical work of his Chicago colleagues. As Greer and Kube [19, p. 112] and Wilensky [38, p. 121] have pointed out, the Chicago sociologists conducted their most intensive studies in the inner city.[2] At that time, these were slums recently invaded by new waves of European immigrants and rooming house and skid row districts, as well as the habitat of Bohemians and well-to-do Gold Coast apartment dwellers. Wirth himself studied the Maxwell Street Ghetto, an inner-city Jewish neighborhood then being dispersed by the acculturation and mobility of its inhabitants [39]. Some of the characteristics of urbanism which Wirth stressed in his essay abounded in these areas.

Wirth's diagnosis of the city as *Gesellschaft* must be questioned on three counts. First, the conclusions derived from a study of the inner city cannot be generalized to the entire urban area. Second, there is as yet not enough evidence to prove—nor, admittedly, to deny—that number, density, and heterogeneity result in the social consequences which Wirth proposed. Finally, even if the causal relationship could be verified, it can be shown that a significant proportion of the city's inhabitants were, and are, isolated from these consequences by social structures and cultural patterns which they either brought to the city, or developed by

---

[2] By the *inner city*, I mean the transient residential areas, the Gold Coasts and the slums that generally surround the central business district, although in some communities they may continue for miles beyond that district. The *outer city* includes the stable residential areas that house the working- and middle-class tenant and owner. The *suburbs* I conceive as the latest and most modern ring of the outer city, distinguished from it only by yet lower densities, and by the often irrelevant fact of the ring's location outside the city limits.

living in it. Wirth conceived the urban population as consisting of heterogeneous individuals, torn from past social systems, unable to develop new ones, and therefore prey to social anarchy in the city. While it is true that a not insignificant proportion of the inner city population was, and still is, made up of unattached individuals [26], Wirth's formulation ignores the fact that this population consists mainly of relatively homogeneous groups, with social and cultural moorings that shield it fairly effectively from the suggested consequences of number, density, and heterogeneity. This applies even more to the residents of the outer city, who constitute a majority of the total city population.

The social and cultural moorings of the inner city population are best described by a brief analysis of the five types of inner city residents. These are:

1. the "cosmopolites";
2. the unmarried or childless;
3. the "ethnic villagers";
4. the "deprived"; and
5. the "trapped" and downward mobile.

The "cosmopolites" include students, artists, writers, musicians, and entertainers, as well as other intellectuals and professionals. They live in the city in order to be near the special "cultural" facilities that can only be located near the center of the city. Many cosmopolites are unmarried or childless. Others rear children in the city, especially if they have the income to afford the aid of servants and governesses. The less affluent ones may move to the suburbs to raise their children, continuing to live as cosmopolites under considerable handicaps, especially in the lower-middle-class suburbs. Many of the very rich and powerful are also cosmopolites, although they are likely to have at least two residences, one of which is suburban or exurban.

The unmarried or childless must be divided into two subtypes, depending on the permanence of transience of their status. The temporarily unmarried or childless live in the inner city for only a limited time. Young adults may team up to rent an apartment away from their parents and close to job or entertainment opportunities. When they marry, they may move first to an apartment in a transient neighborhood, but if they can afford to do so, they leave for the outer city or the suburbs with the arrival of the first or second child. The permanently unmarried may stay in the inner city for the remainder of their lives, their housing depending on their income.

The "ethnic villagers" are ethnic groups which are found in such inner city neighborhoods as New York's Lower East Side, living in some ways as they did when they were peasants in European or Puerto Rican villages [15]. Although they reside in the city, they isolate themselves from significant contact with most city facilities, aside from workplaces. Their way of life differs sharply from Wirth's urbanism in its emphasis on kinship and the primary group, the lack of anonymity and secondary-group contacts, the weakness of formal organizations, and the suspicion of anything and anyone outside their neighborhood.

The first two types live in the inner city by choice; the third is there partly because of necessity, partly because of tradition. The final two types are in the inner city because they have no other choice. One is the "deprived" population: the very poor; the emotionally disturbed or otherwise handicapped; broken families; and, most important, the non-white population. These urban dwellers must take the dilapidated housing and blighted neighborhoods to which the housing market relegates them, although among them are some for whom the slum is a hiding place, or a temporary stop-over to save money for a house in the outer city or the suburbs [27].

The "trapped" are the people who stay behind when a neighborhood is invaded by non-residential land uses or lower-status immigrants, because they cannot afford to move, or are otherwise bound to their present location [27].[3] The "downward

---

[3] The trapped are not very visible, but I suspect that they are a significant element in what Raymond Vernon has described as the "gray areas" of the city [32].

mobiles" are a related type; they may have started life in a higher class position, but have been forced down in the socio-economic hierarchy and in the quality of their accommodations. Many of them are old people, living out their existence on small pensions.

These five types all live in dense and heterogeneous surroundings, yet they have such diverse ways of life that it is hard to see how density and heterogeneity could exert a common influence. Moreover, all but the last two types are isolated or detached from their neighborhood and thus from the social consequences which Wirth described.

When people who live together have social ties based on criteria other than mere common occupancy, they can set up social barriers regardless of the physical closeness or the heterogeneity of their neighbors. The ethnic villagers are the best illustration. While a number of ethnic groups are usually found living together in the same neighborhood, they are able to *isolate* themselves from each other through a variety of social devices. Wirth himself recognized this when he wrote that "two groups can occupy a given area without losing their separate identity because each side is permitted to live its own inner life and each somehow fears or idealizes the other" [39, p. 283]. Although it is true that the children in these areas were often oblivious to the social barriers set up by their parents, at least until adolescence, it is doubtful whether their acculturation can be traced to the melting pot effect as much as to the pervasive influence of the American culture that flowed into these areas from the outside.[4]

The cosmopolites, the unmarried, and the childless are *detached* from neighborhood life. The cosmopolites possess a distinct sub-culture which causes them to be disinterested in all but the most superficial contacts with their neighbors, somewhat like the ethnic villagers. The unmarried and childless are detached from

---

[4] If the melting pot has resulted from propinquity and high density, one would have expected second-generation Italians, Irish, Jews, Greeks, Slavs, etc. to have developed a single "pan-ethnic culture", consisting of a synthesis of the cultural patterns of the propinquitous national groups.

neighborhood because of their life-cycle stage, which frees them from the routine family responsibilities that entail some relationship to the local area. In their choice of residence, the two types are therefore not concerned about their neighbors, or the availability and quality of local community facilities. Even the well-to-do can choose expensive apartments in or near poor neighborhoods, because if they have children, these are sent to special schools and summer camps which effectively isolate them from neighbors. In addition, both types, but especially the childless and unmarried, are transient. Therefore, they tend to live in areas marked by high population turnover, where their own mobility and that of their neighbors creates a universal detachment from the neighborhood.[5]

The deprived and the trapped do seem to be affected by some of the consequences of number, density, and heterogeneity. The deprived population suffers considerably from overcrowding, but this is a consequence of low income, racial discrimination, and other handicaps, and cannot be considered an inevitable result of the ecological make-up of the city.[6] Because the deprived have no residential choice, they are also forced to live amid neighbors not of their own choosing, with ways of life different and even contradictory to their own. If familial defenses against the neighborhood climate are weak, as is the case among broken families and downward mobile people, parents may lose their children to the culture of "the street." The trapped are the unhappy people who remain behind when their more advantaged neighbors move on; they must endure the heterogeneity which results from neighborhood change.

---

[5] The corporation transients [36, 38], who provide a new source of residential instability to the suburb, differ from city transients. Since they are raising families, they want to integrate themselves into neighborhood life, and are usually able to do so, mainly because they tend to move into similar types of communities wherever they go.

[6] The negative social consequences of overcrowding are a result of high room and floor density, not of the land coverage of population density which Wirth discussed. Park Avenue residents live under conditions of high land density, but do not seem to suffer visibly from overcrowding.

Wirth's description of the urban way of life fits best the transient areas of the inner city. Such areas are typically heterogeneous in population, partly because they are inhabited by transient types who do not require homogeneous neighbors or by deprived people who have no choice, or may themselves be quite mobile. Under conditions of transience and heterogeneity, people interact only in terms of the segmental roles necessary for obtaining local services. Their social relationships thus display anonymity, impersonality, and superficiality.[7]

The social features of Wirth's concept of urbanism seem therefore to be a result of residential instability, rather than of number, density, or heterogeneity. In fact, heterogeneity is itself an effect of residential instability, resulting when the influx of transients causes landlords and realtors to stop acting as gatekeepers —that is, wardens of neighborhood homogeneity.[8] Residential instability is found in all types of settlements, and, presumably, its social consequences are everywhere similar. These consequences cannot therefore be identified with the ways of life of the city.

THE OUTER CITY AND THE SUBURBS

The second effect which Wirth ascribed to number, density, and heterogeneity was the segregation of homogeneous people into distinct neighborhoods,[9] on the basis of "place and nature of work, income, racial and ethnic characteristics, social status,

---

[7] Whether or not these social phenomena have the psychological consequences Wirth suggested depends on the people who live in the area. Those who are detached from the neighborhood by choice are probably immune, but those who depend on the neighborhood for their social relationships—the unattached individuals, for example—may suffer greatly from loneliness.

[8] Needless to say, residential instability must ultimately be traced back to the fact that, as Wirth pointed out, the city and its economy attract transient—and, depending on the sources of outmigration, heterogeneous—people. However, this is a characteristic of urban-industrial society, not of the city specifically.

[9] By neighborhoods or residential districts I mean areas demarcated from others by distinctive physical boundaries or by social characteristics, some of which may be perceived only by the residents. However, these areas are not necessarily socially self-sufficient or culturally distinctive.

custom, habit, taste, preference and prejudice" [40, p. 56]. This description fits the residential districts of the *outer city*.[10] Although these districts contain the majority of the city's inhabitants, Wirth went into little detail about them. He made it clear, however, that the socio-psychological aspects of urbanism were prevalent there as well [40, p. 56].

Because existing neighborhood studies deal primarily with the exotic sections of the inner city, very little is known about the more typical residential neighborhoods of the outer city. However, it is evident that the way of life in these areas bears little resemblance to Wirth's urbanism. Both the studies which question Wirth's formulation and my own observations suggest that the common element in the ways of life of these neighborhoods is best described as *quasi-primary*. I use this term to characterize relationships between neighbors. Whatever the intensity or frequency of these relationships, the interaction is more intimate than a secondary contact, but more guarded than a primary one.[11]

There are actually few secondary relationships, because of the isolation of residential neighborhoods from economic institutions and workplaces. Even shopkeepers, store managers, and other local functionaries who live in the area are treated as acquaintances or friends, unless they are of a vastly different social status or are forced by their corporate employers to treat their customers as economic units [30]. Voluntary associations attract only a minority of the population. Moreover, much of the organizational activity is of a sociable nature, and it is often difficult to accomplish the association's "business" because of the members' preference for sociability. Thus, it would appear that interactions in organizations, or between neighbors generally, do

---

[10] For the definition of *outer city*, see p. 98, note 2.

[11] Because neighborly relations are not quite primary, and not quite secondary, they can also become *pseudo-primary*; that is, secondary ones disguised with false affect to make them appear primary. Critics have often described suburban life in this fashion, although the actual prevalence of pseudo-primary relationships has not been studied systematically in cities or suburbs.

not fit the secondary-relationship model of urban life. As anyone who has lived in these neighborhoods knows, there is little anonymity, impersonality or privacy.[12] In fact, American cities have sometimes been described as collections of small towns.[13] There is some truth to this description, especially if the city is compared to the actual small town, rather than to the romantic construct of anti-urban critics [33].

Postwar suburbia represents the most contemporary version of the quasi-primary way of life. Owing to increases in real income and the encouragement of home ownership provided by the FHA, families in the lower-middle class and upper working class can now live in modern single-family homes in low-density subdivisions, an opportunity previously available only to the upper and upper-middle classes [34].

The popular literature describes the new suburbs as communities in which conformity, homogeneity, and other-direction are unusually rampant [4, 32]. The implication is that the move from city to suburb initiates a new way of life which causes considerable behavior and personality change in previous urbanites. A preliminary analysis of data which I am now collecting in Levittown, New Jersey, suggests, however, that the move from the city to this predominantly lower-middle-class suburb does not result in any major behavioral changes for most people. Moreover, the changes which do occur reflect the move from the social isolation of a transient city or suburban apartment building to the quasi-primary life of a neighborhood of single-family homes. Also, many of the people whose life has changed reported that the changes were intended. They existed as aspirations before the move, or as reasons for it. In other words, the suburb itself creates few changes in ways of life. Similar conclusions have been reported

---

[12] These neighborhoods cannot, however, be considered as urban folk societies. People go out of the area for many of their friendships, and their allegiance to neighborhood is neither intense nor all-encompassing. Janowitz has aptly described the relationship between resident and neighborhood as one of "limited liability" [20, chapter 7].

[13] Were I not arguing that ecological concepts cannot double as sociological ones, this way of life might best be described as small-townish.

by Berger in his excellent study of a working-class population newly moved to a suburban subdivision [4].

A COMPARISON OF CITY AND SUBURB

If urban and suburban areas are similar in that the way of life in both is quasi-primary, and if urban residents who move out to the suburbs do not undergo any significant changes in behavior, it would be fair to argue that the differences in ways of life between the two types of settlements have been overestimated. Yet the fact remains that a variety of physical and demographic differences exist between the city and the suburb. However, upon closer examination, many of these differences turn out to be either spurious or of little significance for the way of life of the inhabitants [34].[14]

The differences between the residential areas of cities and suburbs which have been cited most frequently are:

1. Suburbs are more likely to be dormitories.
2. They are further away from the work and play facilities of the central business districts.
3. They are newer and more modern than city residential areas and are designed for the automobile rather than for pedestrian and mass-transit forms of movement.
4. They are built up with single-family rather than multi-family structures and are therefore less dense.
5. Their populations are more homogeneous.
6. Their populations differ demographically: they are younger; more of them are married; they have higher incomes; and they hold proportionately more white collar jobs [8, p. 131].

Most urban neighborhoods are as much dormitories as the suburbs. Only in a few older inner city areas are factories and

---

[14] They may, of course, be significant for the welfare of the total metropolitan area.

offices still located in the middle of residential blocks, and even here many of the employees do not live in the neighborhood.

The fact that the suburbs are farther from the central business district is often true only in terms of distance, not travel time. Moreover, most people make relatively little use of downtown facilities, other than workplaces [12, 21]. The downtown stores seem to hold their greatest attraction for the upper-middle class [21, pp. 91–92]; the same is probably true of typically urban entertainment facilities. Teen-agers and young adults may take their dates to first-run movie theaters, but the museums, concert halls, and lecture rooms attract mainly upper-middle-class ticket-buyers, many of them suburban.[15]

The suburban reliance on the train and the automobile has given rise to an imaginative folklore about the consequences of commuting on alcohol consumption, sex life, and parental duties. Many of these conclusions are, however, drawn from selected high-income suburbs and exurbs, and reflect job tensions in such hectic occupations as advertising and show business more than the effects of residence [29]. It is true that the upper-middle-class housewife must become a chauffeur in order to expose her children to the proper educational facilities, but such differences as walking to the corner drug store and driving to its suburban equivalent seem to me of little emotional, social, or cultural import.[16] In addition, the continuing shrinkage in the number of mass-transit users suggests that even in the city many younger people are now living a wholly auto-based way of life.

The fact that suburbs are smaller is primarily a function of political boundaries drawn long before the communities were suburban. This affects the kinds of political issues which develop and provides somewhat greater opportunity for citizen participation. Even so, in the suburbs as in the city, the minority who participate are the professional politicians, the economically

---

[15] A 1958 study of New York theater goers showed a median income of close to $10,000 and 35 per cent were reported as living in the suburbs [10].

[16] I am thinking here of adults; teen-agers do suffer from the lack of informal meeting places within walking or bicycling distance.

concerned businessmen, lawyers and salesmen, and the ideologically motivated middle- and upper-middle-class people with better than average education.

The social consequences of differences in density and house type also seem overrated. Single-family houses on quiet streets facilitate the supervision of children; this is one reason why middle-class women who want to keep an eye on their children move to the suburbs. House type also has some effects on relationships between neighbors, insofar as there are more opportunities for visual contact between adjacent homeowners than between people on different floors of an apartment house. However, if occupants' characteristics are also held constant, the differences in actual social contact are less marked. Homogeneity of residents turns out to be more important as a determinant of sociability than proximity. If the population is heterogeneous, there is little social contact between neighbors, either on apartment-house floors or in single-family-house blocks; if people are homogeneous, there is likely to be considerable social contact in both house types. One need only contrast the apartment house located in a transient, heterogeneous neighborhood and exactly the same structure in a neighborhood occupied by a single ethnic group. The former is a lonely, anonymous building; the latter, a bustling micro-society. I have observed similar patterns in suburban areas: on blocks where people are homogeneous, they socialize; where they are heterogeneous, they do little more than exchange polite greetings [16].

Suburbs are usually described as being more homogeneous in house type than the city, but if they are compared to the outer city, the differences are small. Most inhabitants of the outer city, other than well-to-do homeowners, live on blocks of uniform structures as well—for example, the endless streets of rowhouses in Philadelphia and Baltimore or of two-story duplexes and six-flat apartment houses in Chicago. They differ from the new suburbs only in that they were erected through more primitive methods of mass production. Suburbs are of course more predominantly areas of owner-occupied single homes, though in the outer districts of most American cities homeownership is also extremely high.

Demographically, suburbs as a whole are clearly more homogeneous than cities as a whole, though probably not more so than outer cities. However, people do not live in cities or suburbs as a whole, but in specific neighborhoods. An analysis of ways of life would require a determination of the degree of population homogeneity within the boundaries of areas defined as neighborhoods by residents' social contacts. Such an analysis would no doubt indicate that many neighborhoods in the city as well as the suburbs are homogeneous. Neighborhood homogeneity is actually a result of factors having little or nothing to do with the house type, density, or location of the area relative to the city limits. Brand new neighborhoods are more homogeneous than older ones, because they have not yet experienced resident turnover, which frequently results in population heterogeneity. Neighborhoods of low- and medium-priced housing are usually less homogeneous than those with expensive dwellings because they attract families who have reached the peak of occupational and residential mobility, as well as young families who are just starting their climb and will eventually move to neighborhoods of higher status. The latter, being accessible only to high-income people, are therefore more homogeneous with respect to other resident characteristics as well. Moreover, such areas have the economic and political power to slow down or prevent invasion. Finally, neighborhoods located in the path of ethnic or religious group movement are likely to be extremely homogeneous.

The demographic differences between cities and suburbs cannot be questioned, especially since the suburbs have attracted a large number of middle-class child-rearing families. The differences are, however, much reduced if suburbs are compared only to the outer city. In addition, a detailed comparison of suburban and outer city residential areas would show that neighborhoods with the same kinds of people can be found in the city as well as the suburbs. Once again, the age of the area and the cost of housing are more important determinants of demographic characteristics than the location of the area with respect to the city limits.

CHARACTERISTICS, SOCIAL ORGANIZATION, AND ECOLOGY

The preceding sections of the paper may be summarized in three propositions:

1. As concerns ways of life, the inner city must be distinguished from the outer city and the suburbs; and the latter two exhibit a way of life bearing little resemblance to Wirth's urbanism.

2. Even in the inner city, ways of life resemble Wirth's description only to a limited extent. Moreover, economic condition, cultural characteristics, life-cycle stage, and residential instability explain ways of life more satisfactorily than number, density, or heterogeneity.

3. Physical and other differences between city and suburb are often spurious or without much meaning for ways of life.

These propositions suggest that the concepts urban and suburban are neither mutually exclusive, nor especially relevant for understanding ways of life. They—and number, density, and heterogeneity as well—are ecological concepts which describe human adaptation to the environment. However, they are not sufficient to explain social phenomena, because these phenomena cannot be understood solely as the consequences of ecological processes. Therefore, other explanations must be considered.

Ecological explanations of social life are most applicable if the subjects under study lack the ability to *make choices*, be they plants, animals, or human beings. Thus, if there is a housing shortage, people will live almost anywhere, and under extreme conditions of no choice, as in a disaster, married and single, old and young, middle and working class, stable and transient will be found side by side in whatever accommodations are available. At that time, their ways of life represent an almost direct adaptation to the environment. If the supply of housing and of neighborhoods is such that alternatives are available, however, people will make choices, and if the housing market is responsive, they can even make and satisfy explicit *demands*.

Choices and demands do not develop independently or at random; they are functions of the roles people play in the social system. These can best be understood in terms of the *characteristics* of the people involved; that is, characteristics can be used as indices to choices and demands made in the roles that constitute ways of life. Although many characteristics affect the choices and demands people make with respect to housing and neighborhoods, the most important ones seem to be *class*—in all its economic, social and cultural ramifications—and *life-cycle stage*.[17] If people have an opportunity to choose, these two characteristics will go far in explaining the kinds of housing and neighborhoods they will occupy and the ways of life they will try to establish within them.

Many of the previous assertions about ways of life in cities and suburbs can be analyzed in terms of class and life-cycle characteristics. Thus, in the inner city, the unmarried and childless live as they do, detached from neighborhood, because of their life-cycle stage; the cosmopolites, because of a combination of life-cycle stage and a distinctive but class-based subculture. The way of life of the deprived and trapped can be explained by low socioeconomic level and related handicaps. The quasi-primary way of life is associated with the family stage of the life-cycle, and the norms of child-rearing and parental role found in the upper working class, the lower-middle class, and the non-cosmopolite portions of the upper-middle and upper classes.

The attributes of the so-called suburban way of life can also be understood largely in terms of these characteristics. The new suburbia is nothing more than a highly visible showcase for the ways of life of young, upper-working-class and lower-middle-class people. Ktsanes and Reissman have aptly described it as

---

[17] These must be defined in dynamic terms. Thus, class includes also the process of social mobility, stage in the life-cycle, and the processes of socialization and aging.

"new homes for old values" [22]. Much of the descriptive and critical writing about suburbia assumes that as long as the new suburbanites lived in the city, they behaved like upper-middle-class cosmopolites and that suburban living has mysteriously transformed them [7; 14, pp. 154–62; 25; 36]. The critics fail to see that the behavior and personality patterns ascribed to suburbia are in reality those of class and age [6]. These patterns could have been found among the new suburbanites when they still lived in the city and could now be observed among their peers who still reside there—if the latter were as visible to critics and researchers as are the suburbanites.

Needless to say, the concept of "characteristics" cannot explain all aspects of ways of life, either among urban or suburban residents. Some aspects must be explained by concepts of social organization that are independent of characteristics. For example, some features of the quasi-primary way of life are independent of class and age, because they evolve from the roles and situations created by joint and adjacent occupancy of land and dwellings. Likewise, residential instability is a universal process which has a number of invariate consequences. In each case, however, the way in which people react varies with their characteristics. So it is with ecological processes. Thus, there are undoubtedly differences between ways of life in urban and suburban settlements which remain after behavior patterns based on residents' characteristics have been analyzed, and which must therefore be attributed to features of the settlement [11].

Characteristics do not explain the causes of behavior; rather, they are clues to socially created and culturally defined roles, choices, and demands. A causal analysis must trace them back to the larger social, economic, and political systems which determine the situations in which roles are played and the cultural content of choices and demands, as well as the opportunities for their achievement.[18] These systems determine income distributions,

---

[18] This formulation may answer some of Duncan and Schnore's objections to socio-psychological and cultural explanations of community ways of life [9].

educational and occupational opportunities, and in turn, fertility patterns, child-rearing methods, as well as the entire range of consumer behavior. Thus, a complete analysis of the way of life of the deprived residents of the inner city cannot stop by indicating the influence of low income, lack of education, or family instability. These must be related to such conditions as the urban economy's "need" for low-wage workers, and the housing market practices which restrict residential choice. The urban economy is in turn shaped by national economic and social systems, as well as by local and regional ecological processes. Some phenomena can be explained exclusively by reference to these ecological processes. However, it must also be recognized that as man gains greater control over the natural environment, he has been able to free himself from many of the determining and limiting effects of that environment. Thus, changes in local transportation technology, the ability of industries to be footloose, and the relative affluence of American society have given ever larger numbers of people increasing amounts of residential choice. The greater the amount of choice available, the more important does the concept of characteristics become in understanding behavior.

Consequently, the study of ways of life in communities must begin with an analysis of characteristics. If characteristics are dealt with first and held constant, we may be able to discover which behavior patterns can be attributed to features of the settlement and its natural environment.[19] Only then will it be possible to discover to what extent city and suburb are independent—rather than dependent or intervening—variables in the explanation of ways of life.

This kind of analysis might help to reconcile the ecological point of view with the behavioral and cultural one, and possibly

---

[19] The ecologically oriented researchers who developed the Shevsky-Bell social area analysis scale have worked on the assumption that "social differences between the populations of urban neighborhoods can conveniently be summarized into differences of economic level, family characteristics and ethnicity" [3, p. 26]. However, they have equated "urbanization" with a concept of life-cycle stage by using family characteristics to define the index of urbanization [3, 18, 19]. In fact, Bell has identified suburbanism with familism [2].

put an end to the conflict between conceptual positions which insist on one explanation or the other [9]. Both explanations have some relevance, and future research and theory must clarify the role of each in the analysis of ways of life in various types of settlement [6, p. xxii]. Another important rationale for this approach is its usefulness for applied sociology—for example, city planning. The planner can recommend changes in the spatial and physical arrangements of the city. Frequently, he seeks to achieve social goals or to change social conditions through physical solutions. He has been attracted to ecological explanations because these relate behavior to phenomena which he can affect. For example, most planners tend to agree with Wirth's formulations, because they stress number and density, over which the planner has some control. If the undesirable social conditions of the inner city could be traced to these two factors, the planner could propose large-scale clearance projects which would reduce the size of the urban population, and lower residential densities. Experience with public housing projects has, however, made it apparent that low densities, new buildings, or modern site plans do not eliminate anti-social or self-destructive behavior. The analysis of characteristics will call attention to the fact that this behavior is lodged in the deprivations of low socio-economic status and racial discrimination, and that it can be changed only through the removal of these deprivations. Conversely, if such an analysis suggests residues of behavior that can be attributed to ecological processes or physical aspects of housing and neighborhoods, the planner can recommend physical changes that can really affect behavior.

A RE-EVALUATION OF DEFINITIONS

The argument presented here has implications for the sociological definition of the city. Such a definition relates ways of life to environmental features of the city qua settlement type. But if ways of life do not coincide with settlement types, and if these ways are functions of class and life-cycle stage rather than of the ecological attributes of the settlement, a sociological definition of the city cannot be formulated.[20] Concepts such as city and suburb allow us to distinguish settlement types from each other physically and demographically, but the ecological processes and conditions which they synthesize have no direct or invariate consequences for ways of life. The sociologist cannot, therefore, speak of an urban or suburban way of life.

CONCLUSION

Many of the descriptive statements made here are as time-bound as Wirth's.[21] Twenty years ago, Wirth concluded that some form of urbanism would eventually predominate in all settlement types. He was, however, writing during a time of immigrant acculturation and at the end of a serious depression, an era of minimal choice. Today, it is apparent that high-density, heterogeneous surroundings are for most people a temporary place of residence; other than for the Park Avenue or Greenwich Village cosmopolites, they are a result of necessity rather than choice. As soon as they can afford to do so, most Americans head for the single-family house and the quasi-primary array of life of the low-density neighborhood, in the outer city or the suburbs.[22]

Changes in the national economy and in government housing policy can affect many of the variables that make up housing supply and demand. For example, urban sprawl may eventually

---

[20] Because of the distinctiveness of the ways of life found in the inner city, some writers propose definitions that refer only to these ways, ignoring those found in the outer city. For example, popular writers sometimes identify "urban" with "urbanity," i.e., "cosmopolitanism." However, such a definition ignores the other ways of life found in the inner city. Moreover, I have tried to show that these ways have few common elements, and that the ecological features of the inner city have little or no influence in shaping them.

[21] Even more than Wirth's they are based on data and impressions gathered in the large Eastern and Midwestern cities of the United States.

[22] Personal discussions with European planners and sociologists suggest that many European apartment dwellers have similar preferences, although economic conditions, high building costs, and the scarcity of land make it impossible for them to achieve their desires.

outdistance the ability of present and proposed transportation systems to move workers into the city; further industrial decentralization can forestall it and alter the entire relationship between work and residence. The expansion of present urban renewal activities can perhaps lure a significant number of cosmopolites back from the suburbs, while a drastic change in renewal policy might begin to ameliorate the housing conditions of the deprived population. A serious depression could once again make America a nation of doubled-up tenants.

These events will affect housing supply and residential choice; they will frustrate but not suppress demands for the quasi-primary way of life. However, changes in the national economy, society, and culture can affect people's characteristics—family size, educational level, and various other concomitants of life-cycle stage and class. These in turn will stimulate changes in demands and choices. The rising number of college graduates, for example, is likely to increase the cosmopolite ranks. This might in turn create a new set of city dwellers, although it will probably do no more than encourage the development of cosmopolite facilities in some suburban areas.

The current revival of interest in urban sociology and in community studies, as well as the sociologist's increasing curiosity about city planning, suggest that data may soon be available to formulate a more adequate theory of the relationship between settlements and the ways of life within them. The speculations presented in this paper are intended to raise questions; they can only be answered by more systematic data collection and theorizing.

REFERENCES

1. AXELROD, MORRIS. Urban Structure and Social Participation, *American Sociological Review*, vol. 21 (February 1956), pp. 13–18.
2. BELL, WENDELL. Social Choice, Life Styles and Suburban Residence, in William M. Dobriner (ed.), *The Suburban Community*, pp. 225–47. New York: G. P. Putnam's Sons, 1958.
3. BELL, WENDELL and MARYANNE T. FORCE. Urban Neighborhood Types and Participation in Formal Associations, *American Sociological Review*, vol. 21 (February 1956), pp. 25–34.

4. BERGER, BENNETT. *Working Class Suburb: A Study of Auto Workers in Suburbia.* Berkeley, Calif.: University of California Press, 1960.

5. DEWEY, RICHARD. The Rural–Urban Continuum: Real but Relatively Unimportant, *American Journal of Sociology*, vol. 66 (July 1960), pp. 60–66.

6. DOBRINER, WILLIAM M. Introduction: Theory and Research in the Sociology of the Suburbs, in William M. Dobriner (ed.), *The Suburban Community*, pp. xiii–xxviii. New York: G. P. Putnam's Sons, 1958.

7. DUHL, LEONARD J. Mental Health and Community Planning, in *Planning 1955*, pp. 31–39. Chicago: American Society of Planning Officials, 1956.

8. DUNCAN, OTIS DUDLEY and ALBERT J. REISS, JR. *Social Characteristics of Rural and Urban Communities, 1950.* New York: John Wiley & Sons, 1956.

9. DUNCAN, OTIS DUDLEY and LEO F. SCHNORE. Cultural, Behavioral and Ecological Perspectives in the Study of Social Organization, *American Journal of Sociology*, vol. 65 (September 1959), pp. 132–55.

10. ENDERS, JOHN. *Profile of the Theater Market.* New York: Playbill, undated and unpaged.

11. FAVA, SYLVIA FLEIS. Contrasts in Neighboring: New York City and a Suburban Community, in William M. Dobriner (ed.), *The Suburban Community*, pp. 122–31. New York: G. P. Putnam's Sons, 1958.

12. FOLEY, DONALD L. The Use of Local Facilities in a Metropolis, in Paul Hatt and Albert J. Reiss, Jr. (eds.), *Cities and Society*, pp. 237–47. Glencoe, Ill.: The Free Press, 1957.

13. FORM, WILLIAM H., *et al.* The Compatibility of Alternative Approaches to the Delimitation of Urban Sub-areas, *American Sociological Review*, vol. 19 (August 1954), pp. 434–40.

14. FROMM, ERICH. *The Sane Society.* New York: Rinehart & Co., Inc., 1955.

15. GANS, HERBERT J. *The Urban Villagers: A Study of the Second Generation Italians in the West End of Boston.* Boston: Center for Community Studies, December 1959 (mimeographed).

16. GANS, HERBERT J. Planning and Social Life: An Evaluation of Friendship and Neighbor Relations in Suburban Communities, *Journal of the American Institute of Planners*, vol. 27 (May 1961), pp. 134–40.

17. GREER, SCOTT. Urbanism Reconsidered: A Comparative Study of Local Areas in a Metropolis, *American Sociological Review*, vol. 21 (February 1956), pp. 19–25.

18. GREER, SCOTT. The Social Structure and Political Process of Suburbia, *American Sociological Review*, vol. 25 (August 1960), pp. 514–26.

19. GREER, SCOTT and ELLA KUBE. Urbanism and Social Structure: A Los Angeles Study, in Marvin B. Sussman (ed.), *Community Structure and Analysis*, pp. 93–112. New York: Thomas Y. Crowell Company, 1959.

20. JANOWITZ, MORRIS. *The Community Press in an Urban Setting.* Glencoe, Ill.: The Free Press, 1952.

21. JONASSEN, CHRISTEN T. *The Shopping Center Versus Downtown.* Columbus, Ohio: Bureau of Business Research, Ohio State, University 1955.

22. KTSANES, THOMAS and LEONARD REISSMAN. Suburbia: New Homes for Old Values, *Social Problems*, vol. 7 (Winter 1959–60), pp. 187–94.

23. REISS, ALBERT J., JR. An Analysis of Urban Phenomena, in Robert M. Fisher (ed.), *The Metropolis in Modern Life*, pp. 41–49. Garden City, N.Y.: Doubleday & Company, Inc., 1955.

24. REISS, ALBERT J., JR. Rural–Urban and Status Differences in Interpersonal Contacts, *American Journal of Sociology*, vol. 65 (September 1959), pp. 182–95.

25. RIESMAN, DAVID. The Suburban Sadness, in William M. Dobriner (ed.), *The Suburban Community*, pp. 375–408. New York: G. P. Putnam's Sons, 1958.

26. ROSE, ARNOLD, M. Living Arrangements of Unattached Persons, *American Sociological Review*, vol. 12 (August 1947), pp. 429–35.

27. SEELEY, JOHN R. The Slum: Its Nature, Use and Users, *Journal of the American Institute of Planners*, vol. 25 (February 1959), pp. 7–14.

28. SMITH, JOEL, WILLIAM FORM and GREGORY STONE. Local Intimacy in a Middle-Sized City, *American Journal of Sociology*, vol. 60 (November 1954), pp. 276–84.

29. SPECTORSKY, A. C. *The Exurbanites*. Philadelphia: J. B. Lippincott Co., 1955.

30. STONE, GREGORY P. City Shoppers and Urban Identification: Observations on the Social Psychology of City Life, *American Journal of Sociology*, vol. 60 (July 1954), pp. 36–45.

31. STRAUSS, ANSELM. The Changing Imagery of American City and Suburb, *Sociological Quarterly*, vol. 1 (January 1960), pp. 15–24.

32. VERNON, RAYMOND. *The Changing Economic Function of the Central City*. New York: Committee on Economic Development, Supplementary Paper No. 1, January 1959.

33. VIDICH, ARTHUR J. and JOSEPH BENSMAN. *Small Town in Mass Society: Class, Power and Religion in a Rural Community*. Princeton, N.J.: Princeton University Press, 1958.

34. WATTELL, HAROLD. Levittown: A Suburban Community, in William M. Dobriner (ed.), *The Suburban Community*, pp. 287–313. New York: G. P. Putnam's Sons, 1958.

35. WHYTE, WILLIAM F., JR. *Street Corner Society*. Chicago: The University of Chicago Press, 1955.

36. WHYTE, WILLIAM F., JR. *The Organization Man*. New York: Simon & Schuster, 1956.

37. WILENSKY, HAROLD L. Life Cycle, Work, Situation and Participation in Formal Associations, in Robert W. Kleemeier, *et al.* (eds.), *Aging and Leisure: Research Perspectives on the Meaningful Use of Time*, chapter 8. New York: Oxford University Press, 1961.

38. WILENSKY, HAROLD L. and CHARLES LEBEAUX. *Industrial Society and Social Welfare*. New York: Russell Sage Foundation, 1958.

39. WIRTH, LOUIS. *The Ghetto*. Chicago: The University of Chicago Press, 1928.

40. WIRTH, LOUIS. Urbanism as a Way of Life, *American Journal of Sociology*, vol. 44 (July 1938), pp. 1–24. Reprinted in Paul Hatt and Albert J. Reiss, Jr. (eds.), *Cities and Society*, pp. 46–64. Glencoe, Ill.: The Free Press, 1957. [All page references are to this reprinting of the article.]

41. YOUNG, MICHAEL and PETER WILLMOTT. *Family and Kinship in East London*. London: Routledge & Kegan Paul, Ltd., 1957.

Myths of American Suburbia

B. BERGER

Editor's Note

In this extract from the first chapter of Working Class Suburb *Berger analyses the sources of myths about American suburbia, which appeared in popular and semi-popular books, magazines and journals during the 1950s. The argument is no different in essence from that presented in the article by Gans but the detailed documentation of an urban myth is valuable. It is perhaps worth remembering that even if 'suburban man' does not exist, suburban wives are still in a distinct structural situation in relation to community facilities.*

IN RECENT years a myth of suburbia has developed in the United States. In saying this, I refer not to the physical facts of the movement to the suburbs; this is an ecological tendency to which all recent statistics on population mobility bear eloquent testimony.[1] I refer instead to the social and cultural ramifications that are perceived to have been inherent in the suburban exodus. Brunner and Hallenbeck, for example, call the rise of suburbia "one of the major social changes of the twentieth century",[2] and the popular literature especially is full of characterizations of suburbia as "a new way of life".

The significance of the past decade cannot be overestimated since it is only in this period that suburbia has become a *mass*

---

[1] In 1953, for example, *Fortune* reported that suburban population had increased by 75 per cent over 1934, although total population was increasing by only 25 per cent; between 1947 and 1953 the increase was 43 per cent. See The New Suburban Market, *Fortune* (November 1953), p. 234. That this trend is continuing is indicated by a recent Census Bureau report showing that between 1950 and 1956 the population of suburbs increased by 29.3 per cent, although their central cities gained by only 4.7 per cent. For a full discussion of this whole tendency, see Donald Bogue, *Population Growth in Standard Metropolitan Areas, 1900–1950*, especially pp. 18–19, tables 13 and 14, p. 30, and table 19, p. 34.

[2] Edmund deS. Brunner and Wilbur C. Hallenbeck, *American Society: Urban and Rural Patterns*, p. 253.

phenomenon and hence prone to the manufacture of modern myth. Suburbanization, however, goes back as far as the latter part of the nineteenth century, when the very wealthy began to build country estates along the way of suburban railroad stations. Improvements in the automobile and the development of good highways after World War I brought greater numbers of wealthy people to suburban areas in the 1920's. The depression of the 1930's slowed the process of suburbanization, but the late 1930's saw the development of some new residential construction at the peripheries of city limits. The big boom in suburban development, of course, came after World War II with the proliferation of "the mass produced suburbs" all over the country, and well within the reach of middle- and lower-middle-income people. And in the last few years, suburbanization of secondary and tertiary industry has followed closely upon residential suburbanization. Carl Bridenbaugh has noted that suburbanization began as far back as the early part of the eighteenth century. "One ordinarily thinks of the suburban movement of the present century as being of recent origin, and it will come as a surprise to many that the flight from the city began in the first half of the eighteenth century—and for the same reasons as today. The differences were in degree only. Just as Londoners moved westward from the City in search of quiet, air, comfort, lower rents, and more room for display, so did Philadelphians cross the northern and southern bounds of the metropolis in a perennial search for the 'green.' . . . That greatest of townsmen, Benjamin Franklin, even moved from High Street to Second and Sassafras, grumbling that 'the din of the Market increases upon me; and that, with frequent interruptions, has, I find, made me say some things twice over.' " [3]

---

[3] See Frederick Lewis Allen's classification of the five stages of suburbanization in The Big Change in Suburbia, Part I. For some pungent commentaries on the early periods of suburbanization in this century, see H. A. Bridgman, The Suburbanite; Lewis Mumford, The Wilderness of Suburbia; H. I. Phillips, The 7:58 Loses a Passenger; Christine Frederick, Is Suburban Living a Delusion?; and Ethel Swift, In Defense of Suburbia. For the beginnings of suburbanization, see Carl Bridenbaugh, *Cities in Revolt: Urban Life in America, 1743–1776*, p. 24.

The literature on suburbanization seems to fall roughly into two categories. Studies of suburbanization by sociologists have been going on for a long time; with few exceptions, however, these have been primarily ecological or demographic in character.[4] On the other hand, studies of and comment on the culture and social psychology of suburban life have, again with a few exceptions, been left largely to popular writers, journalists, and intellectuals.[5] To urban sociologists in general, "suburbs" is a term of ecological reference; ecologists and demographers may often dispute the most useful way of conceiving "suburbs" for the purposes of their work, but the dispute is largely a technical one. "Suburbia," on the other hand, is a term of cultural reference; it is intended to connote a way of life, or, rather, the intent of those who use it is

---

[4] Some of the more recent work includes: J. Allen Beegle, Characteristics of Michigan's Fringe Population; Noel P. Gist, Developing Patterns of Urban Decentralization; Chauncey Harris, Suburbs; Lewis W. Jones, The Hinterland Reconsidered; Leo F. Schnore, The Functions of Metropolitan Suburbs; Leo F. Schnore, Satellites and Suburbs; Leo F. Schnore, The Growth of Metropolitan Suburbs. See also Walter T. Martin, *The Rural-Urban Fringe*.

[5] See, for example, William H. Whyte's famous series of articles, later revised and reprinted as Part VII of his *The Organization Man*; Harry Henderson, The Mass-Produced Suburbs, Part I, and The Mass-Produced Suburbs, Part II: Rugged American Collectivism; Frederick Lewis Allen, The Big Change in Suburbia, Part I, and The Big Change in Suburbia, Part II: Crisis in the Suburbs; John Keats, *The Crack in the Picture Window*; Carl von Rhode, The Suburban Mind; William Newman, Americans in Subtopia, and Maurice Stein, Suburbia, A Walk on the Mild Side; and Phyllis McGinley, Suburbia, Of Thee I Sing. Some of the exceptions, that is, work by sociologists, include John Seeley *et al.*, *Crestwood Heights* . . .; Sylvia Fava, Suburbanism as a Way of Life; David Riesman, The Suburban Dislocation; Nathan Whetten, Suburbanization as a Field for Sociological Research; Ritchie Lowry, Toward a Sociology of Suburbia; and the early works by Harlan P. Douglass, *The Suburban Trend*, and George Lundberg *et al.*, *Leisure: A Suburban Study*; William Dobriner (ed.), *The Suburban Community*. The following references were published too late for consideration here: Andrew M. Greeley, *The Church and the Suburbs*, New York, 1959; Albert I. Gordon, *Jews in Suburbia*, Boston, 1959; Robert C. Wood, *Suburbia, Its People and Their Politics*, Boston, 1959; Thomas Ktsanes and Leonard Reissman, Suburbia-New Homes for Old Values, *Social Problems*, Winter, 1959–60.

to connote a way of life.[6] The ubiquity of the term suburbia in current popular literature suggests that its meaning is well on its way to standardization—that what it is supposed to connote is widely enough accepted to permit free use of the term with a reasonable amount of certainty that it will convey the images it intends. In the last ten or twelve years, these images have coalesced into a full-blown myth, complete with its articles of faith, its sacred symbols, its rituals, its promise for the future, and its resolution of ultimate questions. The details of the myth are rife in many of the mass circulation magazines as well as in more intellectual periodicals and books; and although the details should be familiar to almost everyone interested in contemporary cultural trends, it may be well to summarize them briefly.

ELEMENTS OF THE MYTH

Approaching the myth of suburbia from the outside, one is immediately struck by rows of new ranch-type houses either identical in design or with minor variations in a basic plan, winding streets, neat lawns, two-car garages, infant trees, and bicycles and tricycles lining the sidewalks.[7] Near at hand is the modern ranch-type school and the even more modern shopping

---

[6] David Riesman comments in a melancholy vein that the ecological work on suburbs and the sociopsychological work do not complement each other: ". . . the characteristic situation in sociology today [is] that research in the macrocosmic and in the microcosmic scarcely connect, scarcely inform each other." David Riesman, *op. cit.*, p. 125.

[7] The following characterization is a distillation of the literature cited in note 5, above. Since what follows is essentially a sketch, the literature, in general, will not be cited. Detailed and specific references to this literature *will* be made, however, in appropriate places in succeeding chapters. In a sense, what follows is more than a sketch; it is really a *definition* of "suburbia," for though there is no standard definition of "suburb" in any rigorous sense (see Brunner and Hallenbeck, *op. cit.*, p. 255), "surbubia" almost universally implies a *tract housing development* within commuting distance of a large city. We will use the terms "suburb" to refer to tract housing developments within standard metropolitan areas and "suburbia" to refer to the kind of life that is said to be led in them. We suggest, however, that commuting is an irrelevant aspect of the definition.

center, dominated by the giant supermarket, which is flanked by a pastel-dotted expanse of parking lot. Beneath the television aerial and behind the modestly but charmingly landscaped entrance to the tract home reside the suburbanite and his family. I should perhaps say "temporarily reside" because the most prominent element of the myth is that residence in a tract suburb is temporary; suburbia is a "transient center" because its bread-winners are upward mobile, and live there only until a promotion and/or a company transfer permits or requires something some-what more opulent in the way of a home. The suburbanites are upward mobile because they are predominantly young (most commentators seem to agree that almost all are between twenty-five and thirty-five), well educated, and have a promising place in some organizational hierarchy—promising because of a con-tinuing expansion of the economy with no serious slowdown in sight. They are engineers, middle-management men, young lawyers, salesmen, insurance agents, teachers, civil service bureau-crats—occupational groups sometimes designated as organization men, and sometimes as "the new middle class." Most such occupations require some college education, so it comes as no surprise to hear and read that the suburbanites are well educated. Their wives too seem to be well educated; their reported conver-sation, their patois, and especially their apparently avid interest in theories of child development all suggest their exposure to higher education.

According to the myth, a new kind of hyperactive social life has apparently developed in suburbia. This is manifest not only in the informal visiting or "neighboring" that is said to be rife, but also in the lively organizational life that goes on. Associations, clubs, and organizations are said to exist for almost every con-ceivable hobby, interest, or preoccupation. The hyperactive par-ticipation of suburbanites is said to extend beyond the limits of voluntary associations to include an equally active participation in local civic affairs. This active, busy participation by young families is encouraged by the absence of an older generation who, in other communities, would normally be the leaders. The absence of an older generation is said to have an especially strong effect upon the young women of the community who, thrown back upon their own resources, develop a marked independence and initiative in civic affairs. The informal social life revolves around the daytime female "kaffeeklatsch" at which "the girls" discuss everything from the problems of handling salesmen to the problems of handling Susie. In the evening the sociability (made possible by the baby-sitting pool) is continued with rounds of couples dropping in on each other for bridge, a drink, or some conversation.

This rich social life is fostered by the homogeneity of the suburbanites; they are in the same age range and have similar jobs and incomes, their children are around the same age, their problems of housing and furnishing are similar. In short, they have a maximum of similar interests and preoccupations which promote their solidarity. This very solidarity and homogeneity (when combined with the uniformities of the physical context) are often perceived as the sources of "conformity" in the suburbia; aloofness or detachment is frowned upon. The intenseness of the social life is sometimes interpreted as a lack of privacy, and this lack of privacy, when added to the immediate visibility of deviation from accepted norms, permits strong, if informal, sanctions to be wielded against nonconformity. The "involvement of everyone in everyone else's life" submits one to the constant scrutiny of the community, and everything from an unclipped lawn to an unclipped head of hair may be cause for invidious comment. On the other hand, the uniformity and homogeneity make suburbia classless or one-class (variously designated as middle or upper middle class). For those interlopers who arrive in the suburbs bearing the unmistakable marks of a more deprived upbringing, suburbia is said to serve as a kind of "second melting pot" in which those who are mobile upward out of the lower orders learn to take on the appropriate folkways of the milieu to which they aspire.

During the daylight hours, suburbia, in the imagery of the myth, is a place almost wholly given over to child rearing. Manless during the day, suburbia is a female society in which the young mothers, well educated and without the interference of tradition (represented by doting grandparents), can rear their children according to the best modern methods. "In the absence of older people, the top authorities on child guidance [in suburbia] are two books: Spock's *Infant Care*, and Gesell's *The First Five Years of Life*. You hear frequent references to them."[8]

The widely commented upon "return to religion" is said to be most visible in suburbia. Clergymen are swamped, not only with their spiritual duties but with marriage counseling and other family problems as well. The revivified religious life in suburbia is not merely a matter of the increasing size of Sunday congregations; the church is not only a house of worship but a local civic institution also, and as such it benefits from the generally active civic life of the suburbanites.

Part of the myth of suburbia is the image of suburbanites as commuters: they work in the city. For cartoonists and other myth-makers, this mass morning exodus to the city has provided opportunity for the creation of images such as "the race to make the 7:12," getting the station wagon started on a cold morning, or the army of wives waiting at the Scarsdale station for the 5:05 from the city. A good deal has been deduced about the way of life in the suburbs from the fact of commuting. For father, commuting means an extra hour or two away from the family, for example, with its debilitating effects upon the relation between father and children. Sometimes this means that Dad leaves for work before the children are up and comes home after they are put to bed. Naturally, these extra hours put a greater burden upon the mother, and have implications for the relation between husband and wife.

In commuting, the commuter returns in the morning to the place where he was bred, for the residents of suburbia are apparently former city people who "escaped" to the suburbs. By moving to the suburbs, however, the erstwhile Democrat from

---

[8] Harry Henderson, The Mass-Produced Suburbs, Part II: Rugged American Collectivism, p. 84.

the "urban ward"[9] becomes the suburban Republican. The voting shift has been commented on or worried about at great length; there seems to be something about suburbia that makes Republicans out of people who were Democrats while they lived in the city. But the political life in the suburbs is said to be characterized not only by the voting shift, but by the vigor with which it is carried on. Political activity takes its place beside other civic and organizational activity, intense and spirited.

SOURCES OF THE MYTH

The foregoing characterization is intended neither as ethnography nor as caricature. Brief and sketchy as it is, it does not, I think, misrepresent the typical image of suburbia that, by way of highbrow as well as middlebrow periodicals (as well as some recent books), has come to dominate the minds of most Americans, including intellectuals. It takes scarcely more than a moment's reflection, however, for the perplexing question to arise: why should a group of tract houses, mass produced and quickly thrown up on the outskirts of a large city, apparently generate so uniform a way of life? What is the logic that links tract living with "suburbanism as a way of life"?

If the homes characteristic of suburbia were all within a narrow price range, we might expect them to be occupied by families of similar income, and this might account for some of the homogeneity of the neighborhood ethos. But suburban developments are themselves a heterogeneous phenomenon. The term "suburbia" has not only been used to refer to tract-housing developments as low as $7,000 per unit and as high as $65,000 per unit,[10] but

---

[9] William Whyte has a way of making the phrase "urban ward" resound with connotations of poverty, deprivation, soot, and brick—as if "urban ward" were a synonym for "slum."

[10] "In a single suburb of Chicago, for example, you can buy ranch houses that cost $10,000 or $65,000 just a few hundred yards apart." Russell Lynes, *The Tastemakers*, p. 253. $7,000 was the original price for homes in Levittown, Long Island.

also to rental developments whose occupants do not think of themselves as homeowners. The same term has been used to cover old rural towns (such as those in the Westchester-Fairfield county complex around New York City) which, because of the expansion of the city and improvements in transportation, have only gradually become suburban in character;[11] it has been applied also to gradually developing residential neighborhoods near the peripheries of city limits. Clearly, then, the ecological nature of suburbs cannot justify so monolithic an image as that of "suburbia."

If the image of suburbia is limited to the mass-produced tract developments, perhaps it is the fact of commuting that links suburban residence with "suburbanism as a way of life." Clearly, the demands of daily commuting create certain common conditions which might go far to explain some of the ostensible uniformities of suburban living. But certainly commuting is not inherent in suburban living despite the many students of suburbia who have made commuting an essential part of their definitions of suburbs. *Fortune*, for example, says that, "The basic characteristic of suburbia is that it is inhabited by people who work in a city, but prefer to live where there is more open space, and are willing to suffer both inconvenience and expense to live there." Von Rhode says, "The distinguishing aspect of the suburb is, of course, the commuter." And Walter Martin says, ". . . the characteristics essential to suburban status . . . are a unique ecological position in relation to a larger city and a high rate of commuting to that city." These definitions would exclude the community reported on in this study from the category "suburb," but more than twenty-five years ago, Lundberg noted, ". . . perhaps too much has been made of commuting as a phenomenon unique to the suburb. As a matter of fact, comparatively few people in a large city live within walking distance of their work. From this point

---

[11] The articles by Carl von Rhode and Phyllis McGinley, cited earlier, clearly evoke the image of a Connecticut town on Long Island Sound. It is perhaps all to the good that this kind of suburb has recently been designated an "exurb." See A. C. Spectorsky's diverting book, *The Exurbanites*.

of view a great number of people living in the city are also commuters . . . commuting can certainly not be stressed as a unique
feature or a fundamental distinction of suburban life as contrasted
with urban." [12]

It may have been true that the occupations of most suburbanites
required a daily trip to and from the central business district of
the city; it may still be true, but it is likely to be decreasingly
true with the passage of time. The pioneers to the suburban
residential frontier have been followed not only by masses of
retail trade outlets, but by industry also. Modern mass production
technology has made obsolete many two- and three-story plants
in urban areas,[13] and today's modern factories are vast one-story
operations which require wide expanses of land, which are either
unavailable or too expensive in the city itself. Thus with the passage of time, "industrial parks" will increasingly dot suburban
areas, and the proportions of suburbanites commuting to the city
each day will decrease.[14]

If the occupations of most suburbanites were similar in their
demands, this might help account for the development of a
generic way of life in the suburbs. Or indeed, if suburbs were
populated largely by organization men and their families, then
we could understand more readily the style of life that is said to

---

[12] See The New Suburban Market, p. 129. See also Carl von Rhode, *op. cit.*,
p. 294; Walter T. Martin, The Structuring of Social Relationships Engendered
by Suburban Residence; and George Lundberg *et al.*, *Leisure: A Suburban Study*,
p. 47.

[13] In 1954, *Time* reported, ". . . now industry is seeking the country too, looking for large tracts of open land to build efficient one-story plants. Of 2,658
plants built in the New York area from 1946 to 1951 only 593 went up in the
city proper." Flight to the Suburbs *Time* March 22, 1954, p. 102. For more
detailed reports of this trend see Evelyn Kitagawa and Donald Bogue, *Suburbanization of Manufacturing Activities within Standard Metropolitan Areas.* For tertiary
industry, see Raymond Cuzzort, *Suburbanization of Service Industries within Standard Metropolitan Areas*, and James D. Tarver, Suburbanization of Retail Trade
in the Standard Metropolitan Areas of the U.S., 1948–1954.

[14] What this means, of course, is that increasing numbers of factory workers
will be living in suburbs—not necessarily satellite industrial cities, but new tract
suburbs. Woodbury has noted that the decline in the proportion of production
workers in cities has been matched by increases in suburban areas of the same
cities. See Coleman Woodbury, Suburbanization and Suburbia, p. 7.

go on. Or, lacking this, if organization men, as Whyte puts it, give the prevailing *tone* to life in the suburbs, then we could more readily understand the prevalence of his model in the literature. But there is no ready hypothesis to explain why the occupations of suburbanites should be so homogeneous. It may be true that the typical organization man is a suburbanite. But it is one thing to assert this and quite another thing to assert that the typical tract suburb is populated by organization men and their families and/or dominated by an "organization" way of life.

Clearly then (and with all due respect for the selective aspects of suburban migration), one suburb is apt to differ from another not only in the price range of its homes, the income characteristics of its residents, their occupational make-up, and the home-to-work traveling patterns of its breadwinners, but also in its educational levels, the character of the region, the size of the suburb, the social-geographical origin of its residents, and countless more indices—all of which, presumably, may be expected to lead to differences in "way of life."

But we not only have good reason to expect suburbs to *differ* markedly from one another; we have reason to expect striking *similarities* between life in urban residential neighborhoods and tract suburbs of a similar socioeconomic make-up. Most residential neighborhoods are "manless" during the day; why not? Husbands are at work, and the only men around are likely to be salesmen and local tradespeople. Even in large cities many men "commute" to work, that is, take subways, buses, or other forms of public transportation to their jobs which may be on the other side of town.[15] Also there are thousands of blocks in American cities with rows of identical or similar houses within a narrow rental or price range, and presumably occupied by families in a similar income bracket.[16] Certainly, urban neighborhoods have always had a

---

[15] Webster still prefers to define "commuter" as someone who travels by way of a commutation ticket.

[16] The same fears for massification and conformity were felt regarding these urban neighborhoods as are now felt for the mass-produced suburbs. See Riesman, The Suburban Dislocation, p. 123.

class character and a "way of life" associated with them. Certainly the whole image of "conformity" in suburbia closely parallels the older image of the tyranny of gossip in the American small town.

There is, then, apparently no reason to believe, no ready and viable hypotheses to explain why "suburbia" should be the new and homogeneous phenomenon it is usually conceived to be. What are the sources of the alleged new way of life? Why should the occupations of suburbanities be so homogeneous? Why should there be more conformity? Why should the "social life" be so intense? Why should organizational participation be so wide-spread? Why should the churches be so much busier than else-where? Why should educational levels be so much higher than average? Why should the residents vote Republican? In short, why does "suburbia" set off this chain reaction of images, associations, and ideas that have coalesced into a single myth?

WORKING-CLASS SUBURBS

This is, of course, a large question, and it would be premature to attempt an answer at this point. It is enough for the present to observe that the myth of suburbia flourishes in spite of an apparent lack of logic in its formulation. In continually referring to "the myth of suburbia" I do not mean to imply that the reports on the culture of suburban life have been falsified, and it would be a mistake to interpret the tone of my remarks as a debunking one. I mean only to say that the reports we have had so far are extremely selective; they are based, for the most part, upon life in Levittown, New York; Park Forest, Illinois; Lakewood, near Los Angeles; and, most recently (the best study so far), a fashionable suburb of Toronto, Canada. The studies that have given rise to the myth of suburbia have been studies of *middle-class suburbs*, that is, suburbs of very large cities[17] populated primarily by people in

---

[17] Suburbanization, of course, has not only occurred around our largest cities, but around smaller ones as well: ". . . with the exception of a general

the occupational groups often thought of as making up the "new middle class"—the engineers, teachers, and organization men mentioned earlier.[18] If the phrase "middle-class suburb" strikes the eye as redundant, it is testimony to the efficacy of the myth, for as I have suggested, there is certainly no reason to believe that residence in a new tract suburb in and of itself immediately (or even within a few years) generates a uniquely new middle-class style of life. Nor is there any reason to believe that the self-selective processes of suburban migration are such that suburbs attract an overwhelming majority of white-collar people to them.

These remarks are intended to suggest that the extant image of suburbia may be a distorted one; that its accuracy may be limited to the suburbs of great metropolises which are populated by former residents of the central city who work in its white-collar hierarchies. Thus whereas in most minds, Westchester and Nassau counties in New York, and Park Forest, Illinois, are ideal typical representatives of "suburbia," they may, in fact, be representative only of suburbs of great cities and of a way of life lived by metropolis-bred, well-educated people of white-collar status. If this or something like this is, in fact, the case, then it is clearly a mistake to identify "suburbanism" exclusively with the kind of life that is said to go on in places like these. Large tracts of suburban housing, in many respects indistinguishable from those on

---

tendency for SMA's of one million inhabitants or more to grow at a slightly less rapid rate than SMA's smaller than this, there has been no pronounced or consistent trend for rates of total metropolitan growth to vary with size. . . ." Quoted by Woodbury, *op. cit.*, from Bogue, *op. cit.* David Riesman has observed, "so far as I can see we know almost nothing about the suburbs (old or new) surrounding the smaller cities." David Riesman, *op. cit.*, p. 124.

[18] The Toronto study is frankly a study of a wealthy suburb and is, without doubt, quite reliable. The unanimity about well-studied Park Forest also lends credence to its portrayal. However, Levittown, New York, and Lakewood, California, are more ambiguous cases. One sharp resident of Levittown writes me that suburb is not *only* white collar, but contains plenty of "blue collar, frayed collar, and turned collar people also," and that the different groups have different ways of life. The vast Lakewood development is heavily populated with southern California aircraft workers, and there is considerable doubt that *Newsweek*'s report on Lakewood, so heavily laden with the mobility motif, took adequate account of them.

Long Island and in Park Forest, have gone up and are continuing to go up all over the country, not only near large cities, but near middle-sized and small ones as well. And if, as is not unlikely, many of the residents of these are rural-bred, with relatively little education, and innocent of white-collar status or aspirations, then we may expect sharp differences between their social and cultural life and that of their more sophisticated counterparts in white-collar suburbs.

This is hardly a revolutionary supposition; indeed, the fact that it should have to be asserted at all is still further testimony to the vitality of the myth I have been describing. This study, then, is based upon the most conventional of sociological assumptions: that a "way of life" is a function of such variables as age, income, occupation, education, rural-urban background, and so forth, and that this is as true for suburbs as it is for any other kind of modern comunity. To be more specific, a mass-produced tract suburb, rapidly occupied, has little chance to develop gradually a neighborhood "character" of its own. It is thus quite likely that a mass-produced suburb of, say, Chicago or New York, which attracts a large group of relatively well-educated, white-collar New Yorkers or Chicagoans, is apt to take on the "social character" (in Fromm's phrase) which was incipient while the young suburbanites were still resident in the urban apartments of their parents; the "other directedness" they learned in the city may, in the physical context of the tract suburb, be permitted its full development. On the other hand, as I have repeatedly emphasized, there is no reason to suppose that most suburbs have this character of sophisticated "urbanism transplanted." There *is* good reason to suppose that increasing numbers of unquestionably working-class people will be migrating to new tract suburbs; *not*, it should be emphasized, to new suburbs immediately and visibly characterizable as "working class," but to suburbs which to all intents and purposes look from the *outside* like the fulfillment of the promise of America symbolized in the myth. Large numbers of semiskilled as well as skilled factory workers in strongly unionized heavy industry are clearly able to afford to buy new tract homes in the $12,000 to $1006,0 price range;[19] many are doing so, and presumably even more will be doing so as increasing numbers of factories move out of the city to the hinterlands.

BIBLIOGRAPHY

ALLEN, FREDERICK LEWIS (1954) The Big Change in Suburbia, Part I. *Harper's,* June 1954, pp. 21–28.

ALLEN, FREDERICK LEWIS (1954) The Big Change in Suburbia, Part II, Crisis in the Suburbs. *Harper's,* July 1954, pp. 47–53.

BEEGLE, J. ALLEN (1947) Characteristics of Michigan's Fringe Population. *Rural Sociology,* September 1947, pp. 254–63.

BOGUE, DONALD (1953) *Population Growth in Standard Metropolitan Areas, 1900–1950.* Washington, D.C.: U.S. Government Printing Office.

BRIDENBAUGH, CARL (1955) *Cities in Revolt: Urban Life in America, 1743–1776.* New York: Alfred A. Knopf.

BRIDGMAN, H. A. (1902) The Suburbanite. *Independent,* April 10, 1902, pp. 862–4.

BRUNNER, EDMUND DES. and WILBUR C. HALLENBECK (1955) *American Society: Urban and Rural Patterns.* New York: Harper & Brothers.

CUZZORT, RAYMOND (1955) *Suburbanization of Service Industries Within Standard Metropolitan Areas.* Miami, Ohio: The Scripps Foundation.

DOBRINER, WILLIAM (ed.) (1958) *The Suburban Community.* New York: G. P. Putnam's Sons.

DOUGLASS, HARLAN P. (1925) *The Suburban Trend.* New York: D. Appleton Century Co.

DURKHEIM EMILE, (1947) *The Elementary Forms of the Religious Life.* Glencoe, Illinois: The Free Press.

FAVA, SYLVIA (1956) Suburbanism as a Way of Life. *American Sociological Review,* February 1956, pp. 34–37.

GIST, NOEL P. (1952) Developing Patterns of Urban Decentralization. *Social Forces,* March 1952, pp. 257–67.

GREELEY, ANDREW M. (1958) Suburbia, A New Way of Life. *The Sign,* January 1958.

GREELEY, ANDREW M. (1958) The Catholic Suburbanite. *The Sign,* February 1958.

HARRIS, CHAUNCEY (1943) Suburbs. *American Journal of Sociology,* July 1943, pp. 1–13.

HENDERSON, HARRY (1953) The Mass-Produced Suburbs, Part I. *Harper's,* November 1953, pp. 25–32.

HENDERSON, HARRY (1953) Rugged American Collectivism, The Mass-Produced Suburbs, Part II. *Harper's,* December 1953, pp. 80–86.

---

[19] *Time* reports that 27 per cent of all new American homes fall into the price category represented by the $13,000 house shown at the U.S. exhibition in Moscow in the summer of 1959. *Time,* April 20, 1959, p. 91.

JONES, LEWIS W. (1955) The Hinterland Reconsidered. *American Sociological Review*, February 1955, pp. 40–44.

KEATS, JOHN (1957) *The Crack in the Picture Window*. New York: Ballantine Books.

KITAGAWA, EVELYN and DONALD BOGUE (1953) *Suburbanization of Manufacturing Activities Within Standard Metropolitan Areas*. Miami, Ohio: The Scripps Foundation.

LOWRY, RITCHIE (1955) Toward a Sociology of Suburbia. *Berkeley Publications in Society and Institutions*, Spring 1955, pp. 12–24.

LUNDBERG, GEORGE, MIRRA KOMAROVSKY and MARY A. McINERNY (1934) *Leisure: A Suburban Study*. New York: Columbia University Press.

MARTIN, WALTER T. (1953) *The Rural–Urban Fringe*. Eugene: University of Oregon Press.

MARTIN, WALTER T. (1956) The Structuring of Social Relationships Engendered by Suburban Residence. *American Sociological Review*, August 1956, pp. 446–53.

McGINLEY, PHYLLIS (1949) Suburbia. Of Thee I Sing. *Harper's*, December 1949, pp. 78–82.

MUMFORD, LEWIS The Wilderness of Suburbia. *New Republic*, pp. 44–45. The New America: Living Atop a Civic Mushroom. *Newsweek*, April 1, 1957.

NEWMAN, WILLIAM (1957) Americans in Subtopia. *Dissent*, Summer 1957, pp. 255–66.

PHILLIPS, H. I. (1925) The 7:58 Loses a Passenger. *Collier's*, April 11, 1925 pp. 11, 44.

REISSMAN, LEONARD (1953) Levels of Aspiration and Social Class. *American Sociological Review*, June 1953, pp. 233–42.

REISSMAN, LEONARD (1954) Class, Leisure, and Social Participation. *American Sociological Review*, February 1954, pp. 76–84.

RIESMAN, DAVID (1957) The Suburban Dislocation. *Annals of the American Academy of Political and Social Science*, November 1957, pp. 123–46.

RHODE, CARL VON (1946) The Suburban Mind. *Harper's*, April 1946, pp. 289–99.

SCHNORE, LEO F. (1956) The Functions of Metropolitan Suburbs. *American Journal of Sociology*, March 1956, pp. 453–8.

SCHNORE, LEO F. (1957) The Growth of Metropolitan Suburbs. *American Sociological Review*, April 1957, pp. 165–73.

SCHNORE, LEO F. (1957) Satellites and Suburbs. *Social Forces*, December 1957 pp. 121–7.

SEELEY, JOHN, R. SIM, ALEXANDER and ELIZABETH LOOSESLEY (1956) *Crestwood Heights: A Study of the Culture of Suburban Life*. New York: Basic Books.

SPECTORSKY, A. C. (1957) *The Exurbanites*. Philadelphia. Lippincott.

STEIN, MAURICE (1957) Suburbia, A Walk on the Mild Side. *Dissent*, Autumn 1957, pp. 267–75.

SWIFT, ETHEL (1928) In Defense of Suburbia. *Outlook*, April 4, 1928, pp. 543–4, 558.

TARVER, JAMES D. (1957) Suburbanization of Retail Trade in the Standard Metropolitan Areas of the U.S., 1948–1954. *American Sociological Review*, August 1957, pp. 427–33.

WHETTEN, NATHAN (1951) Suburbanization as a Field for Sociological Research. *Rural Sociology*, December 1951, pp. 319–30.

WHYTE, WILLIAM H., JR. (1953) The Transients. *Fortune*, May 1953, pp. 112–17, 221–6.

WHYTE, WILLIAM H., JR. (1953) The Transients, II—The Future, c/o Park Forest. *Fortune*, June 1953, pp. 126–31, 186–96.

WHYTE, WILLIAM H., JR. (1953) The Transients, III—The Outgoing Life. *Fortune*, July 1953, pp. 84–89, 160.

WHYTE, WILLIAM H., JR. (1953) The Transients, IV—How the New Suburbia Socializes. *Fortune*, August 1953, pp. 120–2, 186–90.

WHYTE, WILLIAM H., JR. (1957) *The Organization Man*. New York: Doubleday Anchor Books.

WOODBURY, COLEMAN (1955) Suburbanization and Suburbia. *American Journal of Public Health*, January 1955, pp. 1–7.

The Pattern of Neighbouring Relations in Dortmund-Nordstadt

E. PFEIL

Editor's Note

    This is an attempt to use standard social survey techniques to assess primary group relationships in a high-density residential area in the heart of a German industrial city. Propinquity leads to both common concern and withdrawal. These are subtle relationships and the study suffers from the lack of participant observation and of the development of such conceptual tools as "role" or "network". However, it provides something of the flavour of a widely quoted study, hitherto not available in English. The author admits that she raises more questions than she answers.

AREA OF INVESTIGATION

Nordstadt, the survey area, in the industrial town of Dortmund, is a closely built-up suburb north of the town centre, where residential areas are mixed with industry. The tenements (*Mietshäuser*) selected for the survey adjoin one another fronting directly onto the streets, without gardens or a green strip in front. Some of the roads carry through-traffic. These tenements have four or five floors, usually with two flats on each floor; the smallest have six, the largest eighteen flats. Seven large blocks of tenements were visited and every sixth household was interviewed. (A block contains all the tenements enclosed by four roads.) The district was heavily bombed during the war, and has since been partly rebuilt.

Sixty per cent of the investigated working population were manual workers, 17 per cent white collar workers (*Angestellte*), 17 per cent self-employed and 6 per cent were government employees (*Beamten*). Half of the manual workers were skilled, mostly working in the foundries. (There are twice as many of the workers employed in the foundries as in the mines.) The government employees and white collar workers are of lower status; the self-employed have their own shops or workshops. If we call this group *kleine Leute*, or lower class, then we have investigated a closely built-up *kleine Leute* quarter, built typically near the town-centre. The investigation, indeed, proves this to be in more than one respect a group which, in its neighbourly behaviour, is probably quite different from the middle class. They are a comparatively well-settled population, more than half were born in Dortmund, four-fifths having lived there for more than twenty years. However, the separate tenements have different degrees of stability, which we must remember when assessing neighbouring relations.

THE TENEMENT AS A NEIGHBOURHOOD UNIT

Taking the tenement as the unit of investigation, neighbourly behaviour is summarized in Table 1. We find that daily exchange of greetings is taken as a matter of course. Participation in mourning a death is general; nobody withdraws. Death overcomes the barriers which are generally between tenement occupants on family occasions.

On occasions like weddings and confirmations, a fifth of the neighbours do not take part because, as they say, these *are* family occasions.[1] But the remaining four-fifths actively take part in such events. How strongly the tenement functions as a unit is shown by the fact that three-quarters of the group said that news of an illness is known all over the tenement immediately. As many said, when a neighbour needs help during illness, someone will make sure that help is given without necessarily taking an active part, whereas at a funeral and on family celebrations everyone is able to take part.

Lending, as the most common form of neighbourly assistance, is also widespread through the tenement, and three-quarters of

---

[1] Of those who refused to participate, a third firmly quoted this as the reason.

TABLE 1. PERCENTAGE SHOWING POSITIVE PARTICIPATION AND NEIGHBOURLY BEHAVIOUR BY TENEMENT BLOCK

Questioned people	Number	Greeting 1	Death 2	Wedding 3	Confirmation 4	Help in sickness 5	Being informed of news 6	Lending 7	Being friendly with families in tenements 8
Whole number in block	274a	98	97	81	80	77	74	72	52
I–III old tenements (1880–1908)	120	97	98	73	73	75	70	70	60
IV–V built by development company 1928–9	62	98	100	91	91	81	84	80	53
VI–VII badly bombed, VII rebuilt	92	99	94	(81)b	80	76	67	68	40
I large tenements from 1908	98	97	97	71	75	73	69	69	60
V medium tenements from 1908	—	(97)	—	—	—	(81)	(96)	(89)	(68)
VII rebuilt large tenements from 1908	35	(100)	—	—	—	(88)	(68)	(71)	(35)
Tenements with less than 10 flats	113	99	100	93	89	81	82	79	53
Tenements with 10 or more flats	153d	97	95	75	73	75	68	68	52

a For 274 investigated we did not use the one-family tenements in Block VI for our investigation on neighbourhood. We discarded vague or wrong answers. Also answers on family-events when they said that they had not yet happened. Also on lending, the answers of families with lodgers or relatives, who would not provide that kind of help. (We will refer to these various groups in the text.)

The relative number, therefore, changes from question to question. Greeting = 269, Death = 269, Wedding = 195, Confirmation = 208, Help in sickness = 254, Being informed of news = 260, Lending = 238, Being friendly = 256.

b When the relative number is below 50, we put the percentage in brackets; a dash signifies under 30.

c Large = 12 flats per tenement, 8 is usual.

d 8 without information on size of tenement.

the occupants are involved. (Three-quarters actually admitted this—but there are signs that there are more who do not admit it.) Thus even though between three-quarters and four-fifths of the sample join in the pattern of neighbourly activities, curiously enough only about half of the sample said that they were involved with any other family in borrowing or lending.

About one in seven of the respondents said that there had not been a death, wedding or confirmation since they had been there.[2] This denial of knowledge of such events suggests they are neither prepared to employ the custom of their previous background, nor have they yet had an opportunity to find out what is expected of them. (They should have been questioned on their attitudes to this.)

As we expected, the intensity of neighbourly relations varies from tenement to tenement (Table 1). The tenements of Blocks IV and V showed a stronger neighbourly attitude in every respect.[3] They were built by a development company in 1928/9, and hardly damaged during the war. These flat-dwellers have been there longer than those of the other blocks. Two-thirds were here before 1948 and only a few have moved in during the last two years. In the tenements of Blocks I–III, half of the families have moved in since 1948, in those of Blocks VI and VII two-thirds.

The greater stability within Blocks IV and V may be due not only to the actual length of residence, but also to the desired length of residence. Seventy-five per cent want to stay (the usual percentage is 45). These moderately sized tenements are favoured (where there are on average eight flats to each tenement). Neighbourly relations are considerably more complex in the tenements with less than ten families than in the larger tenements (Table 1) and the length of stay is significant. Table 2 shows a turning point after two years' residence. The exchange of the time of day

---

[2] Cf. note a in Table 1.

[3] Table 1, columns 3–7; the differences in columns 1 and 2 are without significance; there is full participation almost everywhere. We will refer to column 8.

is the only neighbourly contact which is established immediately on arrival. All other contacts (Table 2, cols. 2–7) are left for a time by those who later on may decide to participate in neighbourly activities. (It is possible, that the waiting period lasts only a year; because of the small numbers, we had to take a two-year period.)

On comparing Blocks I, V and VII, out of the context of their groups, we might expect a greater contrast in neighbourliness because we are dealing with extremes of both type of tenement and length of residence. In fact, Block V with 7 or 5 flats per tenement (3.7 per cent of the occupants having lived there for less than two years) has the highest rating in neighbourliness. Block I, with the largest tenements and with the greatest turnover of occupants amongst Blocks I–III, has ratings no different from those of Blocks I–III as a whole. In Block VII, which has the largest tenements, with about 9 per cent of new occupants who moved in after the rebuilding, we find the same ratings as in Blocks VI and VII as a whole. As the numbers that we are working with in Blocks V and VII are very small, we must in both cases arrive at results which are not statistically significant. Such characteristics as "short length of stay" and "number of flats" were similarly inconclusive and stop us from overestimating the influence of these two factors on neighbourly relations, or from regarding them as the only effective factors. Other factors may well have contributed to closer relations in Blocks IV and V. A check showed that there was no cause to suspect a difference in age as the determining factor. Perhaps one of the reasons is that they are socially more homogeneous, being the tenements for government employees.

We expected people to be friendly in Blocks IV and V and in the small tenements because they have been shown to have the greatest level of neighbourliness, but in fact friendliness is shown to be independent of the size of house or length of residence (Table 1, col. 8 and Table 2, col. 8). Values decrease from Blocks I–III, through IV and V, to VI and VII, that is from the oldest to the most recently built blocks. The number of families

TABLE 2. NEIGHBOURLY CONDUCT ACCORDING TO LENGTH OF STAY (EXPRESSED AS PERCENTAGES—POSITIVE ANSWERS ONLY)

Stay in years	No. of respondents N = 275	Greeting 1	Participation in			Help in sickness 5	Knowledge of news 6	Lending 7	Being friendly with families in tenement 8
			Death 2	Wedding 3	Confirmation 4				
Under 2 years	51	98	87	72	57	77	60	60	54
2 + up to 6 years	82	100	100	82	84	81	79	76	51
6 + up to 20 years	74	96	98	80	83	90	78	73	44
20 + years	64a	98	98	84	83	70	77	75	65

a Three without information on length of stay.

which any one family knows within the tenement is larger in the older tenements—in Blocks I–II: 21 per cent of the families are acquainted with three to all of the other families; in Blocks IV and V, 12 per cent; in Blocks VI and VIII, 11 per cent; in Block VII, the new block, 1 per cent. The analysis shows that the age and social structure of the tenement are the crucial variables: of one hundred interviewed people who have acquaintances in the same tenement, sixty are in Block I, fifty-three in Blocks IV and V and thirty-five in Block VII. The difference is explained by the varied types of occupants.

TABLE 3. CERTAIN STRUCTURAL CHARACTERISTICS
OF THE POPULATION BY BLOCKS

Occupants are	In Block		
	I	IV & V	VII
65 years and over	33	25	13
Old age pensioners	13	11	3
In the flat for 20 years or more	15	13	7

Length of residence is only relevant when combined with age. It is not the recent immigrants who top the scales, but the established group. This is confirmed in the last column of Table 2. The position stabilizes after a length of stay of 20 years, not of 2 years.[4] The next category of relationships with other families in the tenement, that of getting to know people better in a situation which is not bound by customary patterns or habits, demands personal initiative and is distinct from all the other relationships within the tenement. Newcomers to the tenement may be able to make

---

[4] It is difficult to explain why the occupants of 6 to 20 years' standing make up the smallest fraction of families with acquaintances. Examination showed that neither of the sub-groups with few acquaintances are dominant here: we neither have a great number of independent workers, nor refugees. We either have an unrecognized factor somewhere, or there is a chance deviation.

friends relatively easily acting on their own initiative. However, the more likely situation is for them to fit in with the accepted pattern of behaviour of the tenement community, which involves a period of waiting and watching. Friendship is, of course, very slow to develop to its full strength.

Some of the results are based on inadequate data and can only be used with reservation.[5] We must treat them as a basis for further investigation, rather than final results: primary relations between neighbours spread most rapidly when tenements are not too large and the occupants do not change too often, secondary relations where older people have lived for many years. As respondents said, "Everybody knows everybody else, we stick together." "The families living in this house have almost all been here since 1929, they know one another because of the war and the children." (This does not mean that couples without children find it more difficult to make friends, 46 per cent of these know one or more families closely; as many, in fact, as of the families with children. Children can lead to friendship and to animosity.) Neither should we think that young people had less friends in the tenement. They make friends easily and keep together, since in many cases they were born in the town or even in the tenement. Fewest friendships are found amongst the middle-aged (as amongst those who have been there neither a long nor short while).[6]

It is too early to say whether or not this will prove to be the general rule, which will then prove the validity of other material. We have said several times before that we might arrive at chance correlations, by using the small cells of our sample. But differences (like those of primary relations) that all point towards the same conclusion, support one another. Even if every single difference is not significant, we can be fairly certain that there are important differences. However, we are less certain about the exceptional

---

[5] The amount $N = 274$ bears no correlation of a first or second degree.

[6] This contradicts the thought that the 35–65-year-olds, the refugees, are responsible for the lack of integration: they have been here less time than anybody!

situation of being friendly. We find neighbourly relations in Blocks IV and V more intense than we suspected from the answers at first glance. The most active forms of neighbourly help during illness are "baby sitting", "shopping", "washing up" or "doing the washing" (I–III: 38 per cent; IV and V: 65 per cent; VI and VII: 52 per cent). We get a very firm "Yes" to the question about whether daily greetings are exchanged (I–III: 26 per cent; IV and V: 38 per cent; VI and VII: 9 per cent), and there is hardly any evidence of families being excluded from this relationship (I–III: 15 per cent; IV and V: 3 per cent; VI and VII: 14 per cent).

TABLE 4. FRIENDLY WITH NEIGHBOURS BY AGE GROUPS
(Friendly with neighbours in the tenement, in percentages)

Age of husband	Number of families		
	0	1–2	3 and over
Under 35 years	43	38	18
35 up to 65 years	52	35	13
65 and over	32	40	28

Statements of good relations, made spontaneously when the question about exchange of greetings was put, were mostly from Blocks IV and V. Here are a few:

"We have a very nice atmosphere here" (V).

"People in this tenement stick together and everyone is clean. You would not find another house like this in the district. Everyone is helpful and considerate" (IV).

"We all understand one another, which is marvellous!" (IV).

"Everybody is nice, and easy to get on with" (IV).

"We don't know the word fighting in this house" (V).

(Similar remarks about no fighting came from Block I, but also: "Of course, something does happen now and then. But we always help one another when necessary and let byegones by byegones.")

In one case, praise of the house-community in Block IV went like this:

"We have a wonderful sense of community here. We all know each other well. Most birthday parties are held with everyone there."

These remarks carry particular weight as they were unsolicited.

The strength of a good atmosphere in such a community is shown by the reluctance to move away. In spite of many drawbacks in the flats and district, these occupants would rather stay. Good social relationships with the next man, especially for the "small man" (*kleinen Mann*) are very important in the city. The word *Harmonie* was mentioned again and again. The neighbour, and the relationship with him, is one of the main factors in his life. We can recognize the real extent of social relationships only when we consider them from the standpoint of the family. We will then discover further threads in the fabric of neighbourly relations.

THE FAMILIES' CIRCLE OF NEIGHBOURS

Acquaintanceship: Exchange of Greeting, Gossip and Closer Acquaintanceship

Exchanging the time of day between occupants in tenements demonstrates the importance of a shared roof. The newly-arrived family feels that it has moved into a community with a situation in common—a feeling like that in the bombing, or during a fire. It now belongs to a social group in which everyone greets everyone else. It might, at first glance, seem quite pointless to inquire what kind of greeting, but this turned out to be a key-question. Used as the first of the neighbourhood-complex questions, it illuminated the whole idea of neighbourhoods, since a number of respondents gave explanations of their relations with neighbours with their answer, which made some of the later questions unnecessary. Again in cases where the stimulus of the question about the kind of greeting did not release further comment, we got the impression that there was an interest and eagerness for more questions. Hence, if this question can so readily stir people to comment, the daily greetings must be much more than what the critics of city life would have us believe—"A mere convention, without any significance." Convention, yes, but it is also important for social orientation. The two-thirds of respondents who volunteered further information always mentioned friendly relationships. In one case the emphasis was on non-involvement: "We exchange the time of day, but we keep ourselves to ourselves!" This non-involvement does not rule out the greeting, it refers to developments from it. To the question "Do you greet all the families that live on this staircase?" about one-eighth of the sample answered simply "Yes". Animosities between some of the families had led to the greeting being dropped. But sometimes a family is entirely ignored by everybody: "We have nothing to do with them, but the rest of us stick together." This is usually on account of behaviour that is disapproved of. ("Washing clothes on Sunday" or: "That woman is impertinent", i.e. she has put herself, through her behaviour, outside the community.)

But such animosities are exceptions: they do not invalidate the findings as a whole. It is only when people have friends and enemies that they are related to the neighbourhood; only where they have neither one nor the other are they alone, without neighbours. The women show greater involvement, by giving more elaborate answers, than the men, who often answer simply: "Yes".

TABLE 5. INTENSITY OF EXCHANGE OF GREETING (OF BOTH SEXES)

Questioned	Total No.	% Yes	% Emphatic Yes	% Conditional Yes	No	% No
Men	150	61	21	16	2	0
Women	49	76	9	9	4	0
Both	74	66	28	12	0	0
$N =$	273 = 100%	65	21	12	2	0

The women are forced to be involved both positively and negatively. The small, empty flat makes them feel lonely; they need human contact. The men often refuse to see this: they have enough contact during their working hours. The necessary daily contact and involvement with their neighbours—shopping, carpet beating, emptying-out the rubbish—causes the women to have both more friends and more enemies. We see this clearly in their more detailed answers. (In a conversation with both partners, the more dominant of the two would control the direction of the answers.)

Very rarely is a family completely ignored: the double image of the daily greeting is not so much "greeting and not-greeting" side by side, as the ambivalence of the greeting itself. The question concerning the daily exchange causes one family to talk in terms of unity and understanding in the tenement, and another to emphasize the limits of the relationship: "I say, hallo, to everybody: I don't want to know them any better", "We get along, we say hallo, and keep to ourselves", is said over and over again in the Nordstadt and elsewhere. Saying, "Guten Tag, guten Weg und damit Schluss!" ("Good day, safe journey and that's all!") is as common in Westfalia as it is on the Rhine, in Dortmund as in Hamburg, in a mining village as in the industrial village, in the town centre as in the suburb. The relationship has distinct limits: a greeting is a turning towards *and* a turning away. It implies both good manners and social distance. To some people the element of turning towards is the important one, to others that of distance—it is the same with other attitudes of whole tenement communities. The new tenant makes known his position as a potential neighbour when he first moves in and when he first says "Good morning". If he says nothing or is offhand in his greeting he puts himself outside the community. If he appears reserved, this reserve will only be broken with difficulty, in an emergency, or by a fortuitous accident. If he appears friendly, the ground is prepared for further neighbourly relations. It is difficult to gauge the right balance of friendliness and reserve. In the case of further inquiries, one would have to find out to what extent people's names and circumstances are known to the rest.[7] The first sign of an intensification in the relations is the occasional chat after the "Good morning". This particular circle of neighbours at this stage begins to separate from that of the whole tenement; though one respondent said "I talk to everyone", this is not the common practice. Everybody exchanges the time of day; about half are acquainted with other families; the occasional neighbourly chat stands about halfway between the two. These chats draw a larger number of families together than the pattern of close acquaintanceship, but not all are involved to the same degree. Three-quarters of all neighbourly chats takes place on the stairs, an inhospitable spot, but valued because of its neutrality. The roads in the Nordstadt are too busy with traffic to invite chats on the front doorstep: we heard almost nothing of front door chats. Two people chatting in the hall look casual and can continue on their way at any moment, as when they chat in the corner shop or at the milk-cart. The housewives have a chance to meet others from their own and other tenements. The circle of neighbours expands, but it stays loose, particularly if it is not supported by strong "staircase-relations" in one's own tenements. Neighbours are not usually invited into the flat; only a quarter of neighbourly exchange happens in the flat, usually in the kitchen: again we meet the idea of distance. Neighbourly gossip appears to be regarded as a vice by some; we have therefore cause to believe that perhaps more chats are held in kitchens than the women will admit. When both marital partners are questioned they only confess to half the kitchen chats admitted by a separate partner. (Both 13 per cent, wife 28 per cent.)

Admitting people from outside the family into the home is a delicate subject; we may expect silence or a suppression of facts. D. V. Oppen points out the symbolic importance of the front door with a Yale lock, instead of the old open farmhouse-door. If we can trust the very small number of answers from the Nordstadt,

---

[7] W. Dunkhorst has already inquired into the knowledge of names in his parish research. The Structure of the Church Parish in the Industrial Large Town. Diss. FU Berlin, 1959.

we find that manual workers open their kitchens readily to friends; the government employees are the most withdrawn. Not a single wife of a government employee admitted to kitchen gossip: perhaps it does not fit into their ideal of what behaviour in their stratum should be like. (They are not in any way bad neighbours.)

We did not inquire into the subject matter of the talk: the odd remark was dropped: "What would we talk about, if it weren't for the weather!"; the cheapest shops, children and household affairs. H. Klages, who has explored the content of neighbourly conversation, emphasizes that, significantly, politics and "shop talk", subjects discussed with friends of the same political conviction or with colleagues, do not occur in talk between neighbours. Neighbours are reluctant to burden relationships with contrary opinions.

We can, through observing these differentiations, make out the particular laws ruling neighbourly relations. Everyone has to take account of these rules, since they are, to an extent, obligatory.

Still considering the level of acquaintanceship involving chat and gossip, we may mention the rapid spread of news, which we heard about when questioning about help with nursing the sick. "It gets around"; not necessarily from neighbour to neighbour, but finally it reaches everyone's ear through the separate relationships. How actively gossip unites the community in the tenement was shown by a particular event.[8] Gossip is the life-blood of social relationships, and it can unite or divide. "To know someone well" was not precisely defined. From what could be gathered, mutual

---

[8] A daily newspaper in Dortmund published a report on work by the social research centre, in which a few facts had got mixed up. An investigation on married couples, already completed, had been wrongly connected with the current investigation of the "Nordstadt", under the heading: "Who married whom? Social scientists investigate "Nordstadt!" The field-workers, who up to then had been received amiably, suddenly found the doors closed to them, although they had made appointments the day before. In the end thay managed to get a housewife to tell them the reason: "Nobody wanted to be interviewed about things like that!" When the situation had been explained, it was discovered that not nearly all of the occupants took that newspaper, but rumour had spread quickly and the ranks of the community closed against the suspected threat.

visiting by the families in the flats was the determining factor in this, the third degree of intensity in neighbourly relations. [9]

Further investigations on the basis of these findings should try to separate the steps of intensity more precisely: from knowing someone by sight, exchanging the time of day, chat in the street, on the stairs, and in the flat, up to knowing one another well and having both chance and pre-arranged get-togethers. The transitions here are not clearly defined and are therefore hard to distinguish. "To know someone well" tends as much towards the second level of intensity as towards friendship at the fourth level. But friendship cannot be regarded simply as the fourth level of neighbourly relations: it has its own place amongst social contacts.

Every second family has not developed this degree of friendship with anyone in the tenement, and often underlined this by remarks such as: "Going into each other's flats leads to nothing but gossip." "First they come in, then they look into all the saucepans and when they have found out everything about you they go away again!" "We do not pay much attention to other people. *Guten Tag und Guten Weg!* Any more than that leads to trouble." But we must not try to generalize from these colourful statements, because it was only 6 per cent of those who had made no friends, and 3 per cent of respondents who gave answers of this kind, which may arise out of fear and unhappy experiences. They were mostly old widows and old-age pensioners. The old seem to become either friendly and gentle, or embittered and withdrawn. It may not be chance that widows and single old-age pensioners, especially, are amongst those reluctant to open their doors. A feeling of inferiority, because of their shabby belongings, may contribute to this reluctance. The withdrawal of the government employee is due to different motives. In some cases unpopular neighbours may pretend that they want no relations. There is, however, one incident that happened several times during our

---

[9] Only occasionally was a contrary attitude discovered: "I know everybody well, but I don't go in and out of flats!"

investigations elsewhere. Someone said very emphatically that she would not suffer neighbours running in and out, nor peeping into cooking-pots, when the door opened and the woman from the neighbouring flat came in, with the greatest nonchalance, even lifting lids off saucepans on the stove saying: "Well, what are you having for lunch today?" (This teaches the social-researcher that the expression: *Pöttekieken* (Peeping into sauce-pans) is in fact meant literally.)

Contradictions between professed and practised neighbourliness,[10] apparent reserve and actual proximity, were frequently found.

The subjective interpretation of the questions on "knowing the neighbour well" was left to respondents. The answers are as follows (Table 6).

TABLE 6. EXTENT OF CLOSE ACQUAINTANCES
KNOWING

	%
No one in house	45
1 family	26
2 families	8
3–6 families	7
Everybody or almost everybody	7
Indeterminate answers	5 (23)[11]
No answer	2 (23)[11]

It is of course possible that those who said "Nobody" make higher demands on a close relation than those who say "All" or "Almost all". We are on surer ground with answers expressed in numbers, which provide us with a scale. On an overall average each family has 1.6 acquaintances in the tenement; those who actually have acquaintances in the tenement know 2.6 families.

[10] We also have an observation from England of actual behaviour contradicting the outwardly presented cultural idea (refusal of neighbourly relations). J. M. Mogey, *Family and Neighbourhood*, London, 1956.

[11] Extracted from Tables 1 and 2: so we have there for the definite answers slightly higher percentages for the remaining answers than here.

Skilled workers, particularly miners, have more close acquaintances than anyone else. The self-employed workers have least: they say they are too busy with their shops or workshops or that they only know people for business reasons.

Yet how significant is it when they say they know 1–2 families of a tenement community? We heard remarks like: "We are good neighbours, but not too close." It is quite possible to be a good neighbour without being on more friendly terms. For friendliness, apart from the possibility of enriching relations, also involves the danger of destroying the primary ones. A number of people feel that the bounds of neighbourliness have been transgressed with the growth of closer friendship. The need for privacy is very easily understood, under conditions where everyone hears and sees what goes on, where everyone knows the next man's taste in radio programmes; the excessive proximity demands that a distance be preserved between personal spheres.

Georg Simmel raised this basic question: "What degree of spatial proximity or separateness is being demanded or is it endurable, under given forms and contents, by *Vergesellschaftung*?" When you have physical distance the social distance establishes itself automatically; with physical proximity, it has to be *created*; social distance will be emphasized when it does not necessarily arise out of the situation and there is no valid behaviour pattern to follow. Reserve amongst neighbours is not unfriendliness, but a defence barrier against an endless enlargement of the neighbouring circle. It is not isolation as such. Perhaps it is not by chance that people who have no relatives in Dortmund make friends with their neighbours more easily than people who have their family living close-by. But close proximity is not the only explanation of the need for privacy. Another motive is evident in the whole of modern society, more obvious in a large town, because it is ahead in social development—respect for the sphere of privacy. The deliberate keeping of one's distance is not defence against interference, but caused by the idea that certain things are "of the family" alone.

HELP DURING ILLNESS

Contrary to the stereotype of the city-dweller, who might fall ill and die in his tenement without attracting attention, we found the people of Nordstadt well informed about their fellows. They were always prepared to help: three out of four respondents confirmed that news of illness or need travelled fast:

". . . you come to hear of it at once, everybody tells everybody else!"

"We tell people."

The rest thought that it was left to chance who got to know, very few said that they paid no attention. The occupants of small tenements are better-informed than those in the large ones (compare Table 1). Refugees are told less of the news, but they know at once of a neighbour's illness; they are ready to help just as much as any well-established inhabitant of Dortmund.

Again, four out of five take care of sick neighbours; only 18 per cent refuse and they are characteristically the self-employed, with both husband and wife working in the business, or old people who need help themselves. The idea of help for the sick is not burdened with the same ambiguity as borrowing. It is not surprising that people speak about it without hesitation. We don't know how far the idea of having to tend a sick neighbour was influenced by conscious Christian standards and this must be left to guesswork.

This duty is not only recognized by almost everyone, but neighbours hasten to fulfil it. We now arrive at the methodological question of how to judge results which may be prejudiced by the suppression or exaggeration of facts (as we showed in the study of gossip). This evasion is a result in itself. Adroit objective questioning in "intensive interviews" can determine the extent of neighbourliness as it is actually practised, in contrast with earlier claims.

If relatives live within easy reach, all that need be done by neighbours is to send them word; but apart from these cases, real help is given to the rest (77 per cent). Neighbours who are friends, or who live on the same floor are the most likely helpers and the most usual help given is shopping, but flat-cleaning, washing and cooking are mentioned twenty-one times. Thus, there is more help given than simply calling the doctor: only three of our flat-dwellers regarded this as the only active help they would give in case of illness. Here again, we find that the small tenements have more neighbourliness than the others, and that the statements of women are more varied and vivid than those made by men, because helping the sick is almost exclusively women's business.

After illness, the next most important situation in which help is given is confinement. When a neighbour has a baby everybody is helpful: they clean the flat or do the washing. "When my baby was born, neighbours brought me broth and things, cleaned the flat, did the washing; all without having to be asked." Human involvement in the event is another important motive, next to helpfulness.

Births and deaths, and other major family events such as weddings and confirmations, are always certain to arouse general interest. (The city-dweller, too, will stop to watch the bride leave the church after the wedding when he sees the wedding carriages wait outside.) Such occasions break up the family circle, inviting not only help, but also, to a certain extent, participation in the celebration by the neighbours.

NEIGHBOURING PARTICIPATION IN FAMILY EVENTS: BIRTHS, WEDDINGS, CONFIRMATIONS, DEATHS

In a rural community those neighbours who help each other in every case of emergency, would, as a matter of course, share family celebrations. We can quote cases from another study of a mining town where an old woman, whom the hosts had forgotten to invite, appeared with the words "*Ik gehor auch dabi*" ("I should be here too"). Another story concerns a young man, whose wife had come from somewhere else: he only wanted relatives or friends at his wedding because he thought it would be more private, but his father firmly insisted on inviting the neighbours as well. Even in an urban community on the outskirts of a town, neighbours may "simply join" celebrations: "It is customary"—at least at silver wedding anniversaries.

Our Nordstadt dweller does not necessarily join in as a matter of course; he respects the family character of a christening, a confirmation or a wedding: "That is a family celebration" is said by many. Yet he is not indifferent—the concern may take different forms: a card of congratulation, flowers, or a small present; or every family in the tenement might contribute towards a wedding present. We are also told about *Poltern*[12] and the decoration of the tenement with garlands, particularly in the new tenements of Block VII, by families who have not long since moved in! It appears that such customs may be introduced by one or more brave occupants: a few personalities stand out. They are the catalysts of the community.

Before a wedding in any tenement the next-door neighbour collects money for a communal wedding present: her job is to buy and deliver it. Anyone who has grown up in the tenement and who is popular will find that the next-door tenements will also put up garlands over the door to celebrate the wedding. "When the couple is badly off, neighbours provide food, drink and music".

Block I: "Everybody is excited when we have a party in the tenement (*im Haus*). That is a good thing." *Da geht es hier rund* ("We all take part"). Some tenements become family communities on such occasions: From Blocks IV and V: *Da ist alles ein Herz und eine Seele* ("We are all friends together"). But on the whole invitations are not part of neighbourliness in the city, and they are only extended to neighbours who have developed into friends. You are accepted at a party not as a neighbour but as a friend. Only 8 per cent say that they have been invited to weddings in the tenement. A later celebration with the neighbours seems to be more common; they are asked in the day after for coffee and cakes. Using up left-overs is good housekeeping, and everybody likes to

---

[12] The eve of wedding custom of throwing saucepans down the stairs— *Translator's note*.

talk about what happened on the day of the party. Help, congratulations and presents thus being repaid. "We often have marvellous parties." We find the separation of celebration and celebration-with-neighbours mostly in Block IV, but it is mentioned quite often in Block VI.

Apart from sharing typical family festivities, no local, traditional celebrations are customary in the community. Yet several roads join in a children's summer party. The children's play-communities extend far outside the tenement, and their summer party has the same broad basis. Adults in the Nordstadt attend the summer parties, but this does not lead to an adult community of neighbouring streets.

Any barriers between families come down when death hits one of them. Nine-tenths of the families who were present in the tenement at the time of a death describe the help and kindness showed by everyone, the wreath sent by the neighbours and their attendance at the funeral. Others describe further individual acts of kindness: a wreath given by each family, expressions of sympathy and offers of help, which can also happen when the community acts together. The close neighbour, or a family who knew the dead person well, and who knows "which other families outside the tenement to approach", collect the money. "Within the tenement, no one would refuse to contribute."

The concept of neighbourhood here includes chosen neighbours and acquaintances outside the tenement. Relatives and close friends send wreaths individually. In some other tenements, it will always be the same woman who takes on the duty of telling the families in the tenement of a death, thus assuming a neighbourly function. Animosities, too, are forgotten at such times. "People who haven't been on speaking terms, forget it. And when we collect for a wreath, nobody refuses. If it was somebody poor, we collect enough to have some left over. That is put into his hand (probably the hands of the deceased's family)." It is customary to go to the funeral, but not all the members of the community attend. "If the dead person was a woman, the woman goes to the funeral; if he was a man, the man in the family goes."

The women who live next door sometimes help with the meal that is provided for relatives after the funeral (serving coffee). Shopkeepers regard deaths and wedding from a "business point of view"; for instance: "We send a basket of flowers to good customers, a bunch of flowers or a card to others. That's all we do." Not much is left of the rich, colourful customs associated with death in the country districts. There are no communal prayers by the bier, no meal provided by the neighbours. Duty as pall-bearers is always taken on by neighbours in the mining-town, but in the city only when rural kinds of living conditions, with garden plots by the houses, make people into closer neighbours.

In Deusen, great poverty at the early beginnings of the estate (it was built in 1933 as a self-help project for the unemployed, to provide them with a means of growing their own food) may have prohibited the expense of pall-bearers. It is a firm tradition there now to perform this last duty for neighbours. On the Busenberg estate the pall-bearing by neighbours is the old village tradition, but in Deusen it is a new tradition with its origin in local economic necessity. In Nordstadt the funeral parlour takes over.

CONCLUSIONS

We find that the Nordstadt people do have neighbourly ties, even if these are limited by their very nature. Certain areas of neighbourly relations have lost their significance in varying degrees. In some senses, they have retained a number of their functions; in others, they are empty and vague. Not all of the changes are caused by the city environment itself. Here are the contours of an industrial world, in contrast to that of a pre-industrial world. It is not simply the size of town, the density of the population, the traffic or the mentality of the city-dweller which shape neighbourly relations, but the industrial bureaucratic patterns of work and ways of thought. Though size of tenement, i.e., urban living conditions, does influence the intensity of relations, the influence of mobility and the degree of turnover of the population is more significant. The image of the unneighbourly city dweller is left over from the days of cities in their infancy; it is still valid for estates outside the city, if they have the turnover of families that is typical for a period of industrialization. Neighbourly relations, even though on the whole more loosely structured than those in the pre-industrial world, amongst city people and amongst other industrial populations are determined by good manners, rules for behaviour and customs. Here, too, man looks for and finds the neighbour, and here too "lesser and greater assistance" is exchanged. For four-fifths of the Nordstadt population relationships with neighbours are closely interwoven with family life.

Community and Association in a London Housing Estate

RUTH DURANT

Editor's Note
   This classic study of the formation of new secondary groups in response to a new urban situation has been hard for students to find for many years. It should perhaps be considered in the context of urbanization involving dispersal and diffusion and is a forerunner of numerous other studies which have appeared in the last thirty years. The detailed ethnography is interesting for its own sake but it also reveals a pattern which still has great relevance.

"I HAVE known Watling in its early days," an old resident said, "when the buttercups were still growing at the place where are now the big shops, in Watling Avenue." "Mud was in the streets." "No shops, no schools, the children were running wild." "We kids used to have bonfires at the site of present school buildings. I was eight then," a youth told me, who had grown up at Watling and, like many others, missed practically all schooling for two years. Only part of the Estate stood, and only houses had been built. The place was pitch-dark at night. "At that time (1928) there was . . . nothing but bricks and mortar and acres of mud. . . . The main thoroughfares . . . were narrow lanes—little more than footpaths and cart-tracks in part. If one wanted to dance or to attend a concert it was necessary either to make a trip to Central London or to one of the public-houses some distance away."[1]

Nowadays, wandering in the Watling side-streets on mornings and early afternoons, when the children are still at school and, but for occasional aeroplanes coming across from the Hendon

---

[1] Reminiscences in the *Watling Resident*, January 1932.

aerodrome,[2] silence is complete, the scene confronting the early settlers can be easily reconstructed.

It was strange and strenuous for the women, being used to buying all they needed at their doorstep, to travel half an hour or more to Edgware for their shopping. Their neighbours were new and even physically more distant than their old neighbours in town. Having lived in London most or all of their lives,[3] they deprecated the markedly rural aspect of this place, which from the ancient survey of 1321 until the post-war ordnance map had hardly changed its appearance. Moreover, their intrusion into the quiet scene was watched with suspicion and even with animosity by the middle-class households in the districts.

"For the immigrants it was like being in a foreign country, with new friends to make and new difficulties to overcome."[4] Thus for the newcomers the two most important factors were the strangeness and newness of the place, bare of all urban traditions and facilities, and the antagonism of the inhabitants of the district, which was manifested all over Hendon. This point, unfortunate as it is, needs to be stressed, since it has had a vital influence upon the growth of local consciousness. Moreover, it is a factor in no way peculiar to the social development of the Watling Estate, but is typical of the early history of all municipal housing estates which have been built on the fringes of urban areas.

---

[2] The Aerodrome and its noisy activity, immediately adjacent to the Watling Estate, has, in fact, often been the subject of complaint by Watling residents.

[3] The *New Survey of London*, vol. vi, p. 18, reports that still, as in 1881, "the poorest and most congested boroughs of the inner ring have the highest proportion of born Londoners. And these are the boroughs from which most of the tenants of L.C.C. Cottage Estates come." Hence their strong attachment to London.

[4] Another account of this period is given in the *Watling Resident*, March 1935: "Some few of the settlers could not adjust themselves to the new environment and, at the first opportunity, packed up their possessions and returned to town. But the majority of us had the pioneer spirit and got busy in our gardens and put our houses in order. Some of the older inhabitants of the district resented the intrusion of Londoners on their rural retirement, but they soon found us to be decent-living, orderly citizens, and everybody benefited by the increased trade and better public services made possible by the greater number of ratepayers."

Antagonism from without breeds association within; that was repeatedly vindicated at Watling. At first, it made the men and women there conscious of being one class of people, different from those in the neighbourhood. It demonstrated to them that they had common problems from which there was no escape. And outstanding amongst all these problems was the need for a social life of their own; there were hardly any social activities in the neighbourhood to which they could turn. So far as amenities did already exist, they were barred for the council tenants. Watling realized that, although it had physical existence, it still had to put itself on the map, and it chose to do so by developing its own independent social life.

AWAKENING OF LOCAL PATRIOTISM

The *Watling Resident* was the first local paper and preserves till now its local importance. On the first page of the very first number, published as early as May 1928, we find these words:

"When we have been torn up by the roots, and rudely transplanted to foreign soil, as most of us here have been, we are lonely; yet, save in rare instances, we lack the faculty of quickly making friends. Beyond our immediate neighbours we know no one on this great Estate. . . . The Watling Residents' Association hopes to bring together those whom convention forbids to introduce themselves. . . . It asks only that its member be gregarious. . . . It hopes to make him feel that, in being a citizen of Watling, he is a citizen of no mean city, a man of many and worthy friends."

These words were repeated over and over again, orally and in print, by residents on the Estate. They subsequently created slogans expressing the same ambition, 1929: "Soon Watling will be on its own feet and it will be all Watling for Watling."

A year later: "Watling is noted for its civic achievements and will be regarded in the near future as a model and pattern for others to follow."

A tenant on the Estate, who had to leave for personal reasons, bade farewell in the *Resident*: "Hendon will yet be proud of her immigrants from the area of the London County Council."

The New Year's greetings of the Watling Residents' Association, 1930, ran:

"There was a time, not so very long back, when we seemed to think that Burnt Oak was only a place to come home and sleep in, but those times have vastly changed and we are realizing that it is our own little town and we are proud of it. Some of us are working hard to get all to feel what this means and to wake Watling people up to the fact that they must not only be in it but of it."

This ambition could not have arisen if Watling had been nothing but ugliness. But the first inhabitants were pleased by the sight of the lovely trees on the Estate; they liked their new houses; they perhaps realized what the countryside, so unfamiliar at first to themselves, would mean for the health of their children. They started to fight Watling's drawbacks. Thus for four years the Residents' Association led a campaign under the motto: "We want the Watling Garden City."

THE FIRST IMMIGRANTS

We might well ask, who were the people cherishing such ambitions?

A number of factors operated in selecting people as tenants for the cottage estates in general and for the Watling Estate in particular. The people who came to live there show, therefore, certain characteristics. The majority are not, as it is commonly believed, slum-dwellers; on the contrary, at the time of moving to the Estate a considerable number of families had a higher standard of living than comparable groups in the whole London Area.[5] Yet, as has been said, the economic distinction between

---

[5] This comparison is subject to the definitions and findings of the *New Survey of London*.

Watling and London working-class people is in the main caused by special characteristics of the size and the age-structure of their families rather than by the comparison of the income of the fathers. One type of family is better off mainly because the family is small. Another type of family has grown up and there are now several wage-earners who contribute to the budget. A third type, the one-wage-earner family with several children, is poor and will struggle along until the children are grown up. It is mainly the first, but also the second, type of family which account for the "well-to-do" aspect of the Estate. Together they represent 65·5 per cent of families in the sample of present Watling residents.[6] Yet the important economic distinction is between small and large families on the Estate, 52·5 per cent and 47·5 per cent of the sample respectively. The latter, whether they have one or more wage-earners, whether they are poor or better off, belong to the same social group: they represent different stages of the same family life. It is only the group of small families, with one wage-earner, not all the inhabitants, who belong, to use the words of the *New Survey of London*, to "a much higher economic grade" than the average working-class household.

In addition, a number of more subtle factors have operated in the selection of the tenants for the Estate, or rather of those remaining there. Not everybody who moved to the Estate in the early years was forced to come there by the pressure of over-crowding. The new environment was often their deliberate choice. But we must remember that starting life at Watling meant in-numerable hardships, especially true throughout the early years. It required sacrifices of time, money, energy, comfort and, last but not least, of friendships. One can argue that people who could endure all that for the sake of better things to come were dis-tinguished by their mental and moral capacities. Meeting some of the "pioneers" now confirms this assumption. It ought to be borne in mind because it makes it easier to understand both the

---

[6] That is, at the time of their arrival on the Estate, 65·5 per cent of all families belonged to these groups of families, according to our classification.

successes and the failures in the development of Watling's social life.

THE CIRCUMSTANCES LEADING TO CO-OPERATION

But how did social life ever start? The first cottage on the Estate was let in April 1927. From that date until April 1928, 2,100 cottages were let and inhabited. The Estate was finished and the cottages were let by 1930. There were then 3,698 cottages and 320 flats, a total of 4,018 dwellings. Moreover, a great number of people came from the same area. St. Pancras and Islington dominated as places of origin. About 30 per cent came to the Estate under re-housing schemes; not more than 15 per cent as the result of slum clearance; a number came from pre-war block dwellings in Central London. From 1930 onwards very few people arrived under re-housing schemes.[7] And, since the arrivals on the Estate now occur singly, the geographical origin of the people has acquired a more scattered aspect.

These facts imply that especially favourable conditions for neighbourliness were present in 1927–8. The Estate was so much smaller than it is now. A great number of people immigrating during the same period experienced all the difficulties of adaptation to the new environment more or less simultaneously. Moreover, a majority of them had at least a common geographical background of experience.

This factor did not operate in the way one might easily assume—that people found themselves as neighbours in Watling who had been neighbours in Central London, or that they frequently met old friends in the new streets. In fact tendencies to the recovery of old associations were deliberately counteracted. Firstly, the Estate was not built in large, contiguous blocks but rather in patches. Hence the transference of whole London streets to

---

[7] The number of people re-housed on the Watling Estate after being displaced under slum-clearance, street-improvement, education or other schemes, is given for 1927–34 as 867; for 1934–5 as 21. *L.C.C. Housing Estates Statistics.*

Watling was physically impossible. Secondly, it was the policy of the L.C.C. in the early days wherever great numbers of people came from the same area "to break them up," thus making continuation of old friendships unlikely. When they came to the Estate the new arrivals thus faced the fact that the only social group preserved for them in its integrity was the family.

Yet, if they did not find old intimate friends in the streets of Watling, they saw faces which somehow seemed familiar. "Have I not seen her before?" they used to ask themselves. They continually encountered people whom they actually had not met but whom they easily might have met in London. They seemed so familiar to each other because they had indeed been distant neighbours previously. There was a mutual recognition amongst the immigrants "so rudely transplanted into foreign soil" of not sharing the territory for the first time but of being "compatriots" of long standing. And whoever has been a stranger in a strange place will testify to the relief in being in the company of people whom one might have met at home: it does not matter greatly whether one actually has known them before. The common background assures similar reaction to the new environment.

The problem was, therefore, not to find congenial people to associate with but "who would speak the first word?" We can take it for granted that a woman did, or rather the women. Indeed, particular circumstances compelled the women to establish relationships with each other. For the men only one aspect of their lives had changed, their home. They continued their jobs, at the same place, with the same routine and with the same fellow-workers. The women, having changed their homes, had to build up entirely new lives. Everything was not only new but also so much more difficult than previously: the shops so far away; the neighbours strange; no schools for their children. Loneliness pressed on the women much harder than on the men. They first began to nod to each other over the garden fence; and so the first meeting-place at Watling was the back garden, then not so much a garden as a dismal strip of ground. Of course, the children, living in the same street, soon started to play with each other.

The men met at first in the tube. Although, for the majority, the place of work had not changed, the daily journey to town had become infinitely more strenuous; so the early workmen's trains functioned as a common meeting-ground. They found no room to sit, but there was time to talk. As with their wives, the men who lived in the same street used to get to know each other in going to, and returning from, the station. Yet the fact that people met casually in back gardens and in tube compartments does not tell the whole story of the origin of local social life.

The Estate, it has to be remembered, was still nothing but an assembly of households, and for many people the family has remained the only social group of which they felt themselves to be an integral part. They have never got beyond that stage. They arrived; they had great trouble in rearranging their domestic habits, and the education of their children. So far as this functional adaptation to the new environment required it, they even developed some new interests and entered into some new associations. They settled down; "cultivated their garden"; bought a wireless set; subscribed to those local societies which promote horticulture, provide nursing services and facilitate saving and borrowing money. They belonged to families of a kind which was less frequent amongst the immigrants prior to 1930 than afterwards. They were interested in a distinct type of local organization, one which caters for family needs only.[8] But it would be wrong to conclude, therefore, that these families actually founded these organizations, or that chance meetings of residents from the same street did it. They prepared the ground. Only when another, less parochial, type of person had appeared were those local societies really established.

---

[8] A qualification has to be made so far as the Watling Horticultural Society is concerned. It was founded by people who had an interest not only in their own gardens, but in the development of all Watling into a Garden City. And although the ordinary member of this Society confines himself to his own private horticultural ambitions, its officers have retained their general interest in the Estate.

THE PIONEERS OF SOCIAL ORGANIZATIONS

It has had varying implications that at the beginning of Watling's history the family was the only social group which was intact. Many families remained self-contained; others possessed within themselves the potentialities of wider social groupings.

The "pioneers" of local social life (they use this term if they talk about each other even now) were without exception people who had previously had a share in some sphere of public life. Many of them had served through the War and were members of ex-service associations; some were keen trade unionists, some active members of the Conservative or Labour Party. Now, they threw their houses open to receive their fellow immigrants. Incidentally, few women played a prominent part during the early years on the Estate; most, having large families and young children, were too overburdened with housework. The one who distinguished herself most, and is now called "Granny" by everybody on the Estate, had grown-up children and, it seems, an extremely sensible husband. She knew how to manage her shopping cleverly, and the women in her street soon followed her example in this and other matters. She had been an active member of a political party for years and she had attended a settlement in London. Her sons discovered on the Estate friends from London, whom they brought into the house. Since all of them were engaged in social affairs, she herself was soon involved.

*   *   *   *   *

In December 1927 a letter appeared in the *Hendon and Finchley Times*, full of complaint and even offence against the new Estate. Six Watling people came together to discuss in what form they should protest. They decided that it was not only necessary to answer this letter in the Press, but, moreover, to form a "Residents' Association" which should in future safeguard and promote the interests of all the tenants on the Estate. They called a public meeting in a small local church hall on 5th January 1928. The hall was packed, 250 people attended. At a second public meeting, in a larger hall, which was even more packed and "even livelier than the first," the name and rules of the new Association were approved.

(1) That the Association be known as the "Watling Residents' Association."
(2) That its objects be:

    (*a*) Promotion of the interests of the residents on the Estate, and
    (*b*) for their well-being in such social and other activities as may be found necessary.

Thus the stage was reached where Watling itself became the unit of association.

ANTAGONISM FROM WITHOUT

Watling at that period looked very much like a colony, a community of people of similar origin and outlook settling in foreign territory. But this analogy fits only partly. A real colony consists of men of varied physical and psychological make-up. That very different types of people were living at Watling, different in spite of their common background, does not, therefore, impair the "colonial" aspect. But there were other factors: however unlike each other the colonists may be, they are united by the one impulse—to settle. At Watling this unanimity of purpose was absent. Further, a colony is a place far from the mother country; with each year that passes, the colonists become more conscious of the distance. Watling was from the outset near to London, and ever since it has been brought nearer still. Transport connections have become more varied and faster. The countryside, which formed a gap, separating the metropolis and the new estate, has been built over; they are now connected by an uninterrupted line of streets. Indeed, as Watling grew older, it more and more lost the likeness of a colony and acquired many characteristics of a suburb.

The various stages of this development merit description.

In January 1928, at the time of the foundation of the Watling Residents' Association, the "colonist" type was still predominant in local affairs. The most urgent question of the moment was how to overcome the strangeness of the physical neighbourhood, and how to break the antagonism or the snobbishness of its inhabitants.

There is ample evidence of Watling's feelings in the latter respect. From the *Resident*:

"I hear people from the immediate neighbourhood passing disparaging remarks about our youngsters. It galls me and makes my blood boil. Police Court cases are seized on and much capital is made of them.

". . . They (the children) will turn out fine, strong, healthy citizens that anyone would be proud of."

Sometimes it was not so much antagonism, as the patronizing attitude adopted by Mill Hill and Hendon people, which gave offence. At a quarterly meeting of the Watling Residents' Association in November 1929, the following resolution was passed:

"That this meeting of the W.R.A. strongly resents the use of the word 'charity' as applied to Watling, reported to have been used at the last Council Meeting of the Hendon Urban District Council, and calls for the immediate withdrawal of the offending words."

Another incident of similar kind is reported in the *Resident* in October 1932:

"The Deputy Charter Mayor of Hendon . . . said at the Luncheon on Charter Day, 20th September 1932, at the Town Hall, speaking of Watling: 'They have the material, they have the mentality; it is up to us to mould them'."

There can be no doubt that some reacted against certain criticisms and administrative measures with an exaggerated susceptibility. Yet that was hardly avoidable in the circumstances. [9]

---

[9] An incident which occurred in June 1929, might be mentioned. The *Resident* reported (July 1929): "We have received information of a petition, signed by the Lady residents of —— Avenue, Mill Hill, protesting against an alleged nuisance caused by Watling children. This petition has been forwarded

Even in 1937, when I told people in Hampstead or Hendon that I was working on the Estate, I often heard: "How horrible!" "Little Moscow." A teacher who works at one of the Watling schools confirmed my experience. "Everywhere in Golders Green and Edgware," she said, "there is great snobbishness about the Estate."

In a Watling central school, which draws about half of its pupils from the Estate, a class of forty-four girls, 11–12 years old, were asked whether they liked the Estate and what they thought of living there. They were a very bright and pleasant lot of girls. They did not reflect a moment when asked. Twenty-one of them lived off the Estate, and of these seventeen immediately answered that they did not like Watling. "Why not?" "It is dirty." "It is rough." "Not everywhere, Miss, but some parts are rough." Of those who actually lived on the Estate, four did not say anything, fifteen confessed that they liked it a lot and did not wish to move, four said just the contrary. "And why don't you like the Estate?" "Oh, Miss, if somebody has taken a cat, they say the Watling children have stolen it."

Not everybody in the neighbourhood was snobbish or narrow-minded. There have been a few especially notable exceptions. Mill Hill School, the most prominent local institution, and the Mill Hill Historical Society received the new neighbour Watling with the greatest friendliness. Surely, if they thought that the inhabitants would conform excellently to the traditions of the place, everybody could have followed their judgment.[10] They

---

to the local Council, local police, the headmasters of local schools and to Scotland Yard. . . . Had some foul murder been perpetrated in this delectable Avenue? . . . Having on our staff a very clever sleuth who invariably puts the police on the right track in these difficult cases, we sent him post-haste to the scene of the crime, suitably disguised. . . . Eventually we learned from our sleuth with utter dismay that Scotland Yard are tracking down the mysterious disappearance of some flowers from the front gardens in that particular Avenue. You can imagine our terrible disappointment."

[10] Not all Watling's friends in the neighbourhood are of the same pattern. Here is a letter to the Editor of the *Resident*, published as recently as March 1935. It may pass without comment:

certainly used their influence in order to bring about a better understanding between Watling and the neighbourhood. The first step was frank discussion on this very difficult subject. In March 1929 the Mill Hill Literary and Debating Society debated on "The Watling Estate and what it means to Mill Hill." "Unfortunately," said the *Resident*, "the actual question was not satisfactorily answered, or any definite decision arrived at as to what our Estate does mean to our neighbours. The inevitable question of snobbery arose during the debate as regards Mill Hill's attitude towards us. . . ."

" 'THOSE WATLING PEOPLE!'

'Dear Sir,

"It is with some trepidation that I take upon myself the liberty of writing to your most estimable magazine, and should there be any remarks which may appear to the reader to be a little 'high hat' I trust they will forgive me and endeavour to look at this letter in the light of a friendly criticism of a very worthy and trying section of the community.

"Often it has been said in my hearing. 'Oh, those Watling people!' I wonder why people pass remarks like that. Is it because they are so very perfect and so very pleased with themselves that no one—perhaps because they happen to be less endowed with this world's goods—could possibly have the same ideas, aims and respect for themselves as this type of person?

"On many occasions it has been my pleasure to employ for household duties young ladies from the Watling Estate. In practically every case I have found them to be most diligent in their duties, kind to my children and exceptionally clean.

"Is it, I wonder, that a small part of the inhabitants of the Estate take no interest in themselves or their families that these remarks are so often passed by Mill Hill people? I rather think it is, but it is, I know, the endeavour of the inhabitants of the Watling area to improve themselves.

"If I may say so, the fault lies in the inferiority complex that some of the Watlingites have. May I suggest that if you dear people would only for a short space of time imagine that you are equally as good as Mill Hill people, and in many cases infinitely better, you would in time develop a superiority complex and forge right ahead.

"It is a wonderfully organised estate, and, with the improvements the inhabitants are making, it ought to be a model estate, and no doubt in time Millhillians will say: 'Those too sweet people of *our* wonderful council estate.'

"I know it hurts to be termed inferior, but even the greatest man on earth founded our faith on His very inferiority. I say this with all reverence.

"Good-bye and keep bucking up your ideas.

"A MILLHILLIAN."

Frankness did not stop there:

"At a June meeting of the Hendon Council, Watling affairs were to the fore. Councillor Pugh[11] said: 'I feel that there is a definite feeling against Watling on the part of some members of this Council, but I hope the members will try to shake off that Anti-Watling complex which they seem to have developed.' "[12]

As time went on, Watling got used to the people outside, and they got used to Watling.

"We have our internal and external critics," says an editorial on 'These Watling People,' in the *Resident*, May 1930. "The others from outside point to one or two outstanding acts of the individual and condemn all for one. We would like to take them on a tour of the Estate and open their eyes. And yet, why should we trouble. Rather shall we carry on and create fresh records."

ASSOCIATION WITHIN

It was this spirit in which the Watling Residents' Association was formed. The day of its foundation may be regarded as the birthday of local patriotism. Its history is representative of the development of Watling's self-consciousness.

The Residents' Association was not only the first organization of any kind which was formed on the Estate, but it remains the only one devoted entirely to local interests. People had first to pay tribute to the fact that their needs were subject to common conditions and, therefore, required common solutions, before they could cater for special interests and hobbies.

The most common and most urgent need was to communicate with each other. Hence the first meetings of the Association were packed, as hardly any since. The Association established itself foremost as an organ of communication, and it founded the *Watling Resident*, a monthly publication. It had spectacular success. The first issue had a circulation of 1,637 copies; four months later, an edition of 2,000 copies was actually sold out three days after publication. Another four months later, in December 1928,

---

[11] Councillor for the Burnt Oak Ward.
[12] The *Resident*, August 1932.

record sales were achieved: 2,467 copies had been purchased. In March 1929 the peak of this development was reached with 2,636 copies. Moreover, the actual circulation of the *Resident* was much higher during that period than the figures of cash sales indicate. It was the practice of the circulation manager during that period to visit every month the people in the road which was just being occupied. "Where I could not effect a sale I gave them a back copy," he said in an interview. "If they did buy the book next month I offered them a whole set of back issues at a very reduced price." In that way the *Resident* reached nearly every house on the Estate during the summer and early autumn months of 1928. Systematic visiting of newcomers to the Estate was thus assured, and they were informed of all previous events of common interest. Even now the early volumes of the *Resident* make good reading, not only for people who have themselves lived on the Estate. This journal is indeed a full and very lively chronicle of the development of local social life.

The Association, through its journal, thus served as a "link uniting all Watlingites."

But it had other important tasks to fulfil. As its statutes declare, it wanted to promote "the interests of the residents on the Estate," and that meant foremost to urge the provision of schools, of transport and of postal facilities, the laying-out of playing-fields and of the central park: in short, the establishment of the innumerable services belonging to the ordinary routine of urban life. Rent problems had to be discussed with the L.C.C.; questions of municipal representation with the Urban District Council; cases of distress with the local Relieving Officer. In other words, the provision of amenities for the Estate needed speeding up and personal difficulties of residents needed adjustment. The Association started this work with great vigour and, after having been in existence only five months, it could publish in the first number of the *Resident* a report of its activities which indicated considerable achievements. Indeed, no other period in the lifetime of the Association is distinguished by an equal display of energy and consequent success.

Thus the Association acted as Watling's representative. How well it understood its task can best be demonstrated by the fact that it had a clear picture of its own limitations. It urged that Watling should have proper local government representation— that the Estate should become a ward. It urged in vain, for the present Burnt Oak ward is not confined to the Watling boundaries: it includes some streets in the neighbourhood of the Estate. But whilst emphasizing very rightly that Watling needed to be a municipal entity in order to be adequately represented in local government affairs, the Association itself conducted numerous successful negotiations with official authorities. Its representations were, as a rule, courteously received; although it never had a very large number of members and was a purely voluntary body, it was treated as a semi-official institution.[13] The sole concern of the people who ran the Association was to tackle local problems, and thus they virtually formed a nucleus of local government.

"The Estate wants finishing off," was over and again repeated by the Association, and they voiced that need for three and a half years. For it was not before the summer of 1931 that Watling's institutional equipment was nearing completion. To cite only a few stages: in September 1928 the first permanent school opened on the Estate; in January 1930 all the children not attending school through lack of accommodation, by then only 163, were absorbed in local schools; in August 1931 Watling secured a central school. Watling's park was finished in Spring 1931. The Association stopped criticism and registered its gratitude. In June 1931 the *Resident* addressed the Hendon Urban District Council with these words: "Whatever our neighbours think of us, we at least do appreciate both the magnitude of the task Watling presents to you (Hendon) and the way you are tackling it."

In acting as Watling's advocate before official bodies, the Association followed the precedent of community associations on other housing estates. These "cousins" were continually

---

[13] "The Association has the official recognition of the L.C.C. and the H.U.D.C. as the official organisation to communicate with in connection with the improvements and amenities of the Estate."—*Resident*, June 1923.

referred to in the early volumes of the *Resident*. Correspondence with them was exchanged. In April 1930 officers of the Association attended the first conference of delegates from new estates. The Watling people were conscious that they had to learn from the experience of the others. They felt that they had to combine with the new municipal estates all over the country in order to further their common interests.

The Association, therefore, functioned as an organ of communication in four different directions. It brought the people on the Estate together. It interpreted Watling to the neighbourhood and safeguarded its reputation, at the same time keeping it informed of Hendon's public opinion. It represented the Estate before official and voluntary bodies, and it helped in equipping it with social services. It established contact with Community Associations on other estates, and it made Watling share their experiences and their hopes.

Later the Association attempted a fifth task, to affiliate all the neighbouring organizations. It wanted to become the focus of local corporate life. In the early years this ambition was quite superfluous, since the Association was the sole centre of social activity on the Estate. It rapidly produced sub-committees and sub-sections which catered for the interests, hobbies and worries of the members and their members. It, therefore, acted not only as a link between people and institutions, but it created social institutions itself.

The *Resident* actively promoted interest in the Estate amongst the tenants. It held competitions on "How I would make Watling brighter" and "Which is the nicest road on the Estate?" It distributed maps of Watling amongst the people. It published a series of articles by a Mill Hill historian on the early history of the district. They met with great success. It also gave accounts of local rambles. It described, under the title "Citizens of Watling," residents who had interesting jobs or experiences. It produced a serial story in which the life of a family in the period immediately after its arrival on the Estate was most realistically described. The moral of this story was a call for participation in local social life.

The Association tried to remedy difficulties of individual families. A distress committee was formed at a very early stage. It was arranged that the children of mothers who were absent from home because of illness were given hospitality by other Watling women. The offer of free legal advice has been open to Watling residents since 1929.[14] Those institutions which were not set up to deal with a special problem but to serve a permanent need have survived till the present day.

A district nursing association was started in May 1928, by the same people who had founded the Association. It was an urgent need, since Middlesex had no county nursing association. A horticultural sub-committee of the Association began work during the same year.

The Association catered for sports, hobbies and entertainment as well as for family needs. In the field adjacent to Burnt Oak station, which has now been built over, the first "Fête and Gala" was held at Whitsun 1928, and became an event so memorable that the "pioneers" refer to it immediately when they talk about old days at Watling. Realizing that the Estate was bare of all entertainment at the time, that everybody felt lonely and was anxious to be sociable, one can easily imagine that such a Fête meant much more to the residents than an ordinary suburban social means to its public.

A "children's league" was started in 1929, later it became the "black cat circle," and after four months it had 700 members. In the same year the Association said: we want a Watling theatre. A dramatic sub-section was formed, it was called "The Guild of Players." This group published articles on its ideal of a "People's Theatre," conducted play-reading circles and gave Watling its first evening of dramatics in April 1930. Soon afterwards the first public lectures were held. A whole week of local entertainment, "Watling Week," which has become an annual event, was first organized by the Association in 1929. Its purpose was to start a building fund; "All Watling for a Watling Hall."

---

[14] It is interesting to note that in 1931 the Association opened a Census Assistance Bureau which dealt, in one month only, with 130 inquiries.

For the Association had no house of its own, not even a cottage, not even a hut. Its earliest activities had to take place off the Estate. Later, when churches, church halls and schools had been built on the Estate, from the spring of 1928 onwards, it took advantage of their hospitality.

Thus all the activities of the Association seemed disjointed. And whilst the park had been laid out, schools had been established, numerous organizations put on their feet, the Association itself was still without a building signifying its existence.

Its officers had early realized the need for a "Watling Centre". In the second number of the *Resident*, they describe in detail their ideal for such a place. It has remained an utopia; the Watling Centre of 1937 cannot be compared with the dream centre of 1928. Difficulties because of the lack of headquarters soon became apparent. The *Resident* said as early as August, 1928: ". . . the Committee alone cannot put life into an Association . . . the first business of the associates of an Association is to associate. This is difficult until there is a house in which to associate for indoor pleasures, and ground on which to associate for outdoor pleasures."

The statement that there was not enough life in the Association signalled a whole period of similar complaints. "What is wrong with the Association?" asked the *Resident*, for the first but not for the last time, in August 1928. Membership dwindled. In May 1928 the Association had 400 members, in May 1929 only 94. The number of people attending general meetings was dwindling too—"a sure sign of loss of interest." Sub-sections disaffiliated and have remained independent.[15] In October 1928 the *Resident* repeated its warning: "Do not let us get a disjointed tangle of societies and clubs on the Estate." Where co-operation had been, competition now set in.[16] Rivalry even influenced the domestic life

---

[15] E.g., the Horticultural Society disaffiliated in March 1929, the Loan Club in September 1931.

[16] An old resident commented: "In the early days there was much more corporate life on the Estate, the various sections have broken off and have become self-contained."

In July 1931 the *Resident* addressed "A Word to the Horticultural Society": "Watling's Horticultural Society has a membership of 800 or thereabouts . . .

of the Association; there was continuous quarrelling amongst its officers and disturbance of its work in consequence.[17] In fact, the whole fabric of local corporate life was similarly torn, never to be quite mended again.

SOCIAL STRUCTURE AND COMMUNITY LIFE

All these events happened during the period just described. The change is obvious. At the end of this early period, in the summer of 1931, the Estate had acquired much of the likeness of a town and had lost much of its earlier resemblance to an intimate community of people. The people themselves had become more like strangers to each other.[18] In other words, a housing estate which is faced with its specific problems is more likely to develop social consciousness and keeness for local unity than a modern town pursuing its daily routine.

But it has to be remembered that a housing estate will never exactly resemble an ordinary town; a number of important differences remain which at least offer the possibility of its being

will it be believed that for some unscrutable reason the Watling Horticultural Society and the Watling Association regard each other with suspicion and (it must be said) with jealousy? Yet such is the case, and so we have the spectacle of the Community Association and the most successful Watling Society keeping up, as a religious observance, this absurd kind of blood feud."

[17] See the *Resident*, November 1930 (p. 12):

"We have to report some very heavy engagements on the Watling Front. . . . The impasse in the internal affairs of the Watling Association is common knowledge and gossip. . . . We must rebuild. The important work and excellent opportunities of the Association are forgotten and lost sight of. They must be revived and put to the front. The Association is not alone in this unfortunate position, but we have knowledge of other bodies on the Estate who have suffered casualties in October. . . . Our only regret is that years of work by fine little bands of pioneers in their various bodies should ever be in danger of being destroyed."

[18] To quote from interviews:

"There was much more loyalty to the Estate in the early days, people were proud of living here."

"In the early days everybody wanted to do something."

"In the early days the meetings were packed, now the interest has diminished."

"In the early days we had people at the doorstep of newcomers to the Estate, welcoming them and enrolling them as members of the Association. That does not happen now."

favourably distinguished by the intensity of local social life. Indeed, so far as Watling is concerned, this seems to have been achieved. Its development was positive as compared, first, with the institutional bareness of Watling's early life, and second, as compared with the dreary social existence of suburbia. It was negative when its temper and tempo are set against Watling's early keenness on its own behalf. Whilst new instruments of corporate activity had been created, the old communal enthusiasm had markedly waned.[19]

One set of causes had been primarily responsible for this result: forces inherent in the development of the Estate itself were destructive of community life. Growth of local organizations necessarily means decline of ambition to secure them. This is an obvious fact which needs no elaboration. Moreover, at first the desire to equip the Estate with amenities was common. There was no difficulty in getting various groups of people to agree on a plan of campaign. Later, it was more difficult for them to agree on the administration of existing amenities, especially since new residents had arrived who had not shared the failures and successes of the early struggle.[20] Moreover, there was no institution whose

---

[19] The steadily declining sales of the *Resident* are indicative of the development:

SALES OF THE "RESIDENT"

Date	Number of houses inhabited on the Estate	Number of copies sold	Percentage of all homes reached by *Resident*
July 1928	2,468	2,000	81
March 1929	3,978	2,636	66
March 1930	4,018	1,591	39
March 1933	,,	1,451	36
March 1934	,,	1,143	28
March 1935	,,	1,042	26
March 1936	4,032	956	24

[20] This was, for instance, brought out by the fact that most of the early members of the Association lived in the oldest part of the Estate. In consequence there were soon complaints that "the majority of the Committee men lived in the same area."—*Resident*, October 1928.

authority was recognized by all people and to which a final appeal could be addressed.

On the contrary, the growth of Watling inevitably led to greater differentiation of opinion amongst its inhabitants. Sufficient people had arrived to form branches of established parties and societies. Customary partisanship and rivalries began to mark the social life on the Estate.[21] This influence was particularly felt, since each of the early pioneers had a well-developed *Weltanschauung* and began to be acclaimed as a representative of the opinions to which he adhered. There is no doubt that the officers of the Association fought against being pushed into factional disputes. But they were hardly able to escape, since the type of organization which represents religious and political interests became increasingly influential in local affairs.

Thus, where only one type of organization had been previously, three can now be distinguished. The dominant type caters for narrow family needs only: it is largely self-contained and in no way promotes community spirit. The second represents political and religious interests: its impact is mainly to foster rivalry. Only the third, at whose expense the previous two had grown, serves common local objectives, and attempts co-ordination.

The following are the most prominent of the local societies catering for family needs:

---

[21] This process is summarized in an editorial in the *Resident*, written on the occasion of its fifth birthday, May 1932:

"Watling has grown from a few houses, lots of building, unmade roads, railway tracks, lanes and open fields, that were here when No. 1 was published, to a finished estate. . . . The stages in the material growth of Watling have had their effects on us all in various ways. At first, when there were no shops and many grievances, we were all very chummy and discussed together the many failures of the powers that be. Then as the estate grew to completion there came to be too many people for us all to know each other. Sections and ambitions and vanities and difficulties arose, and we found ourselves in groups and cliques, often at cross-purposes one with another. Most of our voluntary organisations have been through a period of turmoil and internal strife. Can we now say that this period is coming to an end? That Watling is gradually getting ready to go forward as a united community?"

Name of Society	Year of foundation	Total membership during 1936	Total
Horticultural Society	1928	approx. 500	
District Nursing Association	1928	„ 3,000	} 4,820
Loan Club	1928	„ 1,320	

Amongst others, the following national organizations have branches on the Estate. Membership of most of them has remained stationary:

Name of Society	Year of foundation	Total membership during 1936	Total
Old Comrades' Association	1928	approx. 150	
Burnt Oak Townswomen's Guild	1929	„ 150	
Watling Women's Co-operative Guild	1929	„ 100	} 800
Burnt Oak Labour Party	1929	„ 250	
Burnt Oak Conservative Association	1928	„ 150	
Local Churches	1927–30	„ 1,000*	

*(average number of adults in congregations)

The third type of society is represented only by the Watling Association, founded in 1927; with a total membership of 809 during 1936.

Economic and social differentiation was a further result of Watling's growth. In the early period, the major difficulties were common to all people. For many, however, adjustment to their environment meant to become acutely aware of their individual worries. The financial burden of higher rent, more fares and instalment fees on furniture weighed heavily. The weariness of long train journeys made itself felt. Poverty loomed larger than loneliness. People were too worried to develop social interests, and often too tired to seek entertainment. Just when communal life was most in need of their support, when local societies were in their infancy, the economic crisis set in and endangered the existence of innumerable households. For at least one-quarter of all families the margin of comfort was extremely small. That means that illness or unemployment, or the loss of a wage-earner, completely upsets their carefully balanced budgets. Hence the crisis not only enhanced the difficulties of needy families but it also pushed more households into that category.

Simultaneously, it sharpened the cleavage between poor and well-to-do people on the Estate. There were among the small families of the civil servants, transport workers and other people in secure positions, a considerable number who were not immediately affected by external influences, such as the crisis. In fact, they profited from the fall in prices and felt richer, whilst the others became poorer. Thus complaints about snobbishness and also apathy were repeatedly heard during the same period.[22] None of these tendencies was very beneficial to social development.

A further factor created and accentuated differentiation. From 1928 immigration to the Estate slowed down; it became subject to vacancies only. Although large in total, immigration henceforth became an individual event, problems of adjustment to the Estate an individual experience for each particular family, and their solutions became individualistic too. People either completely shut themselves up in their homes, or they went to one of the existing local societies which competed for their favour. Each of these, whether it provided politics, garden seeds or nursing services, was now a closed unit. Hence, by joining, the newly acquired member was helped rather than hindered in becoming "self-contained".

---

[22] On snobbishness—a letter to the *Resident*, February 1931:

"Are there snobs in Watling? There is a tendency on the part of certain groups of people to regard themselves as the 'aristocracy' of the Estate, because they happen to wear clean collars, pressed trousers, and speak with a tolerable air of assurance."

On apathy—the *Resident*, September 1932:

" 'Watlingitis,' common disease after 8–10 months' residence on this Estate. The patient is attacked with a sudden desire to do nothing, see nothing, help no one and go nowhere."

Moreover, it became increasingly difficult for the residents to identify this place with their existence. They realized that, sooner rather than later, they would have to leave it again: the individual family was so mobile. During the ten years which have passed since the first houses were occupied, the total number of families who have lived on the Estate is nearly twice its maximum capacity. One out of every two families which have ever come to the Estate moved elsewhere before the end of ten years. Almost every second of the families stayed there less than five years. Watling belonged to only one part of their day, and merely to a passing period of their lives.

The remainder of the families, who stayed there five years or more, were equally subjected to the influence of removals. They experienced frequent changes of neighbours. Since 1929, fluctuation of membership has hampered the progress of all local organizations. Thus it was difficult for any family to associate Watling with plans for their children.

In the circumstances, it seems to have been inevitable that the growth of the Estate and the constant turn-over of its population would make differences of income, of social status and of outlook apparent. Common objectives tended to wane and, consequently, the desire for common action and common enjoyment lessened. "We have gone into our shells," said an old resident. However, since all Watlingites are wage-earners and parents, their most pressing problems are still alike. Would it not, therefore, be the task of a Community Association to bring the fact of the common way of living into their consciousness? Could we not assume that the process of disintegration might thus have been counteracted? In fact, however, local unity almost completely dissolved away, and we can see some obvious reasons why the Residents' Association was not able to prevent it.

A hall, with adequate financial backing, would have done much in assisting the Association to keep its early importance and so to modify, at least, the development described. Headquarters of its own would have been the monument of its early achievements. Subsections, which otherwise tended to obstinacy and independence, would have been united under one roof. Equally, other local organizations would have found a home and co-ordination would have been so much easier a task. The perpetual complaint that the Association's Executive merely interfered with the work of the sub-sections would have ceased, just as it has since the building of the Watling Centre. The Executive would have had the job of running the Centre, the importance of which would have been acknowledged by the sub-sections. Supervision would have been possible without giving rise to protests of meddling. The practice of multiplying membership fees by charging a subscription for each separate sub-section would not have arisen. People would have paid their fees as members of the Centre, not as members of a sub-section. This practice, so expensive for the individual family, especially in a time of economic difficulties, had deterred many from joining.[23] As members became scarce, competition amongst the sections became intensified; finally they broke with the parent Association. The existence of a Centre able to house all the main associations on the Estate would have prevented the clashing of dates at their functions, a fact which caused much heart-burning. Mutual relations were continually strained by the Association's being financially dependent on its sub-sections. The possession of a building would have provided the parent Association with their own source of income and, at the same time, the sub-sections with the accommodation which they needed and for which they were willing to pay. Indeed, not so much the "Association" but the "Centre" would have linked them and represented their common interest.

"The Centre is the heart of Watling, keep it beating." In 1939 these words strike the eye of the visitor to the building. Yet the Association had no headquarters until September 1931, when it rented a cottage, and no larger building of its own until January

---

[23] E.g., *Resident*, September 1929:

"Is it not possible to co-ordinate some of the activities that do now exist on the Estate? We have the position that in order to belong to all the societies now in existence a family would have to pay out in subscriptions the sum of 10s. per annum."

1933. By that time the Estate had acquired its routine. All other local organizations were well established. The Centre was almost the last building of public importance to be built.

Watling's corporate life had shown symptoms of anaemia prior to that event: the facts enumerated seem to provide the diagnosis.

Urban Ward Associations in Japan

INTRODUCTION

By Professor R. P. Dore, London School of Economics

By the middle of the eighteenth century Tokyo—or Edo as it was then called—was probably, with over a million inhabitants, the biggest city in the world. But it was a city to which the common description of pre-industrial towns as a congeries of villages might well apply. Small territorial segments of 200–300 households called *chō* or *chōnai* were in some respects analogous to the nucleated hamlet settlements of rural Japan in that they had a distinctive name, a distinctive sense of identity and a distinctive organization for the exercise of limited powers of self-government. Their wealthier householders took turns in acting as *chōnai* officials, supervising the maintenance of the family census registers, the collection of taxes and water rates, the subsidization of the fire brigade, the handling of vagrants and foundlings, the payment of night watchmen. Although recent research[1] suggests that the population was more residentially mobile than ideal-typical pictures of the contemporary economy might suggest, nevertheless, for a good proportion of families whose househeads were independent artisans or merchants home was at the same time their place of work, and the *chōnai* was in some real sense a community containing within it most of the important social relations in which they were involved.

These *chōnai* units have retained their identity two hundred years later, despite the transformation of Tokyo into a modern metropolis, over 85 per cent of whose male population work outside their homes for wages or salaries. Postal addresses still take

---

[1] See R. J. Smith, Aspects of Mobility in Pre-industrial Japanese Cities, *Comparative Studies in Society and History*, **5,** iv, July 1963.

the form of house-lot numbers within a *chōnai* area—to the considerable frustration of foreigners who expect streets, not areas, to have names and numbers to follow some rectilinear order. One can still find an unfamiliar house—by visiting the hut of the *chōnai* policeman and consulting his map and set of household registers, not very different from the household registers kept by *chōnai* secretaries two centuries ago.

In most parts of Tokyo the formal political organizations of the *chōnai* atrophied in the late nineteenth century as the new metropolitan and borough[2] governments took over most of their functions. They were increasingly resurrected, however, from the turn of the century as local governments saw advantage in having small local organizations to co-operate in public health programmes. The part the *chōnai* organizations played in dealing with the aftermath of the great earthquake disaster further stimulated their revival in the twenties. By the middle of the next decade their revival was in full swing, deliberately fostered by the government as a means of citizen mobilization for the coming war (just as in recent China similar forms of neighbourhood organization—with, indeed, common historical origins in T'ang China—have been used for purposes of thought-reform campaigns, antifly campaigns, economy campaigns and so on). It was during the thirties that the pattern of the *chōnaikai*—the governing organizations of the *chōnai*—was formalized by state regulation. During the war they were extensively used for rationing and civil defence, the collection of comforts for troops and aluminium saucepans for aeroplanes, the mobilization of flag-waving and send-offs for soldiers, or the provision of captive audiences for the recital of Imperial Rescripts or the performance of Shinto ceremonies.[3]

---

[2] "Borough" is used here as a translation of *ku* for which the Japanese Post Office's official translation is "ward". Their populations range from 117,000 to 706,000. Tokyo Metropolis also includes several satellite cities and rural areas, but in 1960 86 per cent of the population of 9·7 million lived in the 23 central *ku*.

[3] The history and post-war reorganization of *chōnaikai* is described in a thesis by the translator of this article: S. T. Fukawa, Neighbourhood Associations in Japanese Cities and their Political Implications, M.A. thesis, University of London, 1963.

After the war these organizations were banned as instruments of totalitarianism. I have described elsewhere the re-emergence of one such *chōnaiki* and the way it seemed to be working in 1951.[4] By the mid-fifties formal associations had been revived in the majority of Tokyo wards.

To all progressive Japanese sociologists—and almost by definition a Japanese sociologist is expected to be progressive—this revival of *chōnaikai* was to be deplored. They were a relic of the feudal past. The fact that households rather than individuals formed their constituent units was, to begin with, a perpetuation of anti-individualistic familism. The assumption of automatic universal membership was an offence against liberty. And the purposes for which the *chōnaikai* were used were generally deplored. According to the typical stereotype, a *chōnaikai* was composed of a small coterie of conservative and ambitious rogues, and an apathetic rank and file. The latter grudgingly paid their regular monthly contributions, were vaguely grateful for the street lights in the ward's unadopted roads which the contributions helped to pay for and might appreciate the children's parties and outings which the more active *chōnaikai* organized, but generally resented having to contribute to such things as the celebration of the local shrine festival and were diffusely suspicious, though ill-informed, about what happened to their money. The leaders, so the stereotype ran, made a display of "public spirit" as a cloak for less reputable designs. They not only enjoyed a sense of their own importance; they also made use of every opportunity to strengthen their contacts with local dignitaries. Their function as bearers of the *chōnai's* collective tips to the fire brigade, the borough refuse department, and the police (the Crime Prevention Associations mentioned in the following pages may be not unfairly described as mechanisms for channelling tips to the police) allowed them important contacts which improved their chances of aspiring to the position of borough councillor. These contacts might be reinforced by wining and dining—at the expense of

---

[4] R. P. Dore, *City Life in Japan*, 1958.

chōnaikai funds. Their own aspirations, combined with a generally subservient authoritarianism and a flattered sense of their own importance in the existing scheme of things, ensured their docile compliance with the wishes of the authorities". And thus, given their dominance over the mass of apathetic householders, the viability of the corrupt conservatism of Japanese local government politics was preserved.

How differently, so the argument ran, things are managed in the United States. There privacy is respected. A family can keep itself to itself. Neighbourliness is a contract voluntarily entered into. If neighbourhood associations are found they are voluntary societies with all the *gesellschaftlich* purity befitting the primary schools of democracy. They are joined by individuals who share a common purpose which each is clearmindedly and vigorously determined to pursue. It elects its leaders by frank, open, democratic processes very different from the obscure methods of co-option and formal ratifying election of the typical *chōnaikai*. Diffuse obfuscation of the organization's specific purposes is eschewed. There is perfect accounting, perfect honesty and perfect knowledge of the association's affairs on the part of its members.[5]

It is Mr. Nakamura's contention that preoccupation with such stereotypes has prevented Japanese social scientists from seeing what is happening under their noses. He insists that there *is* a new spirit afoot in local politics, at least in the new housing estates of the big cities. The masses are no longer merely apathetic. The large apartment blocks contain householders and housewives who are no longer deferential towards "the authorities" and who *are*

---

[5] The translator of this article, Stanley Fukawa, has recently pursued his studies of neighbourhood associations in the Detroit area. In a recent letter he remarks, apropos of some 70 neighbourhood associations of which he has information: "It is interesting to note how contrary they are to Japanese sociologists' expectations. Most of them have 'family memberships' although they came to have individual voting. Nor were the Detroit *chōnaikai* as uni-functional as any implicitly 'good' (or at least better) American association might be expected to be. About two-thirds were 'wet' enough to have representatives call on sick neighbours and to send flowers to bereaved families, and over half had parties for children. Nine of the seventy even had an annual festival. The Americans, it seems, are not as 'dry' as they are supposed to be."

capable of articulately demanding that local governments do the jobs they are paid for and of creating organizations to make those demands effective. But the organizations they form are likely to be remarkably similar to the old *chōnaikai* in many respects if for no other reason than that people naturally use the social techniques their culture bequeaths to them. And if the form of organization they create is culturally defined as something which also organizes neighbourhood social activities and expresses social solidarity by giving their members wedding gifts and christening presents, then these functions too are more likely to be preserved whatever urban sociologists may have had to say about the inevitable atomization of urban societies. Mr. Nakamura argues, and he does so convincingly, that neither the mere existence of *chōnaikai*, nor the fact thet they retain some of their traditional expressive functions, are necessarily reasons for believing that they must play their traditional role as instruments which permit local oligarchies to batten on the docile ignorance of the masses.

Mr. Nakamura's article was written in 1964. In 1965 the uncovering of financial scandals involving members of the Tokyo Metropolitan Assembly set off a campaign of public protest sufficiently strong to force the dissolution of the Assembly under a special enabling act passed by the national Diet. In the subsequent elections the conservative Liberal-Democratic Party lost its majority for the first time and the Socialist Party emerged with a plurality of seats. It was remarked in press reports that in many areas of Tokyo the *chōnaikai* had notably ceased to operate effectively as vote banks on which conservative councillors could rely.

A RE-EXAMINATION OF CHŌNAIKAI
(URBAN WARD ASSOCIATIONS)

H. NAKAMURA

Recently, *chōnaikai*—those peculiarly Japanese urban neighborhood groups—have come to be the object of sociological and political science research. The characteristics of *chōnaikai* that have been noted in these studies can be summarized as follows:

1. The unit of membership is not the individual but the household.

2. Membership is determined by residence within a defined area and is semi-compulsory.[6]

3. There is no specialization of function. (Other items used to denote this aspect are "all-inclusive and multi-objective", "compound functions" and "multiple functions".)

4. They act as the lowest-level auxiliary bodies in local government administration.

5. They act as the basis for and help to preserve conservative traditions under the leadership of the old middle class.

It seems that behind such descriptions of *chōnaikai* lies the consciousness that these characteristics work in opposition to the trends toward urbanization, modernization and democratization in Japan. Even Dore sees these groups as "institutions which properly belong to the self-contained village".[7] Furthermore, those trends and characteristics which have recently been the object of close attention, such as the tendency for governmental agencies to mobilize existing groups, whatever their supposedly

---

[6] The writer feels he would like to use the term "automatic" instead of "semi-compulsory". It is not a specific individual or a *chōnaikai* officer who compels membership in these groups, membership follows from the character of the *chōnaikai* as a social fact and that of membership as a social norm. It is, in other words, derived from social solidarity and any individual can only be its agent. In the writer's survey, when members were asked why they had joined, many replied, with an air of wonder that I should ask such a question, "Since we moved into this area, is it not natural that we join the local *chōnaikai*?" The *chōnaikai* has become normatively so much a part of local life that neither he who seeks members nor he who is sought to join has any consciousness of compelling or of being compelled. In such a case, it seems better to speak of "automatic" rather than of "compulsory" membership.

[7] R. P. Dore, *City Life in Japan*, p. 286.

specialized functions may be, for the implementation of official policies,[8] the persisting "village" character of Japanese cities, or the reorganization of neighborhood groups by conservative politicians for their own electoral purposes, very frequently involve the *chōnaikai*.

The writer was able to conduct surveys of *chōnaikai* in both Hino and Mitaka in Tokyo Metropolis, both areas which are rapidly becoming suburban cities and which already have a city administration within the Metropolis. Behind the recently proliferating studies of suburban cities in the United States, one senses the assumption that it is here that empirical surveys can detect the leading trends of social change. The writer's aim in his surveys was to see if and to what extent Japanese suburban *chōnaikai* have changed in degree and in substance from those whose characteristics were outlined above.

While the survey was under way, it became apparent that there were many *chōnaikai* that did not fit the description contained in the five points mentioned above, especially points 4 and 5. Furthermore, it also became apparent that the premises, both conscious and unconscious, which underlie the previous characterizations should, with the appearance of these new *chōnaikai*, be re-examined.

The aims of this article are to bring together the underlying assumption of the existing literature, and the writer's criticisms of them to examine these against the Hino and Mitaka survey data, and then to follow this with a re-examination of previous *chōnaikai* studies. Footnotes will indicate the studies which the writer has used. Materials which unquestionably approve of existing *chōnaikai* have not been included as the writer felt them to be beyond the scope of this essay.

---

[8] As opposed to the expected segmentalization of function and the creation of specialized interest groups that present urban theory would lead us to expect in cities, and also opposed to the expected autonomy of existing groups which is deemed integral to the democratic transformation of social structure.—*Translator's note.*

EXAMPLES FROM THE HINO AND MITAKA SURVEYS

Five examples of *chōnaikai* will first be briefly described, one from Hino and four from Mitaka. With the exception of the Inokashira *Chōkai* (*Chōkai* is a varient of *chōnaikai*) all of them have taken the name Jichikai which means literally "self-government association". Nevertheless, they will all be called chōnaikai, for reasons to be discussed below.

Tamadaira Housing Estate Jichikai (Hino)—a Japan Housing Corporation housing estate

Membership: on a voluntary basis. At the time of the survey the membership rate was about 48 per cent of the 2200 households. The constitution of the association makes provision for membership by individuals but in actuality, all members were households.

Activities: campaign to have sewage charges reduced, campaign opposing the invitation of factories to the neighborhood, campaign for the establishment of a nursery, campaign for free medical examinations, the O-bon festival folk dancing, a cultural festival, foreign folk dancing, party to honor the aged, lecture meetings, film presentations, record concerts, etc.

The sewage charge campaign resulted in a revision of the Hino city by-laws. The members refused to pay the charges levied before revision on the grounds that the previous by-laws were invalid. An administrative lawsuit was filed and a court battle ensued.

Co-operation with local government agencies: in Hino, the local authorities have depended very much on *chōnaikai* to help them in local administration, but this new *jichikai* has been very critical of and generally unco-operative toward the authorities. There has been a standing feud between the two which has served to complicate local affairs by affecting relations between the local government and the Hino federation of *chōnaikai* with its hitherto docile member groups.

Local elections: In order to press forward the above-mentioned campaigns the *jichikai* has elected two left-wing candidates to the town assembly.

Officers: as can generally be inferred from the social character of the residents of Japan Housing Corporation housing estates, officers were mainly salaried white-collar workers with university degrees.[9]

Metropolitan Government Housing Development Jichikai (Mitaka)

At the time of the survey there were 40 different lots of Metropolitan Government housing in Mitaka but only those 20 which were represented in the Mitaka Council of Metropolitan Government Housing Development Jichikai are described here. Whereas the other Metropolitan Government Housing Development lots also have *jichikai*, which were formed in order to collect money (for charities and other purposes) and to provide social events (especially a children's festival), the 20 which made up the Council were concerned with negotiating with various government agencies to improve public facilities.

Membership: Complete membership of all households; membership unit is the household.[10]

Activities: Campaigns against both increases in rent and the demands of Metropolitan authorities that those who make more than the maximum salary vacate their flats.[11] Demands for

---

[9] Japan Housing Corporation "housing estates" or *danchi* have minimum income requirements which make these apartment-block communities quite middle-class.—*Translator's note.*

[10] Since all residents of housing estates must co-operate to pay for certain communally-incurred expenses such as street lighting, garbage collection, stairway lighting—it is not difficult to increase the monthly charge by fifty or one hundred yen (a shilling or two) per month to include resident's association dues.—*Translator's note.*

[11] Metropolitan government housing has a maximum income requirement.—*Translator's note.*

sewage construction and better roads. Campaigns against increases in bus fares. Management of "crime prevention street lights",[12] Assistance in collecting for charities, Sanitation measures, festivals, children's parties, congratulation and condolence,[13] etc.

The above-mentioned activities are diverse and do not differ markedly from those of other Metropolitan Government Housing Estate Jichikai. However, the *jichikai* belonging to the Council have put more emphasis on making demands of and negotiating with various administrative agencies. In the matters of eviction and the raising of rents they have stood firm on demands for a recognition of the "basic right of occupancy" and have gained the co-operation of city authorities (i.e. the city has denied the Metropolitan government access to tax rolls). Again, in connection with the campaign against increased bus fares (in which they co-operated with the *jichikai* of other public and Housing Corporation estates) they were able to press forward to the point where the Ministry of Trade and Industry's Transportation Investigation Committee held a public hearing and a representative of the *jichikai* made an official statement opposing the proposed increase.

Co-operation with local government agencies: In Mitaka the *chōnaikai* have not been utilized to the extent that they have been in Hino and their co-operation has been confined to such matters as sanitation (distribution of insecticide to combat flies and mosquitoes), co-operation in collecting for charities and maintenance of street lights (known as *bōhantō*, or, literally, "crime-prevention lights"). In connection with these street lights, the Mitaka Crime Prevention Association must be mentioned.

---

[12] So-called because they were installed to reduce night crime (in Japanese *bōhantō*).—*Translator's note*.

[13] "Congratulation" and "condolence" refers to the widespread practice of making gifts to members on auspicious or tragic occasions such as births, adoptions, marriages, or deaths, by the neighbourhood association on behalf of all members.—*Translator's note*.

As was general in the cities,[14] many *chōnaikai* in Mitaka were first revived after the war as sub-units of the city Crime Prevention Association, one of their main functions being the provision, maintenance and subsidization of these lights. The major offices were monopolized by the conservative "influentials" (*yūryokusha*) and many *chōnaikai* have remained at the same time sub-units of the Association. However, the Metropolitan Government Housing Development Jichi-kai have refused to join the Association, on the grounds that they would not get any return commensurate with the cost of membership, their being no reason to suppose that membership in the Association would alter the extent to which the city subsidizes the provision and maintenance of street lights or to which the police would protect them from crime. Nor have they uncritically volunteered to aid all charities approved by the city. The only firm collaboration with the city is with regard to environmental sanitation, an area in which they themselves benefit greatly.

Local elections: in connection with the opposition to the increase in bus fares, they requested a public statement of support from the city assembly but were unable to obtain this due to strong opposition from two or three assemblymen. This prompted the Mitaka Council of Metropolitan Government Housing Development Jichikai to elect their own representative to the city assembly on a Socialist Party ticket.

Officers: from both blue and white-collar classes.

Shinkawa Housing Estate Jichikai, Mure Housing Estate Jichikai—Housing Corporation estates in Mitaka

Membership: on a voluntary basis (membership rates are at Shinkawa 40 per cent and at Mure 90 per cent). The membership unit is the family.

---

[14] Takagi Shōsaku, *Chihō jichitai to gairō shōmei* (*Local governments and street-lighting*), part 2, *Toshi Mondai* (*Municipal Problems*), vol. 53, no. 3, pp. 78–81.

Activities: Campaign to get the bus route extended into the estates, campaign to have the local property tax reduced, campaign against the increase in fares by a private bus company, measures against the noise created by nearby construction work, improvement of playground facilities. (The above, insofar as they are connected with demands to the administrative authorities, are similar to the activities of the Metropolitan Government Housing Development Jichikai. In the campaign opposing increased bus fares, they worked with the Metropolitan Government Housing Development Jichikai.) They have also undertaken a campaign to improve the service provided by local shop-keepers, children's parties, a cultural festival, dances, a housing estate festival.

Co-operation with local authorities: the Shinkawa housing estate residents have extended no co-operation to local authorities. The Mure residents have co-operated in collecting for the Red Cross and the year-end aid to the poor. Neither is associated with the Mitaka Crime Prevention Association.

Local elections: the residents' associations have not allowed themselves to be used in election campaigns even for left-wing candidates. At the Shinkawa housing estate during a local election all candidates were invited to present their platforms to the estate residents at a special meeting and this was reported in the newspapers as the residents' "sounding-out" of candidates.

Officers: as with the Tamadaira housing estate, mainly university-educated, salaried, white-collar workers.

Inokashira Chōkai

Located in a high class residential area next to the Inokashira Park, it is the largest *chōnaikai* in Mitaka composed of residents of single dwellings.

Membership: In actual fact, many families have not joined, but in principle all families are members and the membership unit is the family.

Activities: Maintenance of crime-prevention lights (is part of the local Crime Prevention Association), donations to charity, environmental sanitation, assistance to the local fire brigade, donations to older neighbouring *chōnaikai* for festival expenses (on the above points further explanations will be added later), film presentations, lecture meetings, parties to honor the aged, children's parties, support of the local *chōkai* baseball team, a monthly two- to six-page newsletter.

Co-operation with local authorities: The *chōkai* has co-operated not only in matters of sanitation, but also in collections for charities. It has joined the Crime Prevention Association. For these activities, as with gifts to the local fire brigade and local festivals, a lump sum is paid and the group is not tied to any *per capita* commitment.

Local elections: the use of the *chōnaikai* in any election is prohibited. One president, who came from one of the few old families which traditionally monopolized the presidency, wanted to stand for a seat in the city assembly but was so strongly opposed by the others on the executive committee that he resigned his post before entering the contest.

Officers: includes many retired and self-employed persons.

This *chōnaikai* differs from the others described here not only in type of officers but also in type of activities. For example, it is co-operative in a sense, toward the authorities, makes donations to the fire brigade and to neighboring *chōnaikai* for festivals. However, this stems from the fact that this is a high-class residential area and there was frequent door-to-door canvassing for donations for many things which could be stopped by turning this function over to the *chōnaikai*. On this point there is, in a sense, an aspect of compromise with traditional practice but there is also on the other hand a strong consciousness that the *chōnaikai* should not be used by the local authorities. The newsletter, which is published solely on income received from advertising, is delivered to all the families in the *chōnaikai* as well as to the authorities, and despite the fact that it reaches only 1800 families has the power of a miniature mass communications organ. The *chōnaikai* itself, is viewed as something which should be done away with but is felt to be temporarily necessitated by the state of local public services. As for its ground rules, as already mentioned, the *chōnaikai* is not allowed to be used by the authorities or converted into an election machine; also, there is an emphasis on making association management less corrupt (especially a strict prohibition against officers utilizing association funds for partying) and on holding meetings more frequently.

Let us now look at the associations just described in the light of the five characteristics supposedly typical of *chōnaikai*, as enumerated at the beginning of this article. In the first place, the membership unit is the family and, except for three housing estates, membership is expected of all households; i.e. is of the "semi-compulsory" kind. The three estates were no different on the second characteristic, however, namely in that membership was limited to residents and anyone who moved so much as a foot outside the area automatically ceased to belong to the association. They all had in common a territorial basis for membership. Thirdly, even though there is emphasis on making demands of administrative authorities, as can be seen in the lists above, the activities ranged widely from the instrumental to the expressive. In other words, as far as the first three characteristics are concerned, there is no difference between *jichikai* and *chōnaikai* and that is my justification for not making a distinction of terminology between them. However, the *chōnaikai*, which have been described, have not generally been compliantly co-operative towards local government administrations and have, on the contrary, placed emphasis on making demands and negotiating for concessions. The only one to have members of the old middle class among its officers was the Inokashira *Chōkai*. With reference to politics, they have either strongly maintained their independence and rejected any attempt to use them in elections or, if they have become involved, they have supported the left-wing. (The writer does not propose to argue the rights and wrongs of *chōnaikai* becoming the machines of left-wing assemblymen. The point here is only that it is contrary to what has been previously asserted about the political complexion of *chōnaikai* leaders.)

The differences on characteristics 4 and 5 are sufficient to warrant calling the *chōnaikai*, described here, a new type. In Hino this new type could be seen only in the Tamadaira housing estate, but in Mitaka, which has advanced more toward becoming a surburban city, it can be seen increasing in numbers not only in the new newcomer residential areas but also in the older areas like Inokashira. And for this reason city authorities have come to take a very cautious attitude toward utilizing *chōnaikai* in their administrative work.

Up to now, the discussion has been confined to the results of the writer's own surveys, but similar trends are occurring, according to one report,[15] in another area of Tokyo Metropolis. Again, in the dormitory towns, which have recently grown up outside Yokohama, it has been reported that in the new residential areas there has been an increase in a type of *chōnaikai* different from what was common in the past,[16] and even Sendai, a city in Northern Honshu has shown similar indications.[17] It has been pointed out that in the so-called conservative re-systematization of the *chōnaikai*—in the interests of conservative politicians—has often involved a change of leadership intended to enhance their effectiveness, men of "locally prominent families" being replaced by men of ability.[18] The change noted by the

---

[15] *Nihon Keizai Shimbun* (*Japan Economic News*), 22 October 1963, evening edition (capital region economy column).

[16] Yokohama-shi Szmukyoku Chzsa shitsu (Yokohama City Investigation Office), *Shimin Seikatsu Hakusho Atarashii Yokohama e no tembo* (*Citizens' Livelihood White Paper: Prospects of a New Yokohama*), pp. 131–2.

[17] Iesaka Kazuyuki *et al.*, Chihō toshi ni okeru shikai giin no katsudō to jūmin soshiki (Activities of a city assemblyman and residents' organizations in a regional city), *Tōhoku dai Nihon Bunka Kenkyūjo kenkyū hōkoku* (*Tōhoku University Japanese Culture Research Centre Research Reports*) special volume, Part 1, pp. 76–84.

[18] Kitagawa and Shimazaki (eds.), *Gendai Nihon no Toshi Shakai* (*Urban Society in Contemporary Japan*), pp. 167–70. Okuda Michihiro, Kyu Chukansō wo shutai to suru toshi chōnaikai: sono mondai ten no teiji (Urban chōnaikai under the old middle class: a presentation of related problems), *Shakaigaku Hyōron* (*Sociological Review*), vol. 14, no. 3. (Reference also is made to what the writer calls the new type of *chōnaikai* in Kitagawa and Shimazaki (eds.), *op. cit.*, pp. 176–8.)

writer is a rather different one—towards a type of local organization less supportive of and even opposed to the conservative political order.

Because what the writer calls the new type of *chōnaikai* has appeared in many places, he began to entertain doubts about the accepted view of their nature and function. He plans to present these below but a few comments should be made beforehand. First, in the new type of *chōnaikai* there is a considerably high standard demanded of public services and secondly, while maintaining a strong independence, they all face difficulty in finding willing and capable officers.

THE CHŌNAIKAI: A RE-EXAMINATION OF ACCEPTED VIEWS

I have noted the appearance of *chōnaikai* not exhibiting the previously mentioned characteristics 4 and 5, but it is the aim of this re-examination to do more than point this out. As mentioned in the Introduction, there seems to be some basic premises lying behind the points previously made and, since the appearance of a new type of *chōnaikai* casts doubt on their premises, they will be reconsidered one by one, utilizing results of the above surveys.

(1) When the five points outlining the character of the *chōnaikai* are enumerated, there usually seems to be some idea that they are mutually related and internally consistent. Modern associations can be thought to be specific-function groups, which individuals join and leave freely and which develop clear aims and independence of outlook. In *chōnaikai*, whose group attributes are quite the opposite, it is only natural to postulate a contrary internal consistency. In a survey of Ushiku-machi in Ibaragi prefecture single-function groups (a transport co-operative and a tax-paying co-operative) were compared to a *chōnaikai* and it was shown that there was a stronger sense of group participation in the former.[19] In this study too, the same sort of internal

---

[19] Soeda Yoshinari, Chiku soshiku no mondai: Ibaragi-ken Ushiku-machi

consistency was assumed—namely, that in multiple-function groups the aims are vague, reasons for participation are unclear, and consequently no self-assertiveness is forthcoming; the group becomes submissive, and consequently susceptible to utilization by the conservative authorities. The proposal to replace the *chōnaikai* by single-purpose groups seems to rest on a similar premise. However, if such a configuration were inevitable, then the new type of *chōnaikai* could never have appeared. The Ushiku survey seems to attest to this inevitability but the objects of comparison were single-purpose groups based on economic interest. The question is: whether, if there had not been a strong economic incentive involved, single-purpose groups based on other interests would have shown the same correlated configuration of the opposite qualities.

(2) As a condition for the continued existence of *chōnaikai*, some have pointed to the continued presence of self-employed workers,[20] whose home is also their workplace,[21] the supposition being that commuters would be less interested in local affairs.[22] The self-employed are suited to office-holding because they remain constantly in the area and in the Inokashira *Chōkai* many were included. However, aside from this *chōnaikai*, none of the others mentioned above had local businessmen or self-employed workers as officers. Hence, it cannot be said that the existence of *chōnaikai* depends on local businessmen nor that urban neighbourhoods are completely blanketed in a *chōnaikai* system controlled by local businessmen. Throughout the report on the Suginami-ku survey[23] (Suginami-ku is a Tokyo borough which

no baai (Local organization in rural communities: the example of Ushiku machi in Ibaragi prefecture), *Shakai Jigyō Daigaku Kenyū Kiyō* (*University of Social Work Research Notes*), vol. 8.

[20] *Asahi Shimbun* (*Asahi News*), 14 October 1962, evening edition.

[21] Dore, *op. cit.*, p. 286.

[22] Okuda Michihiro, Suburbia ni Okeru toshika (Urbanization in suburbia), *Shakaigaku Hyōron* (*Sociological Review*), vol. 13, no. 3 and see also Matsushita, *op. cit.* for what he calls the contrast between "mass conditions" and "village conditions". Tosei Chōsakai (Metropolitan Research Association), *Daitoshi ni okeru Chiiki Seiji no Kōzō* (*The Structure of Neighbourhood Politics in Large Cities*).

[23] Tosei Chōsakai, *op. cit.*

is mainly middle-class and residential) runs the recurrent theme of the lack of interest in local affairs, on the part of commuters, especially those with more education. The writer's surveys also showed a common difficulty in finding officers. Indeed, we may well be safe in assuming apathy if we are talking of the level of consciousness of the average commuter. However, a low average level of interest says nothing about the possibility of a few having more interest, and small numbers have been sufficient to establish the new type of *chōnaikai*.

The criterion for "lack of interest" usually seems to be a contrast with the typical American case[24] but even amongst Americans, who have been called "joiners", it has been said that there is a tendency for voluntary associations, and even labour unions, to become oligarchic.[25] Tocqueville saw the voluntary associations and local self-government together as the bases of American democracy but some political scientists have come to question this.[26] There seems to be no need to refer especially to the Japanese case as being pathological.[27]

(3) The inadequacy of public services has been given as a reason for the existence of *chōnaikai*.[28] The assumption is implied that there is a possibility of eliminating this inadequacy by improving public services with the consequence that the *chōnaikai* should disappear. However, this inadequacy is always a relative

---

[24] Seikatsu Kagaku Chōsakai (Behavioral Science Investigation Association) (eds.), *Chōnaikai Burakukai* (*Urban and Rural Neighbourhood Associations*), pp. 109–11.

[25] B. Barber, Participation and Mass Apathy in Associations, in A. W. Gouldner (ed.), *Studies in Leadership*, and S. M. Lipset, *Political Man* ch. 12 'The Political Process in a Trade Union'.

[26] R. Dahl, *Who Governs*, pp. 311–12, and *Modern Political Analysis*, pp. 58–60.

[27] Okuda Michihiro, Waga kuni ni okeru toshi jumin soshiki no dōkō to mondai ten (Trends and problems in the organization of Japanese urban residents), *Toshi Mondai* (*Municipal Problems*), vol. 51, no. 12.

[28] Dore, *op. cit.*, p. 286, and Burakukai Chōnaikai Zanankai (A discussion on rural and urban neighbourhood associations), *Jichikenyū* (*Research in Self-government*), vol. 36, No. 1. In this discussion Watanabe, for example, said: 'I think if it were not for the exigencies of administration, then *chōnaikai* would cease to exist.'

thing so that, even if services improve, if the level of expectation
rises above this, there will still remain a feeling of dissatisfaction,
and in any non-stagnant society the demand level is constantly
rising. Besides, the ecological changes within the city are always
calling forth demands for new services. With the increase in
population, there is the need to improve schools, a need for new
roads and the repair of old roads with an increase in traffic or a
need to prevent noise. Many such examples can be given but such
unexpected demands will continually arise and, at the least, leave
always a subjective feeling of dissatisfaction with administrative
inadequacies.

If such inadequacies in public services are always present,
chōnaikai will always have some reason for existence, but the
writer does not think that there is a necessary relationship between
the existence of *chōnaikai* and inadequacies in public services.
The *chōnaikai* described earlier emphasized negotiations with
government offices but in both Hino and Mitaka there were many
chōnaikai having nothing to do with local government and placing
emphasis on social activities.[29] The latter type would probably
continue to exist because of their social activities even if there
were no inadequacies in public services.

At this point it is necessary to remember something that
structural-functional analysis tells us, namely that when a
structure X performs a function *x* (for example if a *chōnaikai*
performs the function of making up inadequacies in public
services) we cannot look on *x* as a sufficient reason for the existence
of X. This is because there are structures other than X (for
example Y) which might equally well fulfil function *x*. Why X
rather than Y is the operative structure at a certain time and
place is something which structural-functional analysis cannot
tell us. Unless no other structure but X could perform *x*, we

---

[29] Nakamura Hochiro, Toshi teki hatten to chōnaikai (Urbanistic development and *chōnaikai*), in *Chiiki Shakai to Toshika (Local Communities and Urbanization)*, Kokusai Kirisutokyo Daigaku Gakuho (International Christian University Scholarly Reports) II, A–8. Toshi no Hembō Katei (The Development
Process of Suburban Cities).

cannot speak of *x* as the reason for the existence of X. Consequently, the reason why it should be the *chōnaikai* rather than one of any number of other possible alternative types of organization, which takes on the job of remedying inadequacies in public services, cannot be explained by structural-functional analysis alone and we must consider here cultural factors.[30] In short, the idea, which has guided our observations to this point, is to the effect that the *chōnaikai* is best looked on as a "cultural form" and to the writer this view seems to offer the best opportunity of explaining their existence.[31] Whether they make demands to government agencies on behalf of citizens rather than meekly aiding agencies in their work, or even, like the Inokashira *Chōkai*, try to do away with undesirable elements of traditional *chōnaikai*, the available cultural form of the *chōnaikai* is the pattern which is naturally adopted.

That the *chōnaikai* is not necessarily dependent on inadequacies in public services, but rather exists because it is an established cultural form has been explained. This means that *chōnaikai could* exist without this facilitating condition, but that where this condition exists—that is to say where the supplementation of public services is one of the functions they perform—*chōnaikai* are more likely to be found. In other words, although the inadequacy of public services is a factor which cannot be ignored in the consideration of local public administration, it is by no means the decisive one so far as the existence of *chōnaikai* is concerned.

Conversely, however, the inadequacy of public services is still a positive factor, because it is a facilitating one to the existence of *chōnaikai*, albeit the degree of positiveness is rather small. This

---

[30] Nakamura Hachirō, Mitaka shi no jumin soshiki (Residents' organizations in Mitaka), *Kinkō Toshi no Hembō Katei* (*The Development Process of Suburban Cities*), *ibid.* II, A–10.

[31] Omi Tetsuo, Toshi no chiiki shūdan (Urban territorial groups), *Shakai Kagaku Tōkyō* (*Social Science Research*) vol. 3, no. 1. Dore (*op. cit.*, p. 286) gives as reasons for the existence of *chōnaikai*, the existence of the old middle class and the inadequacies of public services but also adds to this the pre-existence of a traditional *chōnaikai* model. This is close to the view here taken of the *chōnaikai* as a cultural form.

means that up to this small degree *chōnaikai* is provided with more favourable condition to its existence as long as there are needs to supplement public services. Since the needs are, as argued above, unlikely to disappear, the assumption that *chōnaikai* will grow extinct with the improvement of public services loses, rather than gains, its support to the degree, small it may be, that the inadequacy of public services is a facilitating factor.

(4) The further assumption is sometimes made that increasing urbanization will of itself lead to a disappearance of the *chōnaikai*,[32] but this is also doubtful. The Wirthian thesis that local ties inevitably dissolve with increased urbanization has in America itself come under criticism and it is now generally admitted that it is dangerous to generalize simply on the basis of American urban studies alone.[33] The same criticisms can be levelled at this postulate. As shown in the writer's survey results, among those who seem most definitely to have borne the brunt of urbanization and to be most affected thereby in consciousness and attitude (i.e. the white- and blue-collar classes) *chōnaikai* have been formed in fair number—a fact lending credence to such criticism. Therefore, in Japanese cities the *chōnaikai* can be expected to remain as a cultural form, although the majority may be expected to undergo qualitative changes as were described above.

In this event, it would be meaningless to compare them in value-laden terms to single-function American groups. The differences here are cultural differences of the same order as the difference between Western soups and a Japanese bean broth.

(5) When the *chōnaikai* is spoken of as a typical "village" phenomenon[34] of Japanese cities, i.e. their political conservatism, it seems that the consciousness of interest and attitudes of *chōnaikai*

---

[32] In connection with urbanization see the special number of *Toshi Mondai*, vol. 44, no. 10, *Shimin soshiki no shomondai* with articles by Suzuki, Okui and Isomura.

[33] G. Sjoberg, *The Preindustrial City*, pp. 14–15.

[34] The reference is to a frequent characterization of various aspects of Japanese society as "village-like" in the strength of group consciousness, hostility to arts, the society, etc. University departments, political parties, trade unions, are often so characterized by Japanese writers.—*Translator's note*.

members are usually ignored. The *chōnaikai* itself or the adoption of the *chōnaikai* form is taken to be the independent variable and the dependent variable is the maintenance of the conservative social order. Hence, wherever a *chōnaikai* exists there is automatically assumed to be activity to maintain the conservative social order, which means that the sort of *chōnaikai* described at the beginning of this paper are logically impossible to appear. Hence, it is more proper to consider as the independent variable the consciousness of interest and attitudes of the members. Depending on these, *chōnaikai* may be supportive of the conservative social order or in opposition to it, or, indeed, totally irrelevent to politics. Only such a relationship between variables will enable one to understand the appearance of such *chōnaikai* as those surveyed by the writer.

CONCLUSIONS

The foregoing are the writer's doubts concerning established doctrines of the nature of *chōnaikai*. They seem rather obvious doubts on which to base a re-examination, but there are some points that differ radically from previous viewpoints, and, moreover, as far as comparisons with America are concerned, never having lived in the U.S., the writer fears that he may be mistaken, so that on both counts he gladly invites criticism and comment.

Although the writer's main thesis concerns the appearance of a new type of *chōnaikai*, he does not mean to state that all *chōnaikai* are tending toward this type. Such examples as those in Mishima city[35] and groups that have been called "camouflaged territorial groupings"[36] probably still exist, and actually, there were many

---

[35] Hidaka and Kitagawa, *Gendai Shakei Shūdan Ron* (*A Study of Contemporary social groups*), p. 133.

[36] The Japanese term is *gisogata chiiki shūdan*. From Okuda Michiro, Toshika to chiiki shūdan no mondai: Tokyo kinkz toshi ni okeru kirei—(The problem of urbanization and locality groups: examples from Tokyo's suburban cities), *Shakaigaku Hyōron* (*Sociological Review*), no. 35.

chōnaikai in Hino and Mitaka, which were of the old type. It is just that, as new types continue to emerge, it is necessary to widen the scope of the category and, at the same time, to re-examine earlier assumptions.

Some may criticize the writer for ignoring the difference between *chōnaikai* and *jichikai*. It is possible to cite instances[37] where it has been suggested that the two are not the same but even there, common characteristics could be found. These common characteristics are the reason for the writer referring to both as *chōnaikai*.

To sum up, homogeneity or continuity can be maintained in *chōnaikai* structure in the face of change in the functions (in the broad sense including the administrative and political functions) that the structure performs. We have here, therefore, an example of a more general category of what we might call, "structural continuity and functional change"—a process, which, at the micro-level, it is possible to trace in social change in many other areas of society besides *chōnaikai*.

---

[37] Iesaka *et al.*, *op. cit.*, p. 79. Tosei Chosakai, *op. cit.*, pp. 66–77.

Part III

Urban Structure and Social Structure

The Sociology of a Zone of Transition†

J. A. REX

Editor's Note

Professor Rex analyses the urban system in terms of a conflict model and provides an important and distinctive approach to the field. His approach should be compared with that of Professor Gans, who tends to underemphasize the distinctive importance of an urban system. It is interesting that Rex is following the Weberian tradition in the context of an industrial city whereas Weber himself found difficulty in extending his own work beyond an analysis of various forms of pre-industrial city.

IT IS often said nowadays that there is no special urban sociology. What goes on in the city, it is claimed, is merely an expression of general processes at work in a national industrial society. An adequate theory of this society would therefore comprehend within itself the sociology of the city. I believe there is some truth in this view, but I also believe that there are particular processes at work in the concrete urban situation. I propose to illustrate this by outlining a theoretical model which explains something at least of the community structure of what Burgess called "the zone of transition". This model includes three elements: (1) a general theory of housing classes in the city, (2) a theory of ethnic group relations and rural-urban culture change, and (3) a theory of conflict and conflict resolution as between associations in the urban zone of transition.

The theory of housing classes is one which emerges from an attempt to make sense of the processes underlying Burgess's theory of urban zones. Burgess's broad differentiation of the city into four social and cultural zones outside the city centre (a zone of transition, a zone of working men's homes, a middle-class

---

† This paper arises out of the study by John Rex and Robert Moore, *Race, Community and Conflict: A Study of Sparkbrook*, published by the Oxford University Press in 1967.

residential zone and a commuters' zone) may be accepted as a starting point for the analysis of European and North American cities in the inter-war period. The actual physical position of these areas is to a large extent immaterial. What his account of the city principally lacks, however, is a sufficient explanatory theory of why the social and cultural life of these areas is as it is. The general notion of "competition for land use" and the outline of the principal ecological processes such as domination, invasion and succession is too lacking in theoretical bite to give us this. What is needed is an account in terms of the action frame of reference which explains particular kinds of land-use and building use in terms of the action-orientation of typical residents. What follows is an attempt to do this on the basis of research experience in Birmingham. The theory which emerges may in part be generalizable but clearly where important variables in the historical situation differ in other cities other models may have to be developed.

Our starting point then is the sort of industrial settlement with its civic facilities which grew up in England in the nineteenth century. At this stage one sees the first segregation of residential areas determined by position in relation to factories, civic buildings and the prevailing winds. On the one hand one has the homes of the upper middle classes—the captains of industry with good access to central facilities and yet avoiding contact with industrial dirt. On the other one has the grid-iron rows of working-class cottages built in the left-over space and segregated by railway-lines, canals and natural features and in each of these a separate social sub-system with its own way of life develops amongst the residents.

The upper-middle-class way of life is based upon the independence of the family, secure in the possession of its property and not dependent upon neighbourhood and extended kinship. It is expressed in the gracious architecture of large family houses, which although they have long ago been incorporated in the central business district are still structurally sound and help to give style to parts of the city centre.

The rows of red-brick working-class cottages on the other hand were built for rent-paying hands. No concept of family or community life was built into their architecture. Yet perhaps for this reason, though much more because of shared poverty and adversity, these areas came to support a strong extra-familial communal culture which was reflected in the corner shops, the pubs and the chapels, in extended kin groups, neighbourhoods, trade unions, friendly societies and religious congregations. Mutual aid rather than property gave security to the inhabitants of this area and when that mutual aid was expressed in political terms in the socialism of the city hall it was greatly to enhance the power of the established working-classes in their struggle for housing and living space.

Gradually, however, and particularly during the period between 1880 and 1914, a third way of life began to emerge between these two. It was the way of life of growing numbers of white-collar people. In aspiration it was oriented to that of the upper middle classes. True, these people—shopkeepers, minor professionals and privileged employees in industry—paid rent and their quarters were far meaner than those of the gracious upper middle classes. But they were a cut above the small red-brick cottages, and surviving servants' bells in their attics and cellars still testify to the social position of their first tenants. Abandoned by these tenants in the suburban migration of the inter-war period, these houses form a third characteristic type within the city's inner ring.

In the twentieth century, however, the great urban game of leapfrog begins. The types of housing we·have mentioned pass to other residential and commercial uses and support new differentiated styles of life while their original inhabitants open up new desirable housing options further from the centre.

The "captains of industry" together with the most successful professionals settle in larger houses, detached and in their own grounds in the classy inner suburbs. The white-collar people, aided by mortgages, leap still further where the land is cheaper and tend their gardens around one side of their semi-detached houses. And, finally, the working classes, having attained a measure of power in the city hall, have their own suburbs built for them. They are modelled on those of the white-collar people, but are distinguished by the fact that once a week a man from the Council calls for the rent.

These three ways of life and of housing are considered desirable and normal in the city. Less desirable or less normal is the way of life of those who now inhabit the inner zone. They will include some who have bought their own houses, some who occupy houses bought by the Council pending demolition, some who have bought larger old houses but must take tenants to pay their way and some who aspire to nothing more than the tenancy of a room or two.

There will, of course, be some deviants, romantics and intellectuals who actually prefer living in the inner zone, but the persistent outward movement which takes place justifies us in saying and positing as central to our model that suburban housing is a scarce and desired resource. Given that this is so, I suggest that the basic process underlying urban social interaction is competition for scarce and desired types of housing. In this process people are distinguished from one another by their strength in the housing market or, more generally, in the system of housing allocations.

Max Weber, it will be remembered, relativized Marx's view of the nature of social classes by suggesting that any market situation and not only the labour market led to the emergence of groups with a common market position and common market interests which could be called classes. We need only qualify this slightly to include groups differentially placed with regard to a system of bureaucratic allocation to arrive at a notion of "housing classes" which is extremely useful in analysing urban structure and processes.

Some Marxists may argue that such housing classes do nothing more than reflect the class struggle in industry and clearly they are partly right in that there is some correlation between the two. But it is also the case that among those who share the same relation to the means of production there may be considerable differences in ease of access to housing. This is part of the "super-structure" which manifestly takes on a life of its own. A class struggle between groups differentially placed with regard to the means of housing develops, which may at local level be as acute as the class struggle in industry. Moreover, the independence of this process is emphasized the more home and industry become separated.

The following housing-classes may, then, be distinguished in a large British provincial city:

1. The outright owners of large houses in desirable areas.
2. Mortgage payers who "own" whole houses in desirable areas.
3. Council tenants in Council built houses.
4. Council tenants in slum houses awaiting demolition.
5. Tenants of private house-owners, usually in the inner ring.
6. House owners who must take lodgers to meet loan repayments.
7. Lodgers in rooms.

In the class struggle over housing, qualification either for a mortgage or a council tenancy are crucial. They are, of course, awarded on the basis of different criteria. In the first case size and security of income are vital. In the second "housing need", length of residence and degree of affiliation to politically powerful groups are the crucial criteria. But neither mortgages nor council tenancies are available to all so that either position is a privileged one as compared with that of the disqualified. It is likely, moreover, that those who have council houses or may get them soon will seek to defend the system of allocation which secures their privileges against all categories of potential competitors. Thus local politics usually involves a conflict between two kinds of vested interest and between those who have these interests and outsiders.

As with classes generated by industrial conflict, however, there is always some possibility of an individual moving from one class to another. To the extent that individuals feel that such a move is credible, disadvantaged groups come to see the position of the privileged as legitimate and the system of class conflict tends to be transformed into a status system. Potentially class conscious attitudes amongst the housing classes may therefore be blurred.

Before we pass to a discussion of the complications which are introduced into this model by ethnicity and urban-rural culture change, it should be noted that considerable variations in this pattern of housing-class conflict would follow from differences in the economic, political and cultural situation in different industrial countries. The model we have posited assumes the existence of a socialist movement in relation to housing amongst the native working classes, an inability to exercise political power on their own behalf by disadvantaged groups and an aspiration to relatively detached family life in suburban conditions amongst all groups. Where these assumptions do not hold, other conflict and status patterns may emerge. Thus in the American situation "Council housing" does not appear to be an important factor and low-cost public housing is likely to be thought of as part of the destiny of the underprivileged. On the other hand, militancy amongst the disadvantaged in the absence of privileged working-class political power may upset the prevailing pattern. And in many countries the suburban trend may not have the same cultural importance which it has in England so that both middle-class and working-class citizens may prefer flatted accommodation near the city centre.

Such differences as these, however, call for the modification of the basic model which we have elaborated, not for its rejection. What is common to all urban situations is that housing, and especially certain kinds of desirable housing, is a scarce resource and that different groups are differentially placed with regard to access to the available housing stock.

The theory of housing classes, which we have outlined, is a theory which tells us something of the potential bases of conflict. We cannot immediately assume, however, that this will lead utomatically to the formation of organized and class-conscious groups. Any theory of class conflict must further specify the ways in which those with a common "market situation" organize or fail to organize to take action in pursuit of their interests. The business of organization, however, may in any particular case lead to a blurring of the lines of conflict and this is particularly true of the "zone of transition" where the fact that many of the residents are drawn from external cultures introduces another cross-cutting variable into the situation.

The zone of transition is, of course, differentiated from other zones by a particular type of housing-class situation and to that extent its ethnic diversity arises out of the class model we have described. If we define it as the lodging-house area we should note that whatever the ethnic origin of its inhabitants they will be drawn from classes 6 and 7 above. But if, in fact, the native-born population are able to discriminate against the newcomer, then it is certain that these disadvantaged classes will be affected by ethnic differences which divide them amongst themselves.

In point of fact it is desirable, if the ideal type of the lodging-house zone is to have empirical application, to include within it more than just the lodging-houses. In the particular piece of empirical research from which these theoretical conclusions were drawn, the lodging-houses were adjacent to Council slum property and structurally sound privately rented houses. Since the three types of housing were united by common shopping and other facilities, the community structure of the area could only be thought of as the result of interaction between all the housing classes involved.

There were, in fact, four such classes:

1. The lodging-house proprietors.
2. The lodging-house tenants.
3. The slum dwellers.
4. The "respectable" tenants of private houses.

All of these were disadvantaged groups as compared with private and council suburbanites, but there were also important and more complicated conflicts between them.

The first of these and much the most important was the conflict between the lodging-house landlords and tenants on the one hand and their ward neighbours and the City Authorities on the other. The conflict here arose from the fact that their accommodation was accommodation of the last resort and was seen by their neighbours and the authorities to be illegitimate. The landlords, having to pay short-term loans quickly, found it necessary to overcrowd their houses in order to gain as much rent as possible and the tenants, being glad to accept any alternative which gave them a roof over their heads, supported them in this. But the local authorities saw this overcrowding as undesirable from a public health and planning point of view, the slum dwellers resented the wasteful use of houses larger and structurally more sound than their own and the private tenants resented the deterioration of the neighbourhood which overcrowding produced.

Against the background of this conflict, that between lodging-house tenants and landlords and that between private tenants and slum dwellers (the latter conflict like that between private tenants and the lodging-house population being based upon the private tenants' fear of deterioration) seemed less important. But these conflicts were there nonetheless and in certain circumstances might prevent the sorts of alliance which the major conflict implied.

But the housing classes which we have mentioned were, in any case, composed in such a way that allies from the point of view of our model were divided amongst themselves and potential enemies were united. The most important reason for this was that there was diversity within the classes, both with regard to ethnic origin and with regard to the degree to which any individual had been fully socialized into the urban value system.

In order to understand the significance of the immigrant situation as an independent variable, it is useful to elaborate another ideal type. This ideal type assumes that the immigrant is not discriminated against and that his behaviour is affected solely by the degree to which he has adjusted himself to the life of the city. It is, of course, a highly unreal construction since it is of the essence of the competitive urban situation that discrimination does exist. But its value lies in the fact that it explains the deviation in the zone of transition from the pure conflict situation which our class model suggests.

The immigrant newly arrived in the city has necessarily broken or at least attenuated many of his community and kinship ties with his homeland. If he stays in the city and becomes assimilated to its culture and social order he will eventually achieve or at least aspire to the independent conjugal family life of the Council estates and suburbs. The various stages of immigrant adjustment therefore may be conceived as falling between the two points of full integration in his home community and full integration in the city.

The first stage for an individual immigrant is a state of almost complete anomie. Ties with home have been seriously weakened and his sole tie with the host society is the contractual tie of employment. This stage does not usually last for long and leads to the second stage where he looks for those in like condition to himself in order to form an intimate primary sub-community within which he can enjoy relaxed social interaction.

It is, of course, theoretically possible that the immigrant might find this new primary sub-community amongst his native-born hosts. But the barriers of linguistic and cultural differences are usually too great. If the choice is open to him he will turn naturally to those with whom he has the shared linguistic and cultural meanings which are essential to social interaction. He then finds himself a member of a small group which performs important functions for him.

Firstly, it overcomes his social isolation and prevents personal demoralization. Without such a group he would have to satisfy all his needs in the market place. He would have his food in the cafe, his sex in the brothel and he would live in a doss-house. Individuals in the city do sometimes live this way and may survive for a time, particularly with the aid of alcohol and other stimulants, but any attempt to sustain a life of this kind for a long time would lead to mental breakdown or to suicide. It seems to be the case that all men require some kind of intimate primary community to keep them alive and sane.

Secondly, however, the group will do more than this for him. It will not merely use those shared cultural meanings which are already available to facilitate social interaction. It will create new ones. For the individual who talks out his problems with his kin and intimate friends, constructs a social world for himself in so doing. And the rituals of the group will serve to give expression to and reinforce the meanings thus created. Life in the immigrant colony is always remarkable by comparison with other groupings in the city for the emphasis which is placed upon this ritualistic reaffirmation and reinforcement of meanings.

Thirdly, the social network which the group creates will provide the means for solving the individual's personal problems. If he is short of money, if he is unemployed, if he is seeking a house, if he is in trouble with the police, if he has a moral problem or if he needs help in caring for his dependents he will turn in the first place to this group. The aid he needs may ultimately come from some bureaucratic agency but even if it does it may come to him through the mediation of some group member who is skilled in these matters.

In the third stage of his adjustment the individual becomes much less dependent upon this small group. He has friends outside the group with whom he shares new meanings and he becomes less punctilious about adhering to the group's activities and rituals. He begins to solve his own problems and exercises his rights as a citizen going direct to the various civic agencies which can help him without the need for any mediator. Eventually, having created a stable family life of his own and having a secure income and employment he might be able to dispense entirely with any primary community or colony.

The important stage in this adjustment, however, is the second one. It is not, as is often thought, an alternative to becoming fully urbanized. It is a stage on the way. It is not surprising, therefore, that as Oscar Lewis has pointed out, communal social relations become more extensive and intensive during the early stages of the individual's migration. It is inevitable that they should, for the colony is the springboard from which the individual launches himself into the city. It may, of course, be the case that amongst short-term immigrants there will be no progress beyond the colony and that it will simply provide a home from home until his eventual return. But even amongst these groups, if the colony gives sufficient personal security for the individual in the city it may enable him to venture forth into a wider world and establish new contacts.

One thing which is certain, however, is that colony and primary community ties are too important to be broken simply because of economic interests. The landlord and tenant who belong to the same ethnic group cannot see their relationship as based solely on the cash nexus. In fact, the relationship is likely to be greatly modified with the landlord charging far less than the market rent, and the balance of power between the two parties being quite different from what is normal in such circumstances. Hence it is certainly to be expected that as far as the housing-class conflict is concerned, there will be alliances across class lines.

It should now be noted, however, that the zone of transition includes others apart from immigrants who are undergoing a process of urbanization. In a sense all its inhabitants are, for though they are at the back of the queue for housing facilities, the more successful they are the more they will aspire to something like the suburban ideal. And just as the immigrant first uses the ladder of his colony and then kicks it away, so also for the native-born, kinship and neighbourhood are useful supports in the time of adversity, but may be dispensed with as a man becomes successful.

One sub-group amongst the native-born, however, presents special problems. This is the group who have become isolated from their own society through deviance or through personal or family breakdown. They have no colony to turn to and their problems are not easily shared with one another. For the individual in this group very often the most important relationships are those with a social worker. But this alone is not sufficient for the interpretation of their situation and they must look elsewhere for an adequate set of social meanings. Almost certainly they find it in the residue of meanings left over from their former social experience and far from being driven into the community of immigrants, they will be inclined in the presence of immigrants to assert their native culture as strongly as possible. Thus, even though this down-and-out group may share the condition of the immigrants, its affiliation will be to the host society. One cannot expect united action by native and immigrant tenants in such circumstances.

It may now be asked whether, if what we have said about ethnic ties, colonies and sub-communities is true, interaction in the zone of transition is at all affected by the housing classes which we have discussed previously. On this two things may be said. In the first place, the whole process of selection which brings these groups together results from the competition for housing in the city. And, secondly, colonies and similar groupings may take on quite different meanings as a result of the competitive process.

In order to explain the first of these points it is necessary to say something about the way in which the lodging-house area develops. What happens is that some individuals who are denied access to legitimate and desired forms of housing obtain short-term and costly loans in order to buy houses. To make such ventures financially viable they must buy large houses and they must take as many tenants as possible. Since this form of land-lordism is regarded as morally illegitimate by the city, it will most frequently be an outsider who undertakes such an enterprise. He will, it is true, make special provision for tenancies for his own kinsmen and fellow-countrymen, but in the nature of the case he must have tenants from other groups whom he can exploit. These will include both immigrants from other countries than his own and disadvantaged groups from the host society. The lodging-house then will be a multi-racial unit run by foreigners.

Any immigrant group which is prominent amongst the

lodging-house landlords will have a peculiar relationship to the host society. The task which it is performing is socially a vital one for it provides housing for larger numbers who are provided for in no other way. But it is also one which is inconsistent with the ideal values of the society. The group concerned, therefore, becomes a pariah group in the technical sense in which the Jews in Mediaeval Europe were said to be a pariah group because they performed the socially necessary function of usury.

Inevitably, then, inter-ethnic group attitudes are affected by the housing situation. The native residents' attitude to the immigrants does not depend solely upon the fact that they are ethnically different or upon psychologically determined racial prejudice. The immigrant is identified as a man who overcrowds and destroys good houses and it is his position in the housing market which defines his situation for the native.

In these circumstances, immigrant groups must be more than merely a haven of retreat and a cultural home for their members. The immigrants have interests to defend and these interests must be protected by something like a trade union. Hence the system of colonies tends to become structured as a system of conflict groups. Very often, it is true, what set out to be interest-group organizations become colony centres and cultural groups. But equally cultural groups find themselves involved in "trade union" activity on behalf of an economic interest group.

We still have to consider, however, the question of the associational means through which these conflicts are played out. We have indicated that these are a variety of ethnic groups engaged in conflict about housing, but we have still to show how this happens. We have spoken of colonies and conflict and interest groups, but the concrete associations which exist may not set out to be either of these. They are churches, political parties, clubs, immigrant welfare associations, sports clubs and pub clienteles. Our problem is to show the relationship between these and the natural tendency to form "colonies" and economic interest groups which we have described.

What is suggested here is that nearly all associations in the zone of transition, whatever their particular charters may declare their aims to be, do fulfil one or more of the main functions which we have outlined for colonies and conflict groups. These may now be listed as:

1. Overcoming social isolation.
2. The affirmation of meanings, values and beliefs.
3. Administering "pastoral" care to members.
4. The attainment of group goals.

These four functions cannot be sharply separated from one another. Overcoming social isolation depends upon the affirmation and establishment of social meanings and values. The affirmation of values may impose on the individual certain duties whose performance are functional to the attainment of group goals. Participation in goal-attainment activity may assume a ritualistic character whose prime effect is to reinforce values and beliefs. And pastoral care may be concerned with winning the adherence of the individual to a goal-attainment and belief-affirming organization as much as with solving his personal problems. That this overlapping of functions exists follows from the fact that the same organizations are at once colonies and conflict groups. This may be illustrated in the case of the churches and the political parties.

Membership of a religious congregation is one of the main forms of group life available to the inhabitants. It provides a home for those who belong. But the reason why it provides a home is that the assertion of common beliefs and an interpretation of the world is at the centre of its activity. Those who share these beliefs are better able to understand and to interact with one another. The beliefs, however, do more than merely interpret the world. Their point is to change it. Christianity especially provides a rich range of possible beliefs about the relationship between the holy community and the world, and those who affiliate to one of its belief systems thereby come to adopt attitudes of co-operation or conflict towards the various out-groups with whom they are confronted. Finally, in the process of carrying out their pastoral function the churches exercise surveillance over the belief systems of their members and incorporate them more fully into their goal-attainment systems.

The political parties on the other hand appear at first to be concerned with obtaining and using legitimate political power on behalf of interest groups. But as one participates in the life of the party one finds the other functions equally in evidence. For many the party and its social clubs provide a home much in the way the churches do. The enunciation of the party's programme requires a diagnosis of the ills of the world not unlike that offered by the churches. And the councillors or M.P.s surgery performs functions very similar to those of the pastor on his rounds.

What is true of these highly structured organizations is also to a large extent true of more diffuse groupings, such as sports organizations, social clubs and pub clienteles. All of these are marked by a flight of their members from loneliness and isolation, by the affirmation of shared meanings and beliefs, by co-operative group activity and by a concern for their members' welfare. Some may emphasize one function more than another but potentially these organizations may fulfil any of them. Thus we should not be surprised if an immigrant sports and welfare organization becomes a crucially important conflict group any more than we should if a political party becomes primarily a social club.

This merging of functions is of the greatest importance for the conflict model in terms of which we are seeking to interpret the community of the zone of transition. It remains the case that there is considerable potential for conflict between groups and the existence of group goal attainment organizations is central to the structure of the community. But the fact that there is such a variety of organizations and that these organizations also perform other functions means that the conflict will, to some extent, be blurred and muted. Three points may be made to emphasize this.

The first of these is the cathartic function of group membership. In a conflict situation one might expect that the attempt to realize group goals would lead to open conflict and the use of force. And to some extent in the zone of transition it does. But as men organize for the achievement of their goals they are willing to postpone their attainment. They concentrate on the building up of the organization and ensuring the loyalty and doctrinal purity of their fellow members. This may then become a goal in itself and many of the discontents felt in the community may be channelled into ritualistic activity and expression. Thus we should not say that if there is no actual fighting in the streets, consensus has been achieved. The real index of conflict is to be found in the passion of belief and the energy put into organizational activity.

But secondly we have to notice that the residents come to see that there are alternative associational means open to them. If one has a problem one may find that the Catholic priest, the secretary of the immigrant welfare organization, the local doctor, the social worker and the city councillor are all available to deal with it. It remains true that a man will by and large take his problem to his own organization. But this is consistent with some recognition that the associational facilities available belong to the community as a whole. Just as a Labour voter may take a ride to the polling booth in a Conservative car, regarding the car as part of the common electoral facilities, so an individual from any one group may use the facilities which another group provides. It is here that we see the uneasy beginnings of a genuine community structure which transcends the conflict situation. Conflict still exists and may be intense and bitter, but it has begun to take place within a larger ordered structure of organizations.

This use of one's enemy's facilities in this way is the more likely to occur because of a third factor. This is that many of the associations which operate in the area are not merely local organizations. They cannot respond solely to the needs of interests of a particular group and they cannot exclude particular individuals from membership. Thus a Nonconformist denomination whose local native members might find deep satisfaction in affirming predestinarian beliefs and rejoicing in their own election have to accept the fact that their Church also has branches in the West Indies and the West Indian immigrant has a legitimate claim to membership of their church. And the trades unionist who believes in the solidarity of the international working class cannot easily be excluded because he does not share the racial resentments of his comrades in the local party. So organizations find themselves with potentially subversive members and individuals affiliated to organizations often quite inappropriate to the attainment of their goals and interests.

To say that conflict is blurred and muted in these ways, however, is not to deny its existence. What we are trying to do is to follow through our analysis of conflict and to show how it is modified in the process of social interaction. This does not mean that we accept that the community in the zone of transition is forced to reach some sort of value consensus. It does not mean that the various groups achieve a kind of segregated and peaceful co-existence. And it does not mean that with a number of cross-cutting conflicts cancelling one another out an overall stability is realized. The essence of the situation is still that there are a number of ethnic groups engaged in conflict over the allocation of housing, and though their conflict may not be carried through to the point of violence it remains at the centre of the overall interaction system. It is always possible in such a situation that if there were a crisis organizations would become functionally and ethnically specialized and that the lines of the conflict would be more sharply drawn.

There remains, however, one further problem to consider. This is the development of a relatively community-wide organization incorporating all groups. Nearly all community organizations in the zone of transition develop some organization of this kind and it is important that we should understand something of their structure and functioning, of their bases and potential stability.

The kind of community which we are discussing is thought by residents of the city as a whole, as well as by those who live within it, to be a problem community. It is inevitable, therefore, that at some point in its history leading citizens will come together on the basis that "something must be done". Differential developments then occur, depending upon who comes together and what it is they propose to do.

In some cases those who come together simply represent one interest group. If this happens the community organization which is formed may be expected to promote punitive policies against groups other than those to which the organization's members belong. But it is unlikely that such an organization would ever become clearly differentiated from other special interest organizations and make its claim to being a community-wide organization effective. What is perhaps more significant is the possibility that a particular group might come to play a predominant role within the context of a more widely based organization.

One group of individuals, however, is usually in a strategic position to exercise influence in the formation of such organizations. This is the group of professional and semi-professional social workers. They command recognition because they already enjoy some measure of confidence among those who do pastoral work in the various associations and because they have a quasi-official role within the governmental structure of the city. We have seen that colony structures produce leaders who do pastoral work amongst their members and mediate between their members and the bureaucratic agencies. We now see that there is a further group of mediators. The social workers are sufficiently close to the problems of the individuals in the area to have their confidence, but they also bring to these problems a relatively universalistic approach derived from their professional training.

It has, of course, to be recognized that the group of social workers to which we refer here may fall short of achieving these standards of behaviour or of occupying this role. There are a variety of motivations and approaches to social work and the fact that community organizations are likely to be subject to pressures from the various conflict groups makes it less likely that their behaviour will be completely governed by some conception of their professional role. But the fact that such professionalism enters into the situation at all is an important factor and in so far as it does it may help the association to perform two important functions for the local community and for the city as a whole.

The first of these is that of conflict resolution in the zone of transition. In so far as the association co-opts the officials of the various associations to its committees and councils, it confronts them with one another in circumstances where common interests are paramount and this could mean that bargains and contracts will be struck between them. This, we must stress again, does not mean that the basis of conflict will disappear. But it does create the circumstances in which men will at least ask whether there are not less costly ways of pursuing them. And if it were possible for the community organizations to achieve a degree of permanence there might emerge some degree of consensus at least about the legitimate ways in which conflict should be pursued.

The other important function is that of socializing the organization's clients into the wider social system of the city. The organization may be inhibited about doing this by the fact that its charter is to save the local community itself. Nonetheless, its own roots are in the town hall and in various city offices and the mere process of case-work involves facilitating the mobility of some individuals to other parts of the city. Thus, the main role of the association becomes that of maintaining some degree of peace between the various groups while they are still resident in the area, but at the same time facilitating the process of mobility and urbanization which will lead some at least of their clients to move from transit camp conditions to full urban acceptance.

It is not to be supposed, however, from this ideal-type analysis of the role of community organizations that such organizations will automatically arise out of some inherent tendency of the urban social system towards equilibrium. Whether they arise at all will depend upon the availability of individuals motivated to perform this function and, in any case, they constitute a very imperfect mechanism for resolving the built-in tensions which exist. A city is conceivable in which the reasons for these tensions were dealt with at source in a restructuring of the system of housing allocation. But given that there is privilege and discrimination and exploitation of one group by another, and given that the level of life at which many inhabitants of the zone of transition live is nearly intolerable, community organization of this kind is a fall-back social mechanism of potentially considerable importance. It is not surprising, therefore, that it recurs in very different circumstances in European and American cities.

Life in the zone of transition has a very recognizable quality and those who have ever known it recognize it when they see it again. It is a life of squalor, of under-privilege and of conflict and for those who work there professionally it means sitting with clients in dreary church halls, offices and club rooms trying to solve their personal problems and trying to reconcile the attainment of their ends with those of others. It is a world far from the functionally integrated social systems which sociologists are too fond of discussing. Only as sociologists begin to understand it will they begin to understand what the city is like on its underside.

In conclusion, then, we may summarize the central propositions of this essay as follows:

1. Urban development in advanced industrial societies divides men into classes differentially placed with regard to housing.

2. The zone of transition is that area of the city where the least privileged housing classes live, especially the landlords and tenants of lodging-houses.

3. The community life of the zone of transition is shaped by conflicts between these housing classes.

4. Since many of the under-privileged are newcomers to the city their organizations will also perform functions in the re-orientation of men from foreign, traditional and rural societies to urban life.

5. The actual associations such as churches, political parties and clubs will perform important functions in regard to both 3 and 4 above.

6. They will perform these functions relatively imperfectly both because of their functional diversity and because of their responsiveness to outside pressures from parent organizations.

7. Community-wide organizations may arise which have the function for the local community of peaceful conflict resolution and for the city as a whole of mediating and facilitating mobility between its problem areas and the larger urban society.

8. The situation in the zone of transition is a highly unstable one and in any sudden crisis ethnic and class conflicts which are temporarily contained may crystallize and be pursued by more violent means.

These are propositions which relate the study of the urban zone of transition dynamically to a wider concept of the city as a social system.

The Development of Prague's Ecological Structure

J. Musil

Editor's Note

Dr. Musil's careful study provides some understanding of the ways in which the processes at work in a centrally-planned economy affect the form and function of a capital city. His account of the way patterns of segregation grow more or less pronounced, depending on political decisions, is of particular interest and provides a further clue to the nature of an urban socio-ecological system. It also shows the way in which the ecological approach can be modified to fit a system in which land values and rents are of little or no significance.

ECOLOGICAL studies of Central and East European cities are, in comparison with those of other parts of the world, very limited. As far as such studies exist, they are concerned mostly with conditions before World War II, as, for example, Beynon's study on Budapest[1] or Moscheles' demographic and ecological study of Prague.[2] Among the post-war analyses, P. George's and S. Devignes's Greater Prague[3] could be mentioned, as well as Z. Piořo's book on the social ecology of Polish cities.[4] This fact led G. Sjoberg to complain, in his chapter on Comparative Urban Sociology,[5] about the scarcity of ecological and general

---

[1] E. D. Beynon, Budapest: An Ecological Study, *Geographical Review*, **33,** 1943, 256–75.

[2] J. Moscheles, The Demographic, Social, and Economic Regions of Greater Prague, *Geographic Review* **27,** 1937, 414–29.

[3] P. George and S. Desvignes, The Greater Prague, *Annals of Geography*, 1948, pp. 249–56.

[4] Z. Piořo's, *Ekologia spoleczna w urbanistyce*, Warsaw, 1962.

[5] G. Sjoberg, Comparative Urban Sociology. In *Sociology Today, Problems and Prospects*, vol. II, ed. by R. K. Merton, L. Broom and L. S. Cottrell Jr., New York.

sociological studies of cities in Eastern Europe. It is indeed a pity, the more so that in these cities the ecological forces, which formed the pattern of West European and North American cities, were considerably changed and substituted by different ecological processes.

These processes may be illustrated by the example of Prague, during the different stages of its social development over the past 30 years. A long-term study of the ecological patterns of Prague was possible since the basic demographic data of all censuses since 1921 were available for smaller sub-units within the city. Furthermore, it was possible to start with a certain tradition of research on Prague's ecological structure. A close reading of Boháč's study of Prague[6] reveals thoughts and procedures which were later developed by the Chicago School into social ecology.[7] In the thirties the Czech geographer Moscheles[8] employed the results of Prague's census so successfully that her work is still being mentioned in articles on the structure of European cities.

An analysis of the basic demographic data on Prague was made in order to review the changes in the ecological pattern of Prague over the past three decades.

The area of Prague was divided, in the census years 1930, 1950 and 1961, into three concentric zones corresponding to the basic urban structure and to the stages of historical growth of the capital. In 1949 Prague was divided administratively into 16 districts which led to the incorporation of a number of communities which already in effect belonged to Prague; hence it was not possible to use Boháč's five-zone scheme, which certainly was a useful means of analysing the ecological structure. It is, however, interesting that although Moscheles, like Boháč,

---

[6] A. Boháč, *Prague, the Capital. Study of its Population*, 1923.

[7] Comparative survey of studies in the book of J. A. Quinn, *Human Ecology*, New York, 1950, and P. H. Chombart de Lauwe, *Paris and the Parisian Agglomeration*; see also *Studies in Human Ecology*, ed. by G. A. Theodorson, Evanston, 1961.

[8] J. Moschelesová, *op. cit.*

had the detailed statistics of Prague's 45 communities at her disposal, she distinguished between only three zones. This division was justified in that great authorities on Prague, such as J. K. Říha, O. Stefan and J. Vančura, also distinguish three principal concentric zones in Prague: "Above all, it is the inner nucleus of historical character which . . . preserves roughly the character of the walled town. The inner nucleus is surrounded by the first inner ring which occupies Prague's former suburbs of the nineteenth century and roughly also the built-up areas of twentieth-century Prague. Then the second outer ring follows which occupies the outer district of Prague . . .".[9] This zoning corresponds in principle to Dickinson's theory of ecological pattern in West European cities,[10] and it is also used in the following study. Owing to the fact that in some cases the boundaries of communities, which originally belonged to Prague, were to some extent changed in 1949 and 1955, the zones according to which we analyse the data of 1950 and 1961 are not entirely identical with the zones of 1921 and 1930. The differences are, however, so negligible that they cannot affect the relative data on the zones' demographic structure.

THE GROWTH OF THE ZONES' NUMBER OF INHABITANTS

Though the following parts of our study are mainly concerned with the changes which occurred in Prague's demographic structure between 1930–1950–1961, the abundance of historical data on the number of inhabitants in the individual zones made it possible to start from Boháč's demographic study and to complete his retrospective data (which go back to the year 1843) with new data from the period after 1921. The data on the number of inhabitants for the regional unit which forms today's Greater Prague were used therefore in two ways: according to Boháč's

---

[9] J. K. Říha, O. Stefan and J. Vančura, *The Prague of Yesterday and Today*, Prague, 1956.

[10] R. E. Dickinson, *West European Cities*, London, 1950.

original scheme of five zones and according to the division of Prague into three zones.

From Fig. 1, showing either the increase or the decrease of the population of Boháč's zones, it can be readily seen how the proportion of the population in Prague's historical core continuously decreased in relation to the total population of the city.

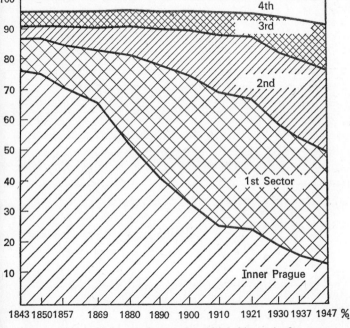

FIG. 1. Growth of the relative number of inhabitants in five zones according to Boháč.

It is also evident that Prague's demographic evolution proceeded in stages. The period from 1843 to 1869 is an era of relative "tranquillity", though there are already the beginnings of the gradual development of new suburbs: the most rapid development occurs, however, in the years from 1869 to 1910. It is interesting that during the period from 1910 to 1947 the first zone's relative number of inhabitants gradually began to decrease, due to the second, and later, the third zone's rapid growth. Prague's development and the growth of its population shifted in the period 1900–37 to the second zone, while in the period 1921–47 the most rapid growth occurred in the third and fourth zones.

The analysis of the demographic development, in accordance with our division of the city into three concentric zones, complements the above conclusions. Table 1 and Fig. 2 show that Prague's population was stabilized shortly before World War II.

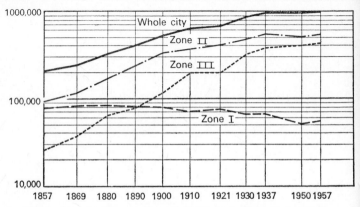

Fig. 2. Growth of the number of inhabitants in Prague's three zones.

Up to that time a relatively rapid growth of the population can be observed. It did not progress at the same speed in all zones, and in the historical core, which comprises today's district Prague 1, it lasted only till 1880. From that year onwards the historical nucleus was gradually losing population and today has about 60 per cent of 1880's population. This decline appears to have occurred all over Europe;[11] it is caused by the transformation of what were originally the residential districts of

---

[11] See the review of the depopulation of inner parts of European cities in R. E. Dickinson, *West European Cities*, London, 1950.

TABLE 1. GROWTH OF THE NUMBER OF INHABITANTS IN PRAGUE'S ZONES

Zones	1857	1869	1880	1890	1900	1910	1921	1930	1937	1950	1957
I	39·00	35·21	27·01	20·45	15·55	11·15	10·80	7·57	6·82	5·39	5·43
II	47·58	49·31	52·53	60·00	61·75	57·27	60·36	56·16	54·57	53·19	52·89
III	13·42	15·48	20·46	19·55	22·70	31·58	28·84	36·27	38·61	41·42	41·68
(100%)	100·00	100·00	100·00	100·00	100·00	100·00	100·00	100·00	100·00	100·00	100·00
$N =$	200,722	239,790	314,442	397,268	514,345	616,631	676,657	848,823	962,200	931,525	981,185

historical centres into central service areas—with offices, shops and so on—and by the decrease of the number of inhabitants in existing dwellings. Characteristically the population of the central area of Prague has higher mortality rates than birth rates and is therefore not capable of natural growth. The centre depends more than any other town district on the influx of new inhabitants.

On the other hand, population growth was most rapid in zone III—from only 26,932 inhabitants in 1857 to 408,982 in 1957 and 448,092 in 1961. The pace of this growth was greatest in the years from 1869 to 1880, 1890 to 1910, 1921 to 1930. Zone II developed more steadily, fundamentally at the same pace as did Prague as a whole. Only in the years 1869–90, thanks to the rapid building of Žižkov, Vinohrady and Holešo-vice-Bubny, did the population grow more rapidly than in Prague as a whole. During this period, Vinohrady, which had in 1869 only 1274 inhabitants, became a town of 52,504 inhabitants. In Žižkov there were only 4336 inhabitants in 1869, while in 1900, there were 59,326. Yet even in this zone from 1937 onwards a decline in the population is to be observed.

The century of Prague's population growth shown in the figures represents a period in which Prague became a city whose area has today a much more uniform population density[12] than was the case several decades ago, but which still shows marks of its uneven and unsystematic growth.

From the ecological point of view the consequences of the irregularly rapid development of the individual zones and the effect of the historical social differentiation of its individual quarters can still be observed today. However, in the two decades between 1930 and 1950 there were signs that the sharp social contrasts between various parts of Prague were disappearing. This was due mainly to decreasing social differentiation and to the stabilization in the capital's growth associated with a smaller

---

[12] Collin Clark, The Location of Industries and Population, *The Town Planning Review*, **35,** No. 3, 1964, 195–218.

influx of new rural population, which influx had been very high in the period 1920–39.

THE POPULATION'S AGE STRUCTURE IN THE ZONES

The analysis of the population's age structure in the individual zones showed very interesting results. Dividing the population roughly into three basic age groups, 0–14, 15–64 and over 65, it appears that Prague's structure was until 1961 also typical of many cities; a small number of children in the centre, the largest number in zone III on the outskirts and, on the other hand, a large number of elderly people in zone I contrasting with their low number on the outskirts. On the map showing the proportion of males aged 0–14 years in Prague's individual communities in 1930 and 1950 it can be clearly seen that this population group gradually declines from the outskirts to the centre. In both investigated periods, (i.e. 1930 and 1950) the age group 15–64 was represented by the greatest number in Prague's historical centre which constitutes zone I.

When comparing the figures of the age structure of the three concentric zones in 1930 and 1950, it can be seen that the differences between zones were in 1950 not as marked as in 1930. The tendency towards a still more homogeneous age structure of the population of the city as a whole is suggested by the 1961 census data. There is almost no difference between the proportion of children in the age 0–14 in the zones I, II and III and the well-known gradient of decreasing percentages of children from the outskirts of the city to its centre almost disappears. Similar trends towards more homogeneity can be seen from data of other age groups.

The more detailed data on the population's age structure, illustrated in Figs. 3 and 4, shows that in 1930 and 1950 the age group 15–24, and in 1950 the age group 25–34 as well, were dominant in zone I. A possible explanation that a larger proportion of men were in the basic military service in this part of the town does not hold because this fact was found to apply to

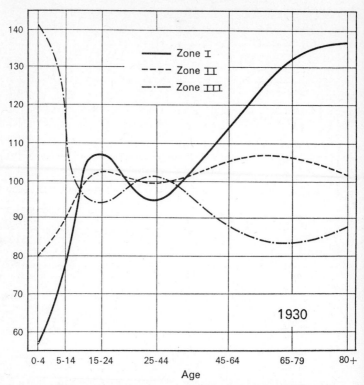

Fig. 3. Population's age structure of Prague's three zones in 1930.
(100 = the average age structure for Prague as a whole.)

men and women alike. This fact is important because the relatively higher number of men and women of child-rearing age does not correspond with a higher number of children, in fact just the opposite is the case. It is therefore evident that Moschelesova's theory that the number of children is in relation to the number of young men in Prague's individual zones is not quite correct. According to her study the number of children is above all a function of the age structure of the zones' population. After a more detailed analysis of the age structure it was found, however, that the area where most of the young men and women

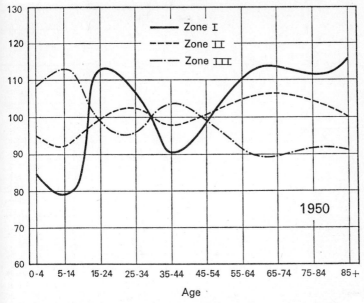

Fig. 4. Population's age structure of Prague's three zones in 1950.
(100 = the average age structure for Prague as a whole.)

live, has the lowest number of children. How may one explain this paradoxical fact?

There can be basically two explanations of this fact:

1. The women's fertility living in this part of the town is lower.
2. In this part of the town there are indeed many young women and men, but they are not married couples in families with children.

No data were or are available for calculating the women's fertility in Prague's zones according to standard demographic methods. The so-called fertility index was therefore calculated, i.e. the number of children aged 0–14 to 100 women aged 15–44. From Fig. 7 and Table 5 below it is evident that in the town centre there were in 1930 and 1961 really fewer children to 100 women of reproductive age than in the other two zones, but because of

TABLE 2. POPULATION'S AGE STRUCTURE OF PRAGUE'S THREE ZONES—1930

Zones	Men			Women		
	0–14 %	15–64 %	65+ %	0–14 %	15–64 %	65+ %
I	10·94	83·45	5·43	9·93	81·80	8·08
II	14·55	80·71	4·63	12·26	81·16	6·44
III	19·44	77·10	3·35	18·55	76·23	5·13
(100%)	16·12	79·56	4·21	14·28	79·49	6·11
N=	65,446	323,151	17,094	63,205	351,833	27,033

TABLE 3. AGE STRUCTURE OF PRAGUE'S ZONES—1961

Zones	Age groups		
	0–14	15–64	65 and more
	%	%	%
I	19·06	70·63	10·32
II	19·12	70·64	10·24
III	20·45	70·35	9·20
All Prague	19·66	70·41	9·93
N=	197,659	707,853	99,867

TABLE 4. NUMBER OF WOMEN TO 100 MEN IN PRAGUE'S ZONES—1961

Zones	Men	Women	Women to 100 men
I	36,848	42,733	115·97
II	205,661	235,097	114·31
III	228,557	256,483	112·21
All Prague	471,066	534,313	113·42

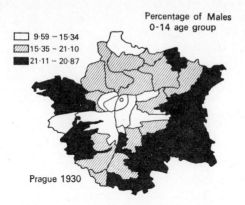

FIG. 5. Proportion of men aged 0–14 to total number of men in Prague's individual communities in 1930.

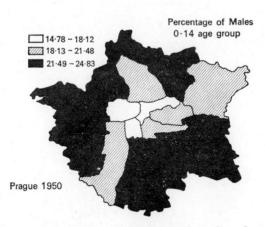

FIG. 6. Proportion of men aged 0–14 to total number of men in Prague's individual districts in 1950.

the nature of the fertility index it is impossible to draw the conclusion that the fertility of women living in Prague's centre was actually lower than that of women living on the outskirts. The fertility index indicates only the number of children to any 100 women aged 15–44, i.e. regardless of whether they are the mothers of these children. However, the data show that the differences between zones are diminishing, as can also be seen from 1961 data.

TABLE 5. FERTILITY INDICES IN PRAGUE'S ZONES—1961

Zones	Number of children	Number of women	Fertility indices
I	3408	16,824	203
II	19,442	89,102	218
III	23,283	98,642	236
All Prague	46,133	204,568	225

The data on the structure of households also helps to explain the small number of children in this part of Prague. Table 6 below clearly indicates that most of the childless households are

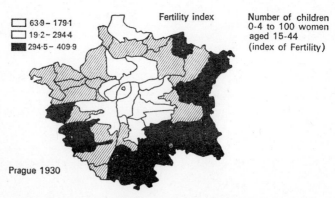

FIG. 7. Number of children aged 0–14 to 100 women aged 15–44 in 1930 in Prague's individual communities.

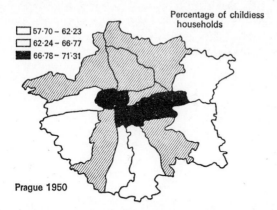

FIG. 8. Relative number of childless households in Prague's individual districts in 1950.

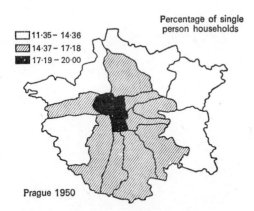

FIG. 9. Relative proportion of single person households in Prague's zones in 1950.

in zone I, a little less of them in zone II and the least of them in zone III. Households with 1–3 children and more family members are, however, concentrated on the town's outskirts.

TABLE 6. HOUSEHOLDS ACCORDING TO THE NUMBER OF CHILDREN—PRAGUE'S ZONES IN 1961

Zones	Total number of households	Childless households %	Households with 1–3 children %	Households with 4 and more children %
I	31,722	70·76	28·85	0·39
II	172,937	70·20	29·44	0·36
III	185,094	68·35	31·18	0·47
All Prague		69·36	30·21	0·43
N =	389,753	270,370	117,782	1601

THE POPULATION STRUCTURE OF THE ZONES ACCORDING TO MARITAL STATUS

The zones also showed marked differentiation from each other in 1930, with regard to the marital status of their inhabitants. It is evident from the data of Table 7 that as well as containing a number of married women and men the town centre also

TABLE 7. PERCENTAGE OF MARRIED MEN, WOMEN AND DIVORCED MEN AND WOMEN IN PRAGUE'S ZONES—1961

Zones	Married men %	Divorced men %	Married women %	Divorced women %
I	53·00	4·50	45·59	6·23
II	55·02	3·48	47·89	5·20
III	54·98	3·20	48·90	4·86
All Prague	54·84	3·43	48·20	5·11
N =	258,371	16,141	257,521	27,352

contained most of the divorced and separated men and women. The table also reveals that the percentage of married women and men increased steadily towards the town's outskirts and, on the contrary, the percentage of the divorced and separated persons kept on increasing from the outskirts to the town's centre. However, the results of the 1961 census, when calculated for the individual zones, do not show the typical gradients demonstrated for 1930 and 1950. This is further evidence of the development towards a more homogeneous population structure of the zones.

TABLE 8. THE STRUCTURE OF THE HOUSEHOLDS IN PRAGUE'S ZONES—1961

Zones	Total number of households	Number of households formed by		
		1 person %	2–5 persons %	6 and more persons %
I	31,722	26·85	71·61	1·54
II	172,937	23·16	75·48	1·36
III	185,094	20·79	77·61	1·60
All Prague		22·34	76·17	1·49
N =	389,753	87,059	296,910	5784

THE STRUCTURE OF THE HOUSEHOLDS

In both the 1950 and 1961 census the number of households and the number of persons per household was published for Prague's individual districts. The relative proportion of households with 1, 2–5 and 6 and more persons in the zones could therefore be calculated. This shows that the town centre is a district in which considerably more single persons lived in 1950, whilst the town's outskirts had an above-average number of larger households. According to the data of 1961 census these differences between individual zones were not so marked, but nevertheless show the same tendency as in 1950

Let us now return to the question of differences between the age structure of individual zones: an explanation of this fact may enable us to understand the basic characteristics of Prague's ecological structure.

It is most probable that the explanation for the small number of children in Prague's historical centre in 1930 and 1950 is related to the fact that considerably fewer married men and women lived here than in Prague's two other zones. This suggests an ecological succession of the population in the central parts of Prague. In view of the fact that there are, as in most other town centres, more opportunities for temporary accommodation, for subtenancies, and the like, young unmarried people who arrive in Prague find their first accommodation possibilities limited to this district. Later, when they marry and settle down, they move, or try to move, farther out from the town centre.

Unfortunately data on the number of dwellings with subtenants in the individual zones are not available because in the 1950 and 1961 censuses the subtenants were not separated from the other occupants of the dwellings; only data for the year 1921 provides information on subtenancies. We mention these older data because from the 1950 data on the excessive number of households with 1 person in zone I it can be deduced that today most of the subtenants are still in this part of Prague.

TABLE 9. NUMBER OF ROOMS TO ONE DWELLING AND PERCENTAGE OF DWELL-INGS WITH SUBTENANTS IN PRAGUE'S ZONES—1921

Zones	No. of occupied dwellings	No. of habitable rooms	No. of rooms to one dwelling	No. of dwellings with sub-tenants	Percentage of dwellings with sub-tenants
I	16,102	47,601	2·96	4,608	28·62
II	101,174	219,140	2·17	22,382	22·12
III	49,285	122,837	2·49	5,871	11·91
All Prague	166,561	389,578	2·34	32,861	19·73

Only larger dwellings, or dwellings with a greater number of habitable rooms, can be sublet. Table 9 shows that the largest dwellings, measured by the average number of habitable rooms per dwelling, were in zone I; then the districts on the outskirts follow; the lowest average number of habitable rooms per house was in zone II. This distribution coincided roughly with the distribution of dwellings with subtenants as ascertained in 1921. As might be expected, their largest number was in the historical centre and systematically decreased towards the town outskirts. The unusually high number of dwellings with subtenants in zone I (28 per cent) was indisputably caused by the housing shortage which Prague suffered after World War I when a very large influx of people to the new capital occurred. It can be justifiably assumed that larger house-building programmes later reduced the number of dwellings with subtenants in the town centre, but the basic proportions with regard to the percentage of these dwellings in the different town zones remained, without doubt, unchanged till today.

The town centre is also, according to the data on mobility published in the Demographic Manual of Prague, a district with the greatest movement of population, an area of temporary and short-time accommodation for young people moving to Prague. It is, however, simultaneously, that part of Prague where most of the old people and old-established inhabitants live. The town centre is a district of social and urban contrasts.

From the theoretical point of view it is evident that the structure and quality of the housing stock influence significantly the spatial distribution of the individual social groups of the population.

THE POPULATION'S SOCIAL STRUCTURE IN THE ZONES

The gradual deterioration of the quality of dwellings in the historical cores after the removal of the town walls and the erection of new town districts at the end of the nineteenth and beginning of the twentieth century led, in central European cities, to significant population movements.

Economically stronger strata of the population began to move to new districts in the suburbs and the urban, underprivileged, classes moved gradually to the historical cores where originally the upper classes used to live.[13] The pace of the "proletarianization" of the town centres and historical cores differed according to local conditions. Prague in the years prior to World War II

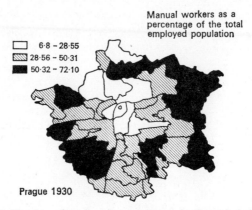

Manual workers as a
percentage of the total
employed population

☐ 6·8 – 28·55
▨ 28·56 – 50·31
■ 50·32 – 72·10

Prague 1930

Fig. 10. Number of workers in percentages in Prague's individual communities in 1930.

was in a situation typical of the unfinished phase of "proletarianization" of the city centre. The number of workers and lower employees was already in the thirties larger in zone I than in zone II, but lower than on the outskirts, which were traditionally working-class districts, in contrast to the American and some West European cities.

Though the tables of the population's social structure in the three zones do not give identical indices (the data of the year 1930 and 1961 show the ratio of individual socio-economic groups to 100 of all inhabitants, whilst the data of 1950 show them out

---

[13] Cf. B. Babánek, *The Changes in the Theories of City Redevelopment*, VUVA, Brno, 1955.

of one hundred of gainfully employed persons), they nevertheless permit comparisons between the zones. It appears that today's social structure of Prague was already formed in the period prior to World War II and that very little of this general pattern has changed during the past 30 years.

In the thirties, in 1950 and 1961 most of the workers and non-manual employees were living in zone III. White collar workers were concentrated in zone II. The analysis of the regional structure of the so-called "self-employed and tenants" in 1930 and "employers" in 1950 had very interesting results. Strictly speaking, they are not identical groups (self-employed and tenants are a wider category than employers) but in reality they represent social groups comprising a predominant part of the upper and middle class.

In each of the periods investigated the percentage of the population in these groups declined from the town centre towards the periphery. This is a further indication of the lack of social uniformity in Prague's historical centre. On the one side the lower class was here relatively strongly represented; on the other side it was a district where many of the middle class lived, particularly small manufacturers and tradesmen.

The data on the economically active population may also be analysed. That category of the population classified in the 1930 census as being in active work evidently does not agree with the

TABLE 10. PROPORTION OF SOME OF THE POPULATION'S SOCIAL GROUPS TO THE WHOLE POPULATION IN PRAGUE'S ZONES—1930

Zones	Self-employed and tenants %	Officials and clerks %	Non-manual employees %	Workers, apprentices %
I	36·79	20·46	16·33	26·41
II	31·19	26·60	16·05	26·16
III	21·81	16·25	18·18	43·75
All Prague $N(100\%)=$	28·21 239,487	22·39 190,012	16·84 142,974	32·56 276,350

TABLE 11. THE SOCIAL STRUCTURE OF PRAGUE'S ZONES—1961

Zones	Workers %	Other employed persons %	Members of co-operatives %	Self-employed persons %	Without data on social group %
I	40·38	52·50	3·10	1·65	2·37
II	39·76	54·76	2·54	0·98	1·93
III	46·77	48·46	2·27	0·74	1·76
All Prague	43·19	51·54	2·46	0·92	1·89
$N(100\%)=$	434,290	518,222	24,689	9203	18,975

category of gainfully employed and unskilled labour which in 1950 formed the group of persons in active work. In spite of this somewhat different classification, the data of both censuses show the differences among the zones, as far as the economic activity of the population is concerned. It is evident, as Table 12 shows, that before and after the war the percentage of the economically active population was highest in Prague's historical centre and decreased towards Prague's outskirts. The higher number of economically active persons in the town centre is the

TABLE 12. ECONOMICALLY ACTIVE POPULATION IN PRAGUE'S 3 ZONES IN 1930 AND 1950

Zones	1930		1950	
	Total of inhabitants	Gainfully employed %	Total of inhabitants	Gainfully employed %
I	64,296	63·97	50,235	51·18
II	476,698	58·76	495,477	46·24
III	307,829	55·99	385,813	43·98
All Prague		58·15		45·57
$N(100\%)=$	848,823	493,575	931,525	424,522

result of the individual zones' age structure. The relatively large number of people of productive age and the small number of children in the town centre when compared with the smaller number of people of productive age, and the large number of children on the outskirts, means that zone I, the town centre, is an area with the highest number of economically active inhabitants.

SPATIAL DISTANCE BETWEEN THE POPULATION'S INDIVIDUAL SOCIAL GROUPS

Data on the social structure of the population of individual districts enables the spatial distance between the main social groups to be measured. It was already evident from data on the relative proportion of social groups in smaller regional units or even zones, that in certain parts of the city there were and still are more workers, while other parts contain more white collar workers. In order to determine more accurately the extent of this social and spatial distance, a number of indices of residential segregation and dissimilarity of occupational origin were calculated.

We employed two of the many possible indices:

(a) The index of dissimilarity which measures differences in the spatial distribution of two social groups.

(b) The index of residential segregation which measures the differences between the spatial distribution of one social group in relation to the remaining population.[14]

In order to be able to calculate these indices, we first calculated the percentages of a certain social group living in the individual regional units. The index of dissimilarity is then the half of the absolute value of the differences between the percentages of the population of two different groups in all regional units.

---

[14] Cf. O. T. Duncan and B. Duncan, Residential Distribution and Occupational Stratification, *The American Journal of Sociology*, **60,** 1955, 493–503.

TABLE 13. INDICES OF DISSIMILARITY OF SOCIAL GROUPS' SPATIAL DISTRIBUTION IN PRAGUE IN 1930 AND 1950

Social group	Social group					
	Clerks		Foremen and non-manual employees		Workers	
	1930	1950	1930	1950	1930	1950
Self-employed, tenants, employers	12·29	8·13	18·50	9·58	25·11	13·28
Clerks	—	—	19·36	10·88	27·45	14·63
Foremen, non-manual employees	—	—	—	—	13·03	5·51

TABLE 14. INDICES OF RESIDENTIAL SEPARATION OF THE POPULATION'S SOCIAL GROUPS IN PRAGUE IN 1930 AND 1950

Year	Social groups			
	Self-employed, tenants, employers	Clerks	Foremen, non-manual employers	Workers
1930	16·60	17·86	9·17	22·14
1950	9·56	12·17	5·97	11·29

If, however, we compare the spatial distribution of one social group with the population of the city as a whole, this calculated index is an index of residential segregation.

The calculation of these indices are given in the Tables 13 and 14. Since we were able to compare data from two censuses (1930, 1950);[15] we can also assess if any considerable population

[15] The data of the 1961 census cannot be used in this comparison because of many differences in the delimitation of city districts in 1930 and 1961.

re-distribution has occurred. The table shows that Prague's structure has changed considerably in this respect. The rank order of the distances between the individual social and occupational groups is the same, but the indices of dissimilarity differ in their absolute value. Though we have to attribute this decrease to the fact that the districts of the year 1950 are in some extent larger than those of 1930, the fact cannot be denied that because of the housing policy of the local authorities a more uniform distribution of all social groups of the population in the Prague area is to be observed.

The highest value of the dissimilarity index in 1930 and 1950 was found between the distribution of the dwelling places of manual workers and white collar workers. The calculated index means that in 1930 27·45 per cent of the manual workers would have had to move to other parts of Prague in order that their distribution would be identical with that of the white collar workers' dwelling places. According to the data of 1950, only 15 per cent of the manual workers would have had to move.

In the thirties, the spatially most isolated group of population were the manual workers, then followed the white collar workers, and the self-employed, while the lowest index of residential separation was found for non-manual employees; their spatial distribution corresponded roughly with the distribution of the entire population. After the war the white collar workers became the most isolated group, but manual workers were already more uniformly distributed in the Prague area. The order of the other groups remained unchanged.

CONCLUSIONS AND DISCUSSION

From this analysis of Prague it follows that the capital of Czechoslovakia—like the majority of European towns of similar size—may be subdivided into concentric zones which differ not only in their physical character but also in the structure of their population. In the pre-war period large differences appeared between the centre and the outskirts of Prague. The outskirts were populated predominantly by families with young children. Compared with the historical core of the city, this area had a more homogeneous social structure, with a predominance of the lower classes.

On the other hand, the centre of Prague was an area where most of the old people, people not living with their family, and also many single-person households were concentrated. This was also an area for the short-term housing of young people who moved to Prague. But within the same area lived established families of the upper and middle classes. The social pattern of the historical core, i.e. of zone I, was very mixed.

The indices of the population structure of zone II were intermediate between the values of indices of the outskirts and the centre. Thus different types of urban population lived in the centre and on the outskirts of Prague.

During the two post-war decades, an important change has taken place, which can be described generally as a trend towards an evening out of the differences between the three zones. These differences have decreased in some respects e.g. the age structure, marital status and fertility indices. This more homogeneous demographic structure of Prague was also confirmed by analysis of birth and death rates, as well as of infant mortality which we do not analyse here because of lack of space.

There are two main causes of this development towards greater homogeneity. The first one is connected with the control of Prague's growth, the second one with the transformation of the nature of ecological processes which operate within Czechoslovak cities.

Prague is probably the only capital in Europe which managed to control its population growth successfully, and hence the number of its inhabitants is now practically the same as before the World War II. Due to the introduction of certain controls, based on the planning of the location of industry and offices, the migration to and from Prague dropped to very low figures, i.e. the number of immigrants per year is about 13,000 (13·0 per thousand inhabitants), and the number of emigrants equals about 9000 persons (9·0 per thousand inhabitants), with the overall mobility rate of 22·0 per thousand inhabitants, which, in comparison with other cities of this size, is a relatively low figure.

These low mobility rates, combined with the fact that most migrants are married people, has important consequences for the ecological structure of Prague. A more stabilized demographic and social structure is emerging; the whole population is rapidly ageing—the inevitable effect of controlling the size of the city—finally the so-called acceptance areas, or transient areas, have almost completely disappeared. Before World War II, as mentioned above, the historical core of Prague was a transient zone: with decreasing migration the differences between zone I and other zones have become less pronounced.

This trend towards greater social homogeneity as shown, for example, by the decreasing dissimilarity indices is related to the mechanisms which account for the spatial distribution of the population in Czechoslovak cities and which are distinct from those described in the classical or neo-classical theories of human ecology.

First of all, the land values and the rents are almost irrelevant for the distribution of socio-economic groups of population.[16] Housing is strongly subsidized from public funds[17] and the rents form—even after a new 1965 Rent Act which increased rents—a comparatively small item in the family budget, that is, an average of 5 per cent of total income. For most inhabitants rent does not determine the choice of housing; there is no close correlation between the size of income and the quality of dwelling inhabited by the households. Thus there is no massive concentration of population groups with lower incomes in dwellings of

---

[16] Land is exempted from the market sphere of the economy.

[17] Incomes from the rents cover roughly one half of all expenses connected with the running and maintenance of the publicly owned housing stock. For more details on the housing policy in Czechoslovakia as compared with the respective policy in Great Britain see Jiří Musil, *Housing Needs and Policy in Great Britain and Czechoslovakia*, Glasgow University, Edinburgh, 1966.

poor quality. If, for example, old people do live in such dwellings this is not exclusively the result of their economic conditions.

Since rents are also not differentiated according to the location of the houses within the city, (so that a dwelling of the same quality and equipment is rented for the same price in the suburb as in the city centre), another economic factor determining spatial distribution of population, according to the classical ecological theory, is excluded.

The influence of economic factors was replaced—especially at a time when most dwellings were built by the State and almost all dwellings of the existing housing stock were under the direct control of Local Authorities—by a housing policy which allocates new dwellings by preference to young families with children, to employees of "key economic branches" and to families living in very bad and unhealthy dwellings. The first two categories contained almost exclusively families with small children. Middle-aged and old people remained therefore in the old housing stock. For this reason there is in Czechoslovakia a strong correlation between the age of houses and the age of their inhabitants, i.e. also between the age of dwellings and the average size of households. The older the houses, the smaller and older the households who live in them.

The result of this housing policy is socially mixed neighbourhoods or districts, and an almost complete disappearance of the social status of some areas of the cities, as an ecological factor. The population, according to housing surveys, does, of course, prefer some parts of a city more than others, but these preferences are determined more by physical and geographical conditions than by social forces.

During the last few years (i.e. after 1960), with the rapidly growing proportion of new houses built in Prague by co-operatives, and with the government's tendency to decrease the housing subsidies, and thus with the increasing importance of market elements in housing, a new combination of forces has started to mould the ecological pattern of Prague. These economic factors, which lost their decisive influence on ecological processes in the post-war period and were replaced by social considerations—as expressed in the housing policy—are gaining more and more in importance at present. This is, however, too short a period to ascertain the effect of these changes in the ecological structure of Prague: nevertheless there is no doubt that they will result in a new social differentiation of the districts of Prague.

Part IV

Urbanization

The Rural-Urban Continuum[1]

R. E. PAHL

Editor's Note
  This paper should be seen simply as a contribution to a continuing discussion, which has carried on in more recent issues of the journal Sociologia Ruralis. *For this reason, the introduction to the discussion of the paper by Eugen Lupri and A. K. Constandse is also included.*

IN A sociological context the terms rural and urban are more remarkable for their ability to confuse than for their power to illuminate.

No one disputes the right of the layman to use these terms to denote different patterns of land use, which are easily observable; what is disputable is the *sociological* relevance of these physical differences especially in highly complex industrial societies. If indeed there are no fundamental sociological differences between urban and rural then those who call themselves rural sociologists may well doubt the basis of their professional identity. Yet the existence of a Society founded to further rural sociology presupposes that there is a distinctive field to study. It is understandable, therefore, that I have many predecessors who have developed this theme in previous conferences and it is difficult to put new gloss on well-worn arguments. I will therefore start simply by reminding you of some of them.

Rural sociologists in the U.S.A. have traditionally led the field both in research techniques and general conceptuzaliation and

---

[1] The section on the Metropolitan Village in this paper was first read at the 1966 Conference of the British Sociological Association at Leicester. I am most grateful to Dr. Derek Allcorn, Prof. Michael Banton, and Prof. Paul Stirling for their critical comments on a draft of this paper. Of course, I alone remain responsible for the opinions expressed.

so perhaps we should give special heed to the warnings they are now giving us. In a recent paper, Fuguitt described the transformation of farming in North America into agribusiness so that, in 1960, 70 per cent of the rural population was not connected with farming and concluded: "If rural and urban sociology are to continue as specialized sub-fields of the parent discipline, distinguished from other sub-fields on a meaningful conceptual basis, the need for new orientations is evident" (Fuguitt, 1963, p. 261). This demand for new orientations is clearly seen in recent discussion of the rural-urban continuum, as the titles of the following papers aptly indicate:

The Rural-Urban Continuum: Real But Relatively Unimportant (Dewey, 1960)
Sociology Uncertain: The Ideology of the Rural-Urban Continuum (Benet, 1963)
Urban-Rural Dichotomies as forms of Western Ethnocentrism (Hauser, 1965).

What Reissman (1964, p. 123) described as 'so-called theories of contrast' are preserved in student textbooks and receive their ritual airing at examination time; however, in Lewis' words "their heuristic value as research tools has never been proven" (1965, p. 491). The various dichotomies and continua, set out below,[2] all appear to be dismissed by Hauser (1965, p. 514) as "catchy neologisms which often get confused with knowledge".

Author	Rural or Non-urban Category	Urban Category
Becker	Sacred	Secular
Durkheim	Mechanical Solidarity	Organic Solidarity
Maine	Status	Contract
Redfield	Folk	Urban
Spencer	Military	Industrial
Tönnies	*Gemeinschaft*	*Gesellschaft*
Weber	Traditional	Rational

---

[2] The table appears in Reissman (1964), p. 123.

For a time these polar typologies, some sanctified with the authority of the founding fathers of sociology, served as a justification for those who have been guilty of what Hofstee (1960) called "Vulgar Tönniesism" or the "uncritical glorifying of old-fashioned rural life". This theme is also discussed by Benet, who attacks the early Chicago school of urban sociology for its ethnocentrism and anti-urban ideology. "As it (i.e. the rural-urban continuum) was a figment of the imagination, and the anti-urban mentality stuck — it being characteristic of European and American folklore to ascribe rural origins to goodness — the thinking about the continuum took some strange forms" (1963, p. 5).

Urbanism as a Way of Life

Perhaps the classic paper for those who stress rural-urban differences is still Wirth's 'Urbanism as a Way of Life' (Wirth, 1938), which was referred to by an American rural sociologist as recently as 1965 as "maybe the most influential article ever to appear in a sociological journal" (Simpson, 1965, p. 133). Certainly in our present context it is difficult to escape from it, and even Dewey, in a somewhat critical article, felt that there was 'evidence' to support Wirth's notion that an increase in the size and density of the population leads to increased anonymity, which, together with the more widespread division of labour, would, in turn, produce social heterogeneity. Under these conditions relationships would, inevitably, become more impersonal and formally prescribed, and prestige would be allocated according to criteria other than personal acquaintance.

Wirth is often criticized for naïvety which is not actually present in his work: he appreciated the arbitrary nature of classifications of settlements related solely to their population size; he understood the implications of technological developments in transportation and communication which extended the city's influence far beyond its physical limits; he also recognized that modes of life which can best be described as urban might appear among people "wherever they may be, who have come under the spell of the influences which the city exerts by virtue of the power of its institutions and personalities operating through the means of communication and transportation" (Wirth, p. 48). Wirth also considers critically other criteria of urban characterization such as density, the occupations of inhabitants, the existence of certain physical facilities, institutions and forms of political organization; he also accepts the great variations between cities and, when moving on to consider their essential characteristics, he adds the crucial caveat 'at least in our culture'. Finally, he is particularly concerned lest urbanism is confused with industrialism and notes that there are preindustrial and feudal cities.

Turning now to recent criticisms of Wirth, and taking care not to impute to him an over-simplified view of the city, we may consider whether "a relatively large, dense, and permanent settlement of socially heterogeneous individuals" (Wirth, p. 50) has any common and distinct patterns of behaviour of its own. These three characteristics have the advantage of being quantifiable so that it might be possible to use them as universals or general referents for the rural-urban continuum. Clearly I am not concerned here with the ranking of various settlements according to service function and their size and spacing: these questions may be of interest to geographers and agricultural economists but their sociological relevance has to be demonstrated.

Wirth claimed that urban life was fundamentally different from that found in a folk society (which he took as his datum). Contacts in the city are "impersonal, superficial, transitory and segmental" so that the urbanite "loses the spontaneous self-expression, the morale and the sense of participation that comes from living in an integrated society" (Wirth, p. 54). The argument will be familiar and I need not go further into it now: the important point that, I think, even Dewey accepts, is that the central areas of large cities are held to be at one polar extreme of the rural-urban continuum.

The Urban Village

There is now an almost overwhelming body of evidence that the central areas of cities differ from what Wirth and many others have suggested. Studies of Bethnal Green, London (Young and Willmott, 1957), Boston (Gans, 1962), Delhi (Bopegamage, 1957), Cairo (Abu-Lughod, 1961), East London (Mayer, 1963), Lagos (Marris, 1961), Medan, Sumatra (Bruner, 1961) and Mexico City (Lewis, 1952), to name but a few, suggest that *urban villages* exist in the centre of cities in which there is a high level of social cohesion based on interwoven kinship networks and a high level of primary contact with *familiar* faces. Lewis showed in Mexico City that peasants adapted to city life much more easily than folk-urban theory might suggest: family life was stable, and indeed family ties increased in importance; religious life became more important, refuting any notions of secularization and various other 'rural' village cultural values persisted in the urban setting. The *vecindad* acts as a shock absorber for rural migrants who live in the city but are not urbanized. In East London, Mayer (1962, p. 590–1) notes that although the work situation might force 'urban' behaviour on the migrants they are not obliged to behave in an 'urban' manner outside working hours: "while some are born 'urban', and others achieve urbanization, none can be said to have urbanization thrust upon them" (p. 591). Mayer uses the word *incapsulation* to describe the situation where migrants live in the city but are not urbanized.

Apart from these urban villages, the central areas of Western cities are by no means homogeneous: they may also include the flats of a cosmopolitan smart set, possibly at very high density but without overcrowding owing to a low room density, and the flats of the unmarried or childless: in particular, many cities have a high student population in these areas; finally, there is a trapped downwardly mobile group 'forced' into the area by the lack of low-rent housing elsewhere. With such a confused mixture of sub-groups and sub-cultures it is difficult to see how the features of size and density could possibly exert a common influence on rich and poor alike. It is also difficult to understand how the city can both be a melting pot and segregate people into distinct neighbourhoods at the same time. A more recent attempt to describe a suburban way of life (Fava, 1956) has also been discredited, largely due to the work of Berger (1960) and, particularly, Dobriner (1963).

Yet perhaps the most thorough and well-argued criticism of the 'urbanism and suburbanism as ways of life' thesis is provided by Gans (1962a), and I owe much to his approach in the argument so far. He maintains that *class* is the most sensitive index of people's ability to *choose*, and that stage in the life-cycle determines the area of choice which is most likely. Gans then concludes "if ways of life do not coincide with settlement type, and if these ways are functions of class and life-cycle rather than of the ecological attributes of the settlement, *a sociological definition of the city cannot be formulated*" (p. 643, my emphasis). By implication this means that sociological definitions of any settlement type cannot be formulated and this would seem to destroy any conception of a rural-urban continuum. As will emerge in the course of my argument Gans, too, suffers from ethnocentrism.

To conclude this section, it does seem that the development of urban villages, characterized by *gemeinschaftlich* relationships, casts doubt on the basis of the rural-urban continuum. There is, nevertheless, an important distinction between high density and interaction with fellow kinsfolk and the high density of transient strangers: areas of rapid neighbourhood change are distinct from urban villages. Residential instability or transience would give rise to many of the characteristics Wirth describes: however, this somewhat Hobbesian situation is restricted to part only of some cities.

The Metropolitan Village

I want to turn now from a consideration of the city population proper, if there be such, to a consideration of the urbanized 'rural' areas around large cities and conurbations. My own research field has been within the London Metropolitan Region, an area within 40 or 50 miles of the centre of London. Here New Towns, Old Towns, Garden Cities, villages and hamlets are related together in a complex whole, which might be described geographically as a *dispersed city*. I have documented this situation in detail in my monograph *Urbs in Rure* and elsewhere (Pahl, 1965, a, b, c): my purpose now is to consider the sociological significance of this in relation to the rural-urban continuum, and to delineate the new 'rural' population.

I say 'new' rural population, but this needs qualification: when Daniel Defoe travelled through Surrey in the early eighteenth century he was struck by the "rich habitations of gentlemen of quality" in the villages. Yet these were not the houses of farmers or members of the landed society, they were "citizen's country houses, whither they retire from the hurries of business and from getting money, to draw their breath in a clear air, and to divert themselves and their families in the hot weather". Defoe welcomed this immigration into rural area "all this variety, this beauty, this glorious show of wealth and plenty is really a view of the luxuriant age which we live in and of the overflowing riches of the citizens".[3] (Sooner or later this same movement hits all European countries: I was struck with similar thoughts when I looked at the summer houses of the rich at Slapy near Prague.)

In Britain, railways and motorcars have now enabled more than just the very rich or propertied class to have a country house—one not just to visit in summer but to which the commuter returns each evening.

For a particular mobile middle-class group the metropolitan village is, to borrow R. E. Park's phrase, 'a state of mind'.[4] In the

---

[3] The quotation comes from Daniel Defoe, *A Tour Through England and Wales* (first published in 1724–6). Everyman Edition (London: J. M. Dent and Sons Ltd.) 1928 edition, Vol. I, p. 168.

[4] The phrase first appeared in Park's paper on the City published in 1916 in the *American Journal of Sociology*. This is reprinted in Park, R. E. (1952), *Human Communities*, and the phrase appears on p. 13.

same way that the urban villagers may be hardly conscious of the city as a whole, so the submerged poor of the metropolitan region—the agricultural workers in their tied cottages—are hardly conscious of the wider environment. Only the middle class have the means and leisure to be able to choose 'places' in which to live. A high degree of personal mobility allows a highly dispersed activity pattern: activities which take people out of the home—shopping, schools, work, recreation, visiting friends and relatives—involve a complex criss-crossing network of journeys. This highly mobile style of life is not dependent on any particular place: it is based on the region. There is something of a paradox here: the people to whom place means least, have a way of life in which choice of living place is very important. However, social contact is maintained with friends and relatives spread over a wide geographical area, although social networks may become more closely tied to the same socio-economic stratum.

In such a situation it is pertinent to ask—where *is* the city and what is its effect? How can this complex metropolitan region or 'Megalopolis'[5] be fitted into the rural-urban continuum? Is it possible to distinguish between the various population elements in terms of 'rural' and 'urban' or are these words so meaningless that we should seek other criteria? In such situations, are the physical surroundings and the spatial constraint simply confusing intervening variables, much in the same way that techniques and technology may confuse the industrial sociologist?

Certainly the commuter village does not fit very happily into the rural-urban continuum, but, since it could be seen as lying somewhere in the middle, it is worth elaborating on it in some detail. In particular we might consider whether there is a 'rural-urban' way of life associated with this specific settlement type. I would like to follow Wirth, who used an enormous wealth of empirical material on which he based his model or ideal-type

---

[5] Cf. Jean Gottman (1961), *Megalopolis—The Urbanized Seaboard of the United States* (New York).

city: my *ideal-type* is based on much less empirical data but I think there is enough to suggest a general pattern.[6]

In order for a metropolitan village to qualify as a 'village' it must simply be considered as such—generally the influential élite will guide the rest. Hence the proportion of agricultural workers or any other objective criterion is not relevant; however, in order to fit the middle-class definition of the situation the village should appear to be socially heterogeneous.

Since, by definition, most of the chief earners commute to work in surrounding towns it is possible to have 'urban' choice in a rural landscape and in a rural settlement type. However, the spatial restraint operates differentially so that the amount of choice becomes more limited further down the social scale. We may thus distinguish some major groupings:

1. Large Property Owners.

   Wealthy landowners who are tied locally by tradition and property but who may have considerable financial and other interests elsewhere. Some of these may be internationally oriented.[7]

2. The Salariat.

   Business and professional people who have defined for themselves à village-in-the-mind and whose place of residence is subjectively an important aspect in the style of life to which they aspire.

---

[6] Apart from my own work in Hertfordshire there is a most useful survey of Kent in four volumes. See in particular: Kent Development Plant Quinquennial Review, 1963, *Report on the Survey and Analysis*, Part Four. Sample survey of Households, Vol. I (Maidstone, September 1964). Among other studies are: Hampshire County Council: *Village Life in Hampshire* (Winchester, April 1966), Cambridgeshire County Council, and East Sussex County Council.

[7] This was noted in the case of the rural areas round Banbury by Stacey (1960). In the case of two of the parishes I studied in Hertfordshire, the main landowner in one came from a long line of merchant bankers; in the other the main landowner, also a banker, had recently died on board ship when returning from Africa. I should add that the area round London is dominated by estates because of the demand from the sixteenth century onward from those who had made money in the city to make that money more respectable by investing in land and have a country seat. (See my *Urbs in Rure*, Ch. II and C. W. Chalklin (1965), Ch. XII.)

3. The Retired Urban Workers With Some Capital.

   Those who choose to come to the settlement to buy or build a house for retirement.

4. Urban Workers With Limited Capital/Income.

   Those who do not particularly want to live in this settlement type but, owing to the high price of urban land, are forced to seek cheaper housing 'in a village'. These are the reluctant commuters and are numerically, maybe, the most important immigrant element in many newly expanded commuter village.[8]

5. Rural Working-class Commuters.

   Those who by inheritance or residential qualifications have the right to a house in the village but who are obliged to seek employment elsewhere. In most metropolitan villages this will be the largest group.

6. Traditional Ruralites.

   This is a small, minority element of local tradesmen, agricultural workers and so on whose residence and employment are both local. There may be close kinship and other links with group 5 and in practice it is difficult to distinguish between them sociologically.

There are, curiously, certain similarities between the metropolitan commuter village and the urban village: segregation and transience may be found in both situations. Local Authorities and private developers build blocks of houses for those of similar socio-economic status in 'rural' as well as urban areas. Transience in a commuter village is found typically in group 2, people who are often obliged to move house on promotion or on changing their jobs. These 'spiralists',[9] as they have been called, may value a small settlement or 'rural society' since they think their wives and families may be able to feel members of a 'community'

---

[8] This is documented in the Kent County Council reports mentioned above.

[9] This term was coined by W. Watson (1964). See his 'Social Mobility and Social Class in Industrial Communities'. In: E. Devons and M. Gluckman (eds.), *Closed Systems and Open Minds* (Edinburgh: Oliver & Boyd).

more easily. There are indications that spiralists are creating this sort of community for themselves, not only in many parts of South East England but also in the West Midlands, Cheshire and elsewhere. The demand for such communities may be an important factor in inter-regional managerial mobility. However, the arrival of group 2 creates fundamental discontinuities of status in the village, particularly between them and group 5. The salariat has a very widely dispersed activity pattern, as I have mentioned, and this is shared to a lesser extent by group 4 (Pahl, 1965b, pp. 54–62). This mobility through the countryside can be seen as an urban pattern—for the essence of the city, to a true urbanite, is choice. The true citizen is the one who can and does exercise choice, and only the middle and upper-class minority has the means and opportunity to choose: thus when the middle-class extends itself from the city into the region then, in this respect, the city has extended itself into the metropolitan region.

Choice as a Way of Life

For sections of the middle-class choice is a way of life—in everything from consumer goods to the friends and kin they want to keep up with and the place in which they live. Thus we have some people who are *in* the city but not *of* it (the urban villagers), whereas others are *of* the city but not *in* it (the mobile middle-class of the metropolitan commuter village).

However, class and life-cycle stage do not explain all: I do not think that my ideal-type commuter village is simply part of the city surrounded by fields, although it may appear to be so in many important respects.

My argument rests on two main points:

1. The small size and social heterogeneity of such a settlement provides more opportunity to learn about the styles of life of status groups which would, in the urban situation, appear more remote.

2. Those of the managerial and professional salariat, who choose to live in a commuter village, do so not merely for the physical surroundings but also on account of a distinctive pattern of social relationships, which they associate with a village. Unlike, say, the suburbs, the village situation involves interaction with other status groups.

With this in mind it is not entirely inappropriate to contrast 'the cosmopolitans' (which we may call the immigrant professional and managerial group) with the locals. The cosmopolitans have defined, as part of the ingredients of their life-styles, the putting down of localistic roots. Almost without exception they are very quick to describe the friendliness and feeling of community in the village (i.e. among themselves). They are equally firm in their objections to new development (generally to house those *forced* out from the towns, but not always) which is inevitably 'out of character'. The 'localist' cosmopolitans are the self-appointed guardians of tradition and rusticity as they define it. (This would seem to me to be a very deviant form of urbanism, if this is what it is. However, it may be a sign of the consciousness of 'regional citizenship'.)

Perhaps most crucial of all is the attitude of the salariat to the manual workers who are forced out to employment elsewhere. In the central city or segregated suburb the middle class would not normally expect to have manual workers and their wives in their clubs and organizations. However, in the village manual workers are seen as props on the rustic stage, which help to define the village situation. If they do not adequately perform the role which has been allocated to them the localistic cosmopolitans become irritated: perhaps they expect deference as one of the rewards of upward social mobility. For example, complaints about the villagers' failure to take an active part in voluntary associations are common. This prevents the amount of mixing necessary in the village-in-the-middle-class mind situation which is felt to be 'a pity'; however this may be a peculiarly middle-class expectation. On the other hand, the localistic cosmopolitans may well provide reasons for not sending their children to the village school or the nearest state secondary school (Pahl, 1963). In this context it is significant that those forced out from the towns did not seem to show this reluctance to use the local schools and, in this sense, may be able to become 'part of the village' more easily. Not only the working-class villagers but also the true, non-localistic, cosmopolitan is criticized by the localistic cosmopolitan for not taking his part in village affairs. Certainly the relationships between the various non-manual categories need to be clarified. I suspect that relations are closer between the localistic cosmopolitans and the deferential locals (church attenders, domestic cleaners) than between the former and other immigrant non-manual groups. If this were the case, here might be another distinctive sociological feature of this settlement type.

Because of the peculiar situation of the metropolitan commuter village not all status groups are proportionately represented. Furthermore, groups which, in the 'normal' urban situation, would be socially distant, are forced into an unusual consciousness of each other. This can lead to an articulation of resentment by the manual workers, whose feelings of relative deprivation may be exacerbated by the proximity of the village situation. Phrases such as 'the posh end', 'snobs', 'not better, just more money' are frequently heard, together with specific comments on salariat life-style—their clothes, cars, haw-haw voices, behaviour in the saloon-bar, and demand to 'take-over' everything. (Elaborated in Pahl, 1965a).

The manual worker responds to this situation by excluding the immigrant as a 'stranger' or 'foreigner' simply because non-acceptance on the basis of length of residence is one of the few ways in which the established working-class can allocate or withhold prestige. The development of alternative 'us' working class values against 'them' may be a further response to the situation forced upon them. I found that in the case of one village, where one farmer owned the whole parish and virtually everyone was connected with the land in some way, it was possible to discern a hierarchy of prestige by the way people spoke of each other. Unsolicited comments about the friendliness of the village and the feeling that it was like a family were very common. At another village, where 45 per cent of a mainly working-class village commute to surrounding towns to work, I have described the tensions within the working class, between the 'rough' and the 'respectable', the council estate and the rest of the village and so on (Pahl, 1964). I suspect the difference is mainly between the deferential and the proletarianized workers: the squire is still an extremely important figure in the village. Finally, however, in my third village, where the estate was broken up after World War I and where is a long tradition of commuting to urban factories, the working class appeared to be less cross-pressured. This was the village where the polarization between 'upper' and 'lower' status groups was the most striking: The salariat in this case were highly visible. It appeared that people had to take sides (this was often put to me); both groups accepted some internal differentiation but united on account of the differences with the other group. It could be described as an industrial strike situation made permanent. The choosers deplore the unwillingness of the manual workers to 'co-operate', and the manual workers dispute the salariat's right to 'run everything'. (Elaborated in Pahl, 1965a).

It seems to me that the *sociologically* most significant feature of this settlement type is the interaction of status groups which have been determined nationally—by the educational system, the industrial situation and so on—in a *small-scale* situation, where part of the definition of the situation, by the localistic cosmopolitans, is some sort of social interaction. They expect a segment of the working class, who may live in a small council estate, to act like 'villagers', that is deferentially—or at any rate to take part in certain well-defined social relationships. Thus I hope it is not too much of a cliché to say that the commuter village of the metropolitan fringe is a social laboratory in which macroscopic changes in structure can be observed in terms of process and interaction. Because such settlements are relatively isolated and because a range of status groups are, for various reasons, likely to be living in close proximity it is possible to observe interaction in a way no longer possible in the increasingly segregated urban areas. It is also possible to construct a typology of communities from the almost completely feudal to the more proletarianized and polarized.[10] Different combinations of status groups will clearly give different local configurations and specific issues such as conflict over local elections, schools and new housing development will vary locally, depending on the different expectations of the 'forced in', the 'localistic cosmopolitans' and so on. I suppose that one of the great attractions of the metro-politan commuter village for the community sociologist is that here, in a necessarily restricted milieu, it is possible to investigate a whole range of social worlds in close juxtaposition. The chances of 'dramatic events', which may be observed and analysed with the traditional methods of social anthropology, are high (cf. Frankenberg, 1966a).

Patterns of Social Relationships

In the same way that the middle-class localistic cosmopolitans value the 'rural' life, so also does the large landowner; on the other hand, his agricultural workers are tied, often reluctantly, to their work place. Where there is a foreman he is in a particu-larly ambiguous position. In '*Westrigg*', a fairly remote Cheviot parish, the forestry foremen complained that they had no friends (Littlejohn, 1963, p. 37). In this area of scattered houses and

---

[10] That is to say the transition from the situation where economic class is just one division among many—as was the case in the village where they des-cribed themselves as members of a family—to the situation where economic class dominates social thought through the cash nexus—typified by those at the mercy of the housing market in the transient zones of cities. A journalistic account of a Cotswold village mentions in passing "the villagers, or *as they like to call themselves*, the working class" (G. Moorhouse, *The Other England*, Harmondsworth (Penguin Books), 1964, p. 66, my emphasis). Whether they be tourists or members of the salariat who come to live in the village the new element helps to crystallize a class situation. However, this is based on bunched status groups and *not* on the ownership of property.

sheep farming the relationship between the classes closely resembles the industrial situation, although apparently the farmers "often congratulate themselves that their relationship to their men is more harmonious than is the case in most industries" [*sic*]. Yet "the existence of the workers' union and the farmers' hostility to it indicates the opposition between farmer and farm worker" (p. 33). It is highly significant that Littlejohn should conclude his study of workers in the 'agricultural industry' (his phrase) thus:

"The most significant social process in the recent history of the parish has been its induction into the wider network. Where this process has advanced to the degree it has in Westrigg the local community becomes less 'an area of common life', than an area within which the individual chooses his associations subject to such barriers as are imposed by social class or physical distance" (Littlejohn, 1963, p. 155).

As Stein has shown in his important and significantly titled survey of American community studies, 'The Eclipse of Community', the processes of urbanization, industrialization and bureaucratization have increased interdependence and decreased local autonomy. Perhaps local milieu-studies in advanced industrialized societies should be undertaken to clarify our understanding of the basic social processes—for example the proletarianization of the agricultural worker. If "the city today *is* society" and "urbanisation is the process of labour—traumatic, perhaps rich in promise—in which modern man and his society are born"[11] then it may indeed be possible to reconsider the rural-urban continuum not in terms of geographic, demographic or economic indices but rather on the basis of *changing social relationships*. This is to some extent forced upon us when both *gemeinschaftlich* and *gesellschaftlich* relationships are found in different groups in the same place.

An attempt to synthesize the British community studies, which ow number between twenty and thirty, has recently been made

---

[11] J. Westergaard in a Review Article on Urban Sociology; *Urban Studies*, Vol. 3, 1 (1966), p. 64.

(Frankenberg, 1966a). Attention was drawn at the last Congress to 'the considerable neglect of intensive, long term community studies' among rural sociologists (Williams, 1964, p. 309). Frankenberg's work is likely to do much to stimulate interest. Modern British communities are arranged along a typological continuum based on economic organization and technology. The familiar dichotomies from classical sociology are resurrected, including Marx's view of the process of proletarianization, which is often neglected in American studies, together with a number of other concepts which are systematically applied to a typology of communities for the first time.

In the context of British studies, Stacey's study of Banbury (1960) is generally held to be in the middle of the continuum: here is the meeting point of the 'traditional', 'local' or 'informal' world with the 'non-traditional', 'cosmopolitan' or 'formal' world. This has arisen because a large-scale bureaucratically-organized industry has put a plant in the town, traditionally dominated by agriculture and some small traditional industries. This complex situation, which Stacey describes, adds other dimensions and a greater depth to what now seem the somewhat superficial formulations of Wirth and Gans. This is because there are *a number of non-overlapping continua*: social class and life-cycle characteristics are inadequate on their own to explain ways of life and patterns of behaviour; the traditional/non-traditional division in Banbury provides another, even more important dimension. The same organization can be viewed quite differently by people with similar class and life-cycle characteristics yet differing on the traditional/non-traditional dimension. For example, in the case of the tennis club the traditionals regarded it as an important arena for a whole range of social relationships, whereas the non-traditionalist viewed it instrumentally as a way of getting a game of tennis. Frankenberg coins the term 'social redundancy' to describe the latent side-functions of behaviour observable among the traditionalists.

Frankenberg's seminal contribution to what he prefers to call the rural/non-rural scale, owing to the lack of adequate urban studies, helps to pose a crucial problem to which I turn, namely this: *Is the rural-urban continuum a typology or a process?* I take this to be one of the fundamental issues which I have been asked to discuss.

RURAL-URBAN CONTINUUM: TYPOLOGY OR PROCESS?

I now want to turn away from Europe to consider some of the empirical material gathered in other parts of the world. Such a comparative perspective is vital if the study of rural-urban differences is to gain in rigour and if new conceptual tools are to be created. Very many studies from all over the world stress fundamental discontinuities between rural and urban life: the continuum does not appear to exist. In India, Majumdar find "two distinct constellations of values".[12] Bailey describes the village of Bisipara and the central administration as being in two worlds, sharing neither the same values nor the same culture. "The social roles of the administrators and the men of the village do not overlap. Even caste is irrelevant" (Bailey, 1957, p. 248). On the Central African copperbelt it is again the *discontinuity* which appears to be so much more important than the continuum. The migrant to the town moves from one social system, with its distinctive social institutions, to a different social system with different social institutions. "It is fallacious, therefore", argues Mitchell (1966, pp. 47–48) "to think of rural institutions as changing into urban types of the same institution". Since an urban social institution is a separate social phenomenon "the behaviour in town of a migrant, when it differs from that in his rural home, is more likely to be a manifestation of 'situational' rather than 'processive' changes". As an example, Watson (1958) has demonstrated in the case of the Mambwe that the tribal and the urban systems can exist side by side, with migrant workers moving between the two worlds.

[12] Majumdar, D. N. (1958), *Caste and Communication in an Indian Village* (Bombay: Asia Publishing House), p. 329. Quoted by Lambert (1962), p. 120.

One of the most striking examples of the coexistence of two different value systems is given by Barclay in his study of Buuri al Lamaab (1964) which is only five miles from Khartoum. He argues that the village is in the process of 'proletarianization' by the influx of propertyless wage earners, who have been forced to seek housing in the village, but who commute daily to Khartoum. In Khartoum they wear western clothes and work as clerks, electricians or handymen: back in the village they change into their *jalibiiyas* and behave as villagers. They live not so much between two worlds as *in* two worlds. In his account of a Turkish village Stirling (1965) discusses the strengthening links between the village and the impersonal large-scale society. A few people leave the village for a new and different social environment. However, "a larger minority live in two scales: an urban migrant workers' world and the village. But for most the village is the only social arena that really matters" (p. 81). In the case of systems of social control Stirling has shown how the informal system of social sanctions in the village world is far more relevant and effective in settling disputes than the legal system imposed by the administration. This is shown particularly in regard to the new Turkish laws on marriage, which are widely different from the informal rules and are largely ignored: as he puts it: "When the law sets out to alter a whole body of related rules built into the informal system, the more it is used as an initiating instrument of social reform, the less efficient it is bound to be as an instrument of social control: and the less it will in fact achieve its aim of reform" (Stirling, 1957, p. 32). Much the same sort of argument is used by Bailey to illustrate the different assumptions of the administration and the village in India (Bailey, 1957, p. 263).

However, one must be cautious not to accept general conclusions too readily: Banton has investigated a distinctive situation in West Africa. He draws attention to the 'urban villages' I have mentioned, and goes on to argue that urban values have permeated the countryside more thoroughly in West Africa than in Central Africa. He believes that the degree of rural-urban continuity must remain open to empirical examination. In situations where migrants come from the same ethnic division or local group they will reinforce each others' attitudes and continuity will be high. Ties will be further strengthened when the immigrants can live together in the same urban locality with a balanced age and sex structure, where jobs are available and they are supervised by their own kin and where pre-migration ties of kinship or clan provide further binding threads (Banton, in press). Kuper has provided an admirably succinct summary of the contrasts between West and South African rural-urban relationships (Kuper, 1965, pp. 15–16). In the South the towns were created by the Whites who needed African labour in the industrial economy. In direct contrast with the 'classless' tribal situation, an urban working-class in structural opposition to the alien white employer emerged in what she describes as "military fortifications of White privilege". In West Africa, by contrast, where the Whites are fewer and generally transient, industrial development is less marked, there is little land alienation and hence the wage-earning population is a relatively small proportion of the total. City–hinterland relationships are ecologically more closely fused, with extended families owning property in both country and town, members living at different times in both or alternatively commuting between them. Kuper concludes "that each society has structural and ethical antecedents of its own which interact with the introduced physical and social attributes of cities associated with modern industry, and so create distinctive types of urbanism. Industrialization cannot be treated as a given change which then produces uniform consequential changes. This approach to society as an integrated social system functionally attaining a new balance after a temporarily disturbing innovation in a vital sector of social life—the economic—is unrealistic. Such a 'before' and 'after' approach ignores the dynamics of simultaneous change, the complexity of uneven sequence, and the nature of structural conflict" (Kuper, 1965, p. 16).

Something of the complexity of the situation is shown in Epstein's extremely valuable study of two villages in South India (1962). From one village, Dalena, commuters into urban factories are involved in two distinct sets of social relations, depending on whether they are with their fellow workers in the town or with the men in the village. "On the one hand through their daily contact with the town they introduce urban values into the village, and on the other hand, through their desire to become full-time farmers and acquire prestige in the village they support the traditional system. The strong pull of farming makes it difficult for them to adjust themselves to the urban environment. It leads them to act as villagers even when in the town and it also tones down their introduction of urban values to the village" (Epstein, 1962, p. 304). Dalena can still be described as an independent social system despite fundamental changes: the hereditary principle has broken down and the nuclear family has replaced the joint family. Although economic changes, consequent upon the introduction of irrigation into the area, have led to changes in the social and political systems the village still retains its social identity. At the second village, Wangala, two miles nearer the town, the introduction of irrigation strengthened the traditional farming economy by providing jobs locally and did not produce such widespread changes in the social and political system as are described in the case of Dalena.

"Dalena's social system changed radically, because the diversification of its economy changed economic roles and relations within the village. Wangala's persisting social system has incorporated many of the cultural changes now characteristic of the wider society: similarly, Dalena's changed system still shows the effects of traditional relations and values" (Epstein, 1962, p. 10). The desire of Dalena's commuters to become full-time farmers and at the same time to live like townsmen both undermines and strengthens the traditional village system. Even though they may bring in urban values, their attempt to translate income earned in the town into social status in the village in terms of traditional values strengthens the established system. Epstein's study illustrates the extreme complexity of the situation in India very well.

In an attempt to draw together the conclusions from the literature on rural India, Lambert feels that the decline of the monopoly of economic power of the landed aristocracy and the growth of a cash economy is the major structural shift from which other changes flow. Yet studies of villages peripheral to the cities do not show any clear pattern. So confusing is the situation "that it is not clear in which way the urban-fringe-rural continuum runs on family types and size, but in any event urban impact is selective within fringe villages and among them" (Lambert, 1962, p. 127).

The problems of relating urban and rural social structure are discussed by Stirling in his study of two Turkish villages. From the town of Kayseri to the village of Sakaltutan was only twenty miles, but the villagers would think of this in terms of 'six hours'. All village women know Kayseri exists and some have been there. However, it would be wrong to see the village ranked completely below the urban system; there is, argues Stirling, a broader span of social distance in the urban ranking system and there are also qualitative differences between the urban and the rural ranking systems. "While town and village may meet for a large number of purposes, official business, temporary urban employment, visits of kinsmen to the village and so on, they do not share a common life. Vertical sociability within rural society is greater than horizontal sociability outside it, and a gulf of mutual strangeness and mistrust is fixed between town and village" (Stirling, 1965, pp. 284–5). Urban and rural ranking systems do not fit easily together. A consciousness of the national ranking system reduces the social autonomy of the village, which finds itself at the bottom of the national hierarchy with a very much lower standard of living than may be available in the towns.

In my attempt to escape from Western ethnocentrism there is a danger that I may have confused the issue. There is one thing that the studies which I have mentioned in Africa, India and

Turkey, all have in common: they all stress that the village community cannot remain the same, in all sorts of complex ways, after the economic frontier has hit it. Furthermore, it is certain that this process will continue and that the integration of villages into the regional and national economic systems will have important but locally different repercussions on their social and political systems. The differences between the Indian villages of Wangala and Dalena which emerged *after* the introduction of a technological innovation into the area provide a salutary reminder that economic development need not necessarily lead to social change. Similarly, the commuters at Dalena in South India and Buuri al Lamaab in the Sudan show that people can be at one end of what we have been referring to as the rural-urban continuum by day and at the other end at night! The differences between West and South Africa point up the dangers of applying ideas of rural-urban continuity or discontinuity, evolved in one area, indiscriminately elsewhere.

Rural communites can be isolated as separate systems for the purpose of academic study, but this is an increasingly unreal exercise. Nevertheless, it seems clear to me that the studies in depth of rural and urban communities in various parts of the world, by social anthropologists, should make one excessively cautious of making the sort of generalizations in which a book like *The Passing of Traditional Society* abounds (Lerner, 1958). The speed of modernization due to the coming of commerce, industrialism, literacy and the media of mass communication is much less dramatic than some would have us believe.

Certainly I can find little universal evidence of a rural-urban continuum, which even as a classificatory device seems to be of little value. Of much greater importance is the notion of a fundamental distinction between the local and the national, which we have noticed in an English commuter village as much as in a remote Turkish village. Bailey describes the situation with regard to his Indian village as follows:

"The village is a community: the administration is an organization. Villages are bound to one another in a complex web of kinship and quasi-kinship and friendship. But their ties with the administration is the single one of *imperium* . . . . . The administrators of the Kondmals have always come from outside, they have a different way of life from the villager. In education, wealth and outlook they are of a different social class. These factors serve to keep the administration and the village as mutually exclusive units. There can be no doubt whether the role of any individual lies in the one or the other. He must be either one of 'us' or one of 'them': he cannot be both" (Bailey, 1957, p. 259).

Differences between the small-scale and the large-scale are enormously important. Stirling claims, perhaps overforcefully, that "people in a small-scale society are bound to fail to grasp the size and diversity of the larger society in which the small-scale society nests" (Stirling, 1965, p. 288). Similarly the large-scale society receives a very distorted view of what is often dismissed as village 'backwardness', adding to the mutual misunderstanding. As the large-scale and the small-scale societies are increasingly brought together, so the opportunity for tension and misunderstanding increases.

CONFRONTATION BETWEEN LOCAL AND NATIONAL: CONCEPTS IN THE PROCESS

I believe that this confrontation between the local and the national, is a crucial and continuing problem and is the common theme or element in my whole discussion. It is this basic situation of conflict or stress that can be observed from the most highly urbanized metropolitan region to the most remote and isolated peasant village. The local and the national can confront each other *in the urban as much as in the rural physical setting*, but quite obviously the rural sociologist is more concerned with predominantly agricultural settlements, largely because of sociologically irrelevent historical and practical reasons associated with the growth of the subject. Furthermore, I believe that there are many similarities between urban and rural sociologists: both are concerned with milieux studies, with social processes in territorially limited settings, and sometimes with the interaction between the national and the local. Since people will always have their lives shaped by a combination of national and local influences and processes a sub-discipline will continue,—and this imples a convergence between rural and urban sociology—under whatever name. It seems likely that rural sociology will develop in this direction, particularly if it shows itself ready to adapt and extend concepts such as role, network and the notion of patron-client relationships, which have proved their usefulness in the study of small-scale societies.

In the past the rural-urban continuum, understood as the process of urbanization, has had a strong physical or spatial bias, as indeed the name suggests. The temporal element in this process has been inadequately stressed; this is perhaps the main reason for the concentration in the past on the *typology* at the expense of the *process*.

Neither the physical characteristics of the settlement nor the occupational structure of the population in themselves lead to social change—that is either fundamental changes in an individual's behaviour to others and their behaviour to him and/or broader, more fundamental, changes in the structure of society, for example in its economic or political system. The case of Wangala in South India is of particular importance in emphasizing that technological change can confirm and strengthen a particular system and indeed prevent more fundamental change. Yet small-scale societies everywhere *are* in the process of change and it is becoming unrealistic and almost absurd to consider distinct 'peasant', 'folk', 'tribal', or 'rural' societies in isolation. This is too well-known to require emphasis. The situation in Europe has been most usefully summarized in the symposium *People in the Countryside* (Higgs, 1966) and there is no case for repeating it here, apart from noting that much of this sort of documentation has been done by workers whose interests are not primarily sociological.

If there is a continuum then it is more likely to have a temporal rather than a spatial basis; furthermore, *if* there is a continuum, then as sociologists we are primarily interested in the social processes which lead to differentiation. However useful economic, geographic or demographic indices may be—and rural sociologists must certainly be grateful to their colleagues for their distinctive viewpoints—it is within a specifically sociological frame of reference that we must work.

With this in mind it is perhaps useful, in this final section, to consider some of the more important elements in the process and to provide some suggestions on the concepts which may be used in the future.

Role and Networks

Aidan Southall has gone so far as to say that the fall in the density of role texture "is the only sociological difference between town and country". He suggests that specific communities might be placed on a continuum "in which the polarities are: the number of persons in a particular area, giving high or low density; the narrow or broad and specific or diffuse definition of roles; the extent of latent role development and of inequality in role distribution and the comparative duration over time of role relationships" (Southall, 1959, p. 29). The rise in the density of role texture fits in with the commonsense notions of the change from rural to urban life but Southall notes that on a continuum of specialization the indigenous Yoruba towns of Nigeria would come at the 'rural' end of the other continuum, whereas the specialized areas of agribusiness in North America would appear at the 'urban' end. However, in the latter case the low population density, itself a product of advances in technology, has sociological significance. Certainly there is a high level of role differentiation, yet the small numbers involved almost inevitably lead to the playing of multiple role relationships by those who know one another well. This will lead to a regeneralization of roles to a level below that of the highly differentiated structure of the wider society. This would be found particularly among the 'locals' or those localistically orientated to the small-scale society.

Banton makes the point that between urban villages or between home and work situations in large industrial cities there may be severe discontinuities so that groups are related to other groups only in a relatively few restricted role relationships. Paraphrasing Durkheim (1964, p. 262) he describes 'opaque partitions' between milieux and sees the level of social interdependence rising in certain social islands and between them falling to a level in general lower than the level in 'village' society (Banton, in press).

Merton's concept of a role set (Merton, 1957) can also be applied in this context: where roles are part of a set certain roles may conflict. Frankenberg (1966a) points out that in a 'rural' situation the high degree of transparency (to use Merton's word) makes it very difficult for the individual to resolve conflicting expectations and this gives rise to special conflict-reducing rituals and practices in the rural area. In the non-rural area conflict may be avoided by spatial and social segregation. Goffman's work on 'Role Distance' (1961) is also highly relevant, particularly when he draws a distinction between role commitment, role attachment and role embracement. With a low density of role texture, efficient enactment of a role is insufficient to provide an identity. Goffman observed that someone employed in the local shop in the Shetland community he studied could not develop a specialized role owing to the transparency of the situation. As he put it, "Here doing is not being" (1961, p. 102).

There is no doubt that role as a concept still has very great potential for refinement in helping to define another continuum. Much, of course, depends on how many roles an individual *perceives* are open to him. Many other ambiguities still remain: in particular in communities with both 'cosmopolitans' and 'locals' the role density may be very different for each group. Furthermore the whole concept of role density may be interpreted in different ways—both many-stranded relationships and highly differentiated relationships could be described in different ways by the same adjective, dense.

The use of the concept of 'social networks' has helped to illuminate the pattern of social relationships in African urban areas. It is possible to create a continuum from the more tight-knit in the 'rural' pole to more loose-knit in the urban situation. However, very often the loose-knit network is due as much to transience and a high degree of previous mobility, as to the urban situation as such, and similarly in urban villages, networks may be as tight-knit as in any rural village. The point is that a detailed study of networks helps to isolate social fields and provides a very useful tool for investigating local communities.

Patron–Client Relationships

How does the local society, with its emphasis on face-to-face relationships and its distinctive norms and values, make contact with the national 'impersonal' and bureaucratic society in which it is incapsulated? To some extent this raises the whole issue of how the studies made by social anthropologists are to be related to the larger issues, such as bureaucratization, with which sociologists concern themselves. We have recently had some very interesting attempts to elucidate the linkages between small-scale and large-scale societies in Mediterranean countries. Kenny describes a system in Spain where the local power élite of the pueblo act as " 'gatekeepers', in that they largely dominate the paths linking the local infrastructure of the village to the superstructure of the outside urban world" (Kenny, 1960, p. 18). These are the 'patrons' who act on behalf of their 'clients' in the village. These patrons may, in turn, be clients to even more powerful patrons in the towns.

The form-filling complexities of officialdom are baffling and frequently arbitrary. To short cut the maze of obstacles thrown up by authority it is necessary to have *enchufe* (i.e. 'plug') so that contact is made with the right people at the right time. It is, says Kenny, "the rule of *amigocracy* . . . The diversity of urban life and regulation by specialized agencies whose equivalent functions in the village would be on an informal level throw up complicated strata of power and authority which can only be dealt with by cultivated friendship and patronage" (1960, pp. 19–20).

This same system is described in more detail by Campbell in his study of a shepherd community in Greece (1964, pp. 230–47, 256–62). Government officials not only have higher status but share no bond of kinship or community with the Sarakatsani, and such is the isolation between their respective worlds that the straight commercial transaction is the only relationship that is possible. "A man's work, affection and moral obligations are almost exclusively contained within the one small group, the commitment of energy, physical resources, or deep affection to an unrelated person is a kind of betrayal" (Campbell, 1964, p. 257). Generally all junior officials are simply bribed for whatever is needed; however, the social distance between shepherds and senior officials is too great for bribing to be possible. Apart from anything else the Sarakatsani are not dressed to walk into a city office and this helps to make them feel inferior. (Stirling also mentioned this in the case of his Turkish villagers (1965, p. 287).) Hence in Greece there is a system of lawyer patronage: "the lawyer becomes obliged to act as a general protector of the shepherd in all his affairs, the shepherd as a good client must show esteem and respect and give his patron the political support on which his power depends. It is not unusual for lawyers to become the godparents of their clients' children" (Campbell, 1964, p. 244). This latter point is also, of course, familiar in the Spanish situation.

The bureaucrat and the villager or shepherd are bound to be distrustful of each other: generally the bureaucratic structure has been imposed on the village from above or outside. The State in rural India, Turkey or Greece is a remote, threatening and, above all, tax-collecting institution; it appears to take much and give nothing. Hence, in Greece and elsewhere, exclusive and particular relationships are established between individual villagers or families and persons in power. Campbell shows that where the gulf of hostility and indifference created by the absence of relationships and difference in status is great the lawyer or other patron has to bridge it, thus introducing "some flexibility into the rigid and uncomprehending administration of village life by a centralized bureaucracy. . . . Patronage is the means through which the local community is linked to the wider national society" (Campbell, 1964, pp. 259–60). This means, of course, that the local society can never offer any collective resistance to the power and authority of the national society since the link between the two is on an individual and not a collective basis.

Quite clearly the implications of the patron–client relationship for the rural sociologist attempting to introduce change are enormous (cf. Hutchinson, 1966). But it would be wrong to assume that this is a distinctive pattern of social relationships at the 'rural' end of the continuum: in Brazil the same pattern continues in the cities (Hutchinson, 1966, pp. 8 and 21) and this is also the case in Southern Italy.[13]

Community Power Structure

Over the past decade there has been a whole series of most interesting studies of community leadership in North America which have certainly not been paralleled in Europe. Very recently there have been comparative studies attempting to relate type of leadership structure to degree of 'urbanism', among other factors. Bonjean found that the greater the influx of population and the greater the community poverty the less visible was the leadership structure. He also found that in less complex communities the leadership structure was also less visible. (Bonjean and Olsen, 1964, pp. 298–9.) Much more comparative work is needed before different patterns of community leadership can even be considered in relation to any continuum. It would seem that this could

---

[13] Research on Southern Italy is being directed by Professor Stirling at the University of Kent at Canterbury. Interesting unpublished work by N. Colclough explores the patron–client relationship in the political structure of Southern Italy.

be an extremely fruitful field for further research, adding a new and valuable perspective to community continua.

CONCLUSION

The notion of a rural-urban continuum arose in reaction against the polar-type dichotomies, but there are equal dangers in over-readily accepting a false continuity. Not only is there a whole series of continua but also there are sharp discontinuities, in particular the confrontation between the local and the national. Whether we call the processes acting on the local community 'urbanization', 'differentiation', 'modernization', 'mass-society', or whatever, it is clear it is not so much *communities* that are acted upon as groups and individuals at particular places in the social structure. Any attempt to tie particular patterns of social relationships to specific geographical milieux is a singularly fruitless exercise.

The action of the national system on the local system may lead to a temporary lack of balance between the two social systems and perhaps also within the local system. One of the defence mechanisms which the local community may develop to link the systems is the patron-client relationship; the restructuring of the pattern of balances in the local system can be analysed through the use of the concepts of role and social network, as Banton (in press) and Epstein (1961), among others, have shown. The restructuring of the local social system in the terms of the national system may result in 'urban villages' or the informal groupings of the workplace.

Education may lead to an understanding by some groups of the broad mesh of the social fabric but may also lead to a conscious acceptance of localistic values. In the case of the ideal-type metropolitan village, a whole range of consciousness and experience is concentrated in one place. It is this overlapping of different meshes which invalidates the notion of a continuum. The different meshes are of different textures, but this is due more to differences between the home and the work situation or between the manual and non-manual worker than to physical differences in the environment or the peculiar occupational structure of the population. The process which I have been discussing in this paper produces a superimposition of different meshes one over another, leading to a much more complex pattern, and also restructures the mesh or system of balances in the local situation.

The rural sociologist's main concern, as I see it, is to explore the impact of the national on the local, using amongst others the analytical concepts I have mentioned. To some extent this will limit him to the manual workers who live in small rather than large settlements but this is a distinctive social field which provides an important social laboratory in which national changes can be studied in detail.

REFERENCES

ABU-LUGHOD, J. (1961) Migrant Adjustment to City Life: The Egyptian Case. *American Journal of Sociology*, **67** (1), 22–32.

BAILEY, F. G. (1957) *Caste and the Economic Frontier*. Manchester: University Press.

BANTON, M. (1965) *Social Alignment and Identity in a West African City*. In: H. Kuper, ed. (1965).

BANTON, M., ed. (1966) *The Social Anthropology of Complex Societies*. London: Tavistock Publications.

BANTON, M. (in press) Urbanisation and Role Theory. In: Edward M. Bruner and Aiden Southall, *Urban Anthropology*.

BARCLAY, H. B. (1964) *Buuri al Lamaab, A Suburban Village in the Sudan*. Ithaca, New York: Cornell U.P.

BAUMERT, G. and E. LUPRI (1963–64) New Aspects of Rural-Urban Differentials in Family Values and Family Structure. *Current Sociology*, **12** (1), 46–54.

BENET, F. (1963) Sociology Uncertain: The Ideology of the Rural-Urban Continuum. *Comparative Studies in Society and History*, **6**, 1–23.

BONJEAN, C. M. and D. M. OLSON (1964) Community Leadership: Directions of Research. *Administrative Science Quarterly*, **9** (3), 278–300.

BOPEGAMAGE, A. (1957) Neighbourhood Relations in Indian Cities—Delhi. *Sociological Bulletin* **6** (1), 34–42.

BRUNER, E. S. (1961) Urbanization and Ethnic Identity in North Sumatra. *American Anthropologist*, **3**, 508–21.

CAMPBELL, J. K. (1964) *Honour, Family and Patronage*. Oxford: Clarendon Press.

DEWEY, R. (1960) The Rural-Urban Continuum: Real But Relatively Unimportant. *American Journal of Sociology*, **66** (1), 60–66.

DOBRINER, W. M. (1963), *Class in Suburbia*. Englewood Cliffs, N.J.: Prentice Hall.

DURKHEIM, E. (1964, first published 1893) *The Division of Labour in Society* (translated by G. Simpson). Glencoe: Free Press.

EPSTEIN, A. L. (1961) The Network and Urban Social Organization. *Rhodes-Livingstone Journal*, **29**, 29–62.

EPSTEIN, T. S. (1962) *Economic Development and Social Change in South India*. Manchester: University Press.

FAVA, S. F. (1956) Suburbanism as a Way of Life. *American Sociological Review*, **21** (1), 34–37.

FRANKENBERG, R. (1966a) *British Community Studies: Problems of Synthesis*. In: Banton (1966), 123–54.

FRANKENBERG, R. (1966b) *Communities in Britain*. Harmondsworth: Penguin Books.

FUGUITT, G. V. (1962) The Rural-Urban Fringe. *Proceedings of American Country Life Association*, 88–98.

FUGUITT, G. V. (1963) The City and the Countryside. *Rural Sociology*, **28** (3), 246–61.

GANS, H. J. (1962a) *Urbanism and Suburbanism as Ways of Life*. In: A. M. Rose, ed., Human Behaviour and Social Processes. London: Routledge & Kegan Paul.

GANS, H. J. (1962b) *The Urban Villagers*. New York: The Free Press.

GEERTZ, C. (1965) *The Social History of an Indonesian Town*. Cambridge, Mass.: MIT Press.

GOFFMAN, E. (1961) *Encounters*. Indianapolis: Bobbs-Merrill.

GUTKIND, P. C. W. (1962) African Urban Family Life. Comment on and Analysis of Some Rural–Urban Differences. Cahiers d'Etudes Africaines, **3** (10), 149–217.

HAUSER, P. M. (1965) *Observations on the Urban-Folk and Urban-Rural Dichotomies as forms of Western Ethnocentrism*. In: P. M. Hauser & L. Schnore (1965), 503–18.

HAUSER, P. M. and L. SCHNORE (1965) *The Study of Urbanization*. London: John Wiley & Sons Inc.

HIGGS, J., ed. (1966) *People in the Countryside; Studies in Rural Social Development*. London: National Council of Social Service.

HOFSTEE, E. W. (1960) Rural Social Organisation. *Sociologia Ruralis*, **1** (2), 105–17.

HUTCHINSON, B. (1966) The Patron-Dependent Relationship in Brazil: A Preliminary Examination. *Sociologia Ruralis*, **6** (1), 3–30.

KENNY, M. (1960) Patterns of Patronage in Spain. *Anthropological Quarterly*, **33** (1), 14–23.

KENNY, M. (1961) *A Spanish Tapestry; Town and Country in Castile*. London: Cohen & West.

KUPER, H., ed. (1965) *Urbanization and Migration in West Africa*. Berkeley & Los Angeles: Univ. of California Press.

LAMBERT, R. D. (1962) *The Impact of Urban Society Upon Village Life*. In: R. Turner, ed., India's Urban Future. Berkeley & Los Angeles: Univ. of California Press.

LERNER, D. (1958) *The Passing of Traditional Society*. Glencoe: Free Press.

LEWIS, O. (1952) Urbanisation Without Breakdown: A Case Study. *The Scientific Monthly*, **75**, No. 1.

LEWIS, O. (1965) *Further Observations on the Folk-Urban Continuum and Urbanization with Special Reference to Mexico City*. In: P. M. Hauser & L. Schnore (1965), 491–502.

LITTLEJOHN, I. (1963) Westrigg: *The Sociology of a Cheviot Parish*. London: Routledge & Kegan Paul.

MARRIS, P. (1961) *Family and Social Change in an African City*. London: Routledge & Kegan Paul.

MAYER, P. (1962) Migrancy and the Study of Africans in Towns. *American Anthropologist*, **64**, 576–91.

MAYER, P. (1963) *Townsmen or Tribesmen*. Cape Town: Oxford University Press.

PAHL, R. E. (1963) Education and Social Class in Commuter Villages. *Sociological Review, N.S.*, **11** (2), 241–6.

PAHL, R. E. (1964) The Old and the New: A Case Study. *New Society* 29, X, 64.

PAHL, R. E. (1965a) Class and Commuting in English Commuter Villages. *Sociologia Ruralis,* **5** (1), 5–23.

PAHL, R. E. (1965b) Urbs in Rure: The Metropolitan Fringe in Hertfordshire. *London School of Economics and Political Science Geographical Papers No. 2.*

PAHL, R. E. (1965c) *Commuting and Social Change in Rural Areas*. Paper read to the Cambridge Meeting of the British Association for the Advancement of Science.

PETRINI, F. (1961) Summary statement on Changing Patterns of Rural Organization. In: *Papers and Discussions of the Second Congress of the European Society for Rural Sociology, Vollebekk, Oslo (Bonn)*.

REISSMAN, L. (1964) *The Urban Process*. Glencoe: Free Press.

SIEGEL, B. J. (1957) The Role of Perception in Urban-Rural Change: A Brazillian Case Study. *Economic Development and Cultural Change*, **5**, 244–56.

SIMPSON, R. L. (1965) Sociology of the Community: Current Status and Prospects. *Rural Sociology*, **30** (2), 127–49.

SOUTHALL, A. (1959) An Operational Theory of Role. *Human Relations*, **12**, 17–34.

STACEY, M. (1960) *Tradition and Change*. Oxford: University Press.

STEIN, M. R. (1960) *The Eclipse of Community*. Princeton University Press.

STEWART, C. T. Jr. (1958) The Urban-Rural Dichotomy: Concepts and Uses. *American Journal of Sociology*, **64** (2), 152–8.

STIRLING, P. (1957) Land, Marriage and the Law in Turkish Villages. *International Social Science Bulletin*, **9** (1), 21–23.

STIRLING, P. (1965) *Turkish Village*. London: Weidenfeld and Nicholson.

WATSON, W. (1958) *Tribal Cohesion in a Money Economy*. Manchester: University Press.

WILLIAMS, W. M. (1964) Changing Functions of the Community. *Sociologia Ruralis*, **4** (3–4), 299–314.

WIRTH, L. (1938) Urbanism as a Way of Life. *American Journal of Sociology*, **44**. Reprinted in: Hatt & Reiss, eds. (1957), *Cities and Society*. Glencoe: Free Press, 46–63.

YOUNG, M. and P. WILLMOTT (1957) *Family and Kinship in East London*. London: Routledge & Kegan Paul.

INTRODUCTION TO THE DISCUSSION—I[1]

EUGEN LUPRI, *Federal Republic of Germany*

THE difficulty which confronts anyone setting out to appraise the usefulness of the concept of the rural-urban continuum is that so much has been written, yet so little has been achieved. The reasons for this dilemma are manifold and complex, and cannot be detailed here.

Pahl has performed a long-overdue service for European rural sociologists in calling attention to some of the basic underlying problems of the rural-urban continuum. Most of his cogent criticisms, with reference to the methodological problems entailed in transforming a potential into an actual continuum, are well taken. He has also provided a lucid and fruitful analysis of the metropolitan village by showing the existence of marked discontinuities. Throughout the paper Pahl argues persistently against the concept of the rural-urban continuum as a valid analytical tool for explaining the key patterns of rural and urban life. In fact, it appears that he considers the construct absolutely useless in almost every respect. The analytical concepts which Pahl has proposed instead—role, social network, patron-client relationship, and, especially, local and national systems— deserve to be taken seriously in their own right. There are, however, a number of points in Pahl's treatment which call for further elaboration and discussion.

Permit me to make a few summarizing statements. The rural-urban continuum as a theoretical frame has not, as Pahl states, been used solely in terms of geographic, demographic or economic indices, but rather it has been rigorously modified recently in view of the observation that social values constitute critical

---

[1] Summary of a critical review, which was published in full in *Sociologia Ruralis*, **7** (1), 1967.

independent variables in accounting for differences among rural and urban structures—familial, religious, and educational. The socio-cultural component needs to be and has recently been taken into account. Likewise, the significance of the temporal or dynamic element has been stressed in recent years.

My position is that rural-urban differences, while clearly diminishing, still remain crucial, even in highly industrialized nations. My own researches into family structure strongly suggest that the extent of rural-urban differences is clearly related to the society's level of economic development. From these findings it appears that internal differences within advanced societies are less, in spite of their greater complexity, than those within less advanced societies.[2]

Recent survey data on West Germany provide further evidence in support of the thesis that rural-urban differences, while vanishing, are still crucial.[3] From a sociological point of view, these differences in economic, social and attitudinal characteristics would seem to be directly related to the different social and cultural contexts of the West German communities. These very different environments still tend to produce different behaviours and attitudes.

Though the findings of many American rural sociologists and social psychologists are by no means consistent, rural-urban differences in regard to various behaviour patterns seem to prevail. These differences are of theoretical significance because generalizations about human behaviour must be tested across space and time. However, rural sociologists need to give more attention to defining the precise limits of their generalization concerning rural-urban variation. Moreover, those who make use of the rural-urban continuum should pay greater heed to the study of changes occurring in other sectors of society, because

---

[2] See Lupri, Eugen (1965), Industrialisierung und Strukturwandlungen in der Familie: Ein interkultureller Vergleich, *Sociologia Ruralis*, **5** (1), 57–76.

[3] These surveys were undertaken by the DIVO-Institut in 1965 and 1966. The results will be published in a forthcoming publication by the present writer.

these may be related to or may in part account for rural-urban variation. National differences which are found should be re-examined in a cross-national setting. In other words, hypotheses about rural-urban differences need to be tested by *comparable* cross-cultural data. Deviations and discontinuities observed in non-Western cultures should be meticulously analysed because their explanation may provide a better understanding of the mechanisms of social change occurring in Western industrialized societies.

The rural-urban continuum may prove to be inadequate for the study of urbanization in non-Western societies. This does not invalidate its usefulness, however, for the study of urbanization in Western industrializing nations. The rural-urban continuum is not a theory of urbanization but, at best, a conceptual framework within which certain rural-urban differences may be meaningfully interpreted. However, such a mode of analysis is only an intermediate step toward the final definitive conceptual formulation necessary for analysing and dealing with social systems whose constituent members have both 'rural' *and* 'urban' characteristics.

Advancement in any science depends on developments in both theory and empirical research, and on a close connection between them. Pahl should be commended for pointing out some important discontinuities. His position is particularly meritorious for his emphasis upon the study of the interaction between, and the reciprocal relationship of, the local system and the national system. The precise role of the analytical concepts, by means of which this process is to be analysed, awaits precise specification and clear formulation. Pahl deserves credit also for calling to our attention the need for a reformulation of current approaches to the study of social change. He has, in an admirably succinct and clearly stated exposition, directed our attention anew to the problems of social change, a study of which represents the *raison d'être* of our discipline. At the very least it is hoped that his excellent paper will serve to stimulate theoretical thinking and empirical research along the lines he has suggested.

INTRODUCTION TO THE DISCUSSION—II

A. K. CONSTANDSE, *The Netherlands*

Dr. Pahl has presented to us an excellent paper. With admirable clarity, displaying an extensive knowledge of the relevant literature, he has demonstrated that the traditional concept of the rural-urban continuum is more an obstacle than a help in our work. Of course, this conclusion as such is not new, as Dr. Pahl himself has shown in his review of recent literature. Any sociologist who has used the concept in his work, has come sooner or later to the finding that one or more elements did not fit in the construct. Whatever the criteria chosen for characterization may be, there is always the case to be found of an urban group behaving 'rural' and of a rural group being 'urban', or, worst of all, one finds rural and urban characteristics within one group or individual.

With the description of the situation in 'urban villages' and with the examples taken from studies made in the developing countries, in which all sorts of discontinuities between the urban and the rural come into the view, Dr. Pahl has found strong support for his statements. It is clear that a typology of settlements, from the small to the large, can never form the basis for a continuum which classifies social structures.

I do not feel the slightest desire to say anything in defence of the rural-urban continuum, but the paper is challenging enough to provoke criticism from someone who basically agrees.

The first remark concerns the use of the terms 'typology' and 'process' in relation to the continuum. I do not see the contra-distinction which Dr. Pahl makes here. The continuum, it should not be forgotten, is neither a typology, nor a process, but only a line with two ends, which can be used as a yardstick for measuring a continuity; it can be used horizontally, for a typology, and vertically for a process. If attempts to produce typologies with the help of a unidimensional continuum do not succeed, this is no reason to be against typologies as such, nor is it a reason to be against a continuum as such, it is the combination of the two, which is wrong. Mr. Pahl throws away *with* the rural-urban continuum the typology of settlements. He proposes to study roles and networks, and he sees the opposition of the local and the national as the most interesting problem. He wants us to study, in fact, the processes of change, of urbanization, differentiation, modernization, etc. Nobody will dispute the significance of the framework which Dr. Pahl gives here for important studies. But, in my view, he enters a new and different field of study in the last part of his paper, simply because he is only interested in the process and not in the typology.

My question is whether, because a typology and the continuum do not fit, the typology as such becomes uninteresting. Indeed, it is time that the rural-urban continuum is burnt and forgotten, but is one allowed to say that 'any attempt to tie particular patterns of social relationships to specific geographical milieux is a singularly fruitless exercise'?

Is there not a sociology which gives particular attention to ecological variables? Dr. Pahl himself gives examples of situations where particular forms of settlement lead to social structures which differ from those which are urbanized to the same degree (the agribusiness areas in North America). Agriculture (think about 'Westrigg'), enforces certain patterns of social relationships on people. That all the subjects in a community do not cherish the values of rural life, that workers and landowners are in opposition in this respect, does not alter the facts. Why should we make such a problem of the settlement patterns in new areas and land reform regions, if there was no relation between these patterns and the social organization?

Of course, it is possible that Dr. Pahl wants to leave this field to geographers and ecologists. If so, then I fear I have reopened the tiresome and disheartening discussion on the borderlines between social sciences. That is not my intention.

I have so many vested interests in rural sociology, that the second remark I want to make will not be surprising. I agree completely that urban sociologists and rural sociologists study the same problems with the same methods and with the same theory. But if one should go so far as to say that rural sociology will continue just because it happens to exist, I doubt it. It is true that if the study of rural life had to start today it would probably not institutionalize itself in agricultural schools and land grant colleges. But, on the other hand, it remains true that wherever agriculture has an important impact on social life, there are certain peculiarities to be observed, which demand special knowledge and special training on the part of the sociologist who studies them. The rural sociologist does not study a society which is basically different from the urban society; he studies that part of society which changes with the global society, but in its own specific way, because of the intervening variable, which is agriculture.

Further, I think, that the similarities between the urban and the rural sociologist are so striking to Dr. Pahl because he restricts the field of the rural sociologist to that of community studies. The rural sociologist may, and does, work, however, in other fields also: he studies religion, the family, the farm (which is, the enterprise), policies, political life, labour, land tenure, etc., on the micro-level as well as on the macro-level. Rural sociology, in my opinion, is a different kind of specialization compared to urban sociology. The urban sociologist studies milieux, the rural sociologist studies in principle everything that is sociologically relevant as long as it is in one way or another related to agriculture.

I must remark again that I am basically in complete agreement with Dr. Pahl; I only wanted to say that we should be careful not to throw away too many things along with the rural-urban continuum.

R. E. PAHL, *United Kingdom* (*Reply*)

I feel honoured by the interest which my paper has aroused
in the distinguished contributors to the discussion. Inevitably,
I cannot do full justice to all the points they have raised now:
indeed some of the issues which have been touched upon are so
fundamental and wide ranging that it would be presumptuous
of me to try.

Dr. Constandse's sympathetic treatment of my paper is most
generous. He questions my distinction between a typology and
a process: I think an emphasis on process is justified since the
usefulness of a typology as a classificatory device is necessarily
limited. Typologies occupy a place in the early development
of a science before a knowledge of process enables us to erect
models and evolve laws, as such they are means to an end and
not an end in themselves. I still maintain that attempts to tie
patterns of social relationships to specific milieux are fruitless:
for example, in Africa the enormous range of variation in social
organizations with similar environmental conditions and farming
systems, is astonishing. In the face of such ethnographic diversity
the case for environmental determinism appears slight. Ecologists
have given us some useful descriptive models, but they have
failed to provide an adequate explanatory framework for the
patterns they describe. Hence my emphasis on process: it is
not surprising that ecologists are forced to undermine their
position by incorporating what they refer to as socio-cultural
variables into their work.

My emphasis on community studies is also in question. This
was to some extent forced upon me, both by the terms of reference
of the paper and the existing assumptions and available literature
on the rural-urban continuum. I agree that as specific milieux
cease to be the only arena of most of an individual's social
relationships so rural sociologists will be driven from place-
oriented studies to occupation-oriented studies. Indeed, some
contributors wanted me to pay more attention to agriculture.
The parallel in this case would then be not with the urban

sociologist but with the industrial sociologist. In the same way that those interested in coal miners or steel workers have to understand the technology in a specific technical system, so those interested in agricultural workers must have special knowledge. I do not see the need for any continuum in dealing with different occupations. However, I am certainly more ready to accept occupational than environmental determinism.

I am also grateful to Dr. Lupri for his careful consideration of my paper. I certainly accept that there may be certain statistical data which, in some areas, appear to correlate with settlement size. However, it is, of course, necessary to show by the necessary statistical techniques that such variations are not reflections of social class differences, and similarly that data relating to one occupational category heavily represented in small settlements are not paralleled by other occupational categories which may appear proportionately less important in larger places.

On the national/local interaction perhaps I would do better to refer to large-scale and small-scale, the difference between face-to-face society and the bureaucratic society, the difference between what actually goes on and what is expected to go on (studies such as A. W. Gouldner's *Patterns of Industrial Bureaucracy* illustrate the tensions very well). I certainly think that a continuing dialogue between the social anthropologist and the sociologist is necessary, and a more rigorous investigation of the importance of *scale*, and the way that patterns of social relationships at different levels are related, are needed.

Migrancy and the Study of Africans[1] in Towns

P. Mayer

Editor's Note
It is unfortunate that it was not possible to include other papers on urbanization. However, Mayer's paper stands out as one of the most important contributions to the study of the process of adjustment to an urban system in Africa. There are a variety of forms of urbanism in modernizing nations but the mechanisms of adjustment may show less diversity. Mayer has begun the task of comparative analysis and many more such studies are needed.

THE study of African town populations may be said to raise some special theoretical issues in those many areas of Africa where labor migrancy prevails. These are areas where, by and large, the African "town population" is not clearly distinct. It still mostly consists of Africans who are spending parts of their lives in town, in between periods spent in the rural hinterland, and who continue thinking of the hinterland, rather than the town, as their permanent "home" because of the greater security there.

One kind of theoretical challenge raised by this phenomenon of migrancy has recently been taken up with marked success. That is, the ongoing nature of the urban social systems has been successfully distinguished from the temporary or shifting nature of the migrant personnel. This is one of the greatest single theoretical contributions made by a recent notable series of studies of Rhodesian Copperbelt towns (e.g., Epstein, 1958; Mitchell, 1960a; Gluckman, 1960). These studies demonstrate that African urban systems, such as trade unions, can and should

---

[1] My thanks are due to Professor J. C. Mitchell of the University College of Rhodesia and Nyasaland, who kindly read the manuscript before publication and made valuable suggestions.

be studied as urban systems in their own right, independently of the fact that the migrant members are recruited from rustic (tribal) life and keep melting away into it again. As Gluckman has it (1960, p. 57), "an African miner is a miner." His activities at work, and the relations he forms at work, need to be considered in relation to an industrial context, not a tribal one.

Thus the Copperbelt work has seemed to forswear "relating the urban African to his tribal background," if by this we mean considering his connections with tribal systems in the hinterland. It has recognized the validity of tribes as categories of interaction *within* the town setting, but has mostly avoided "explaining" town-located phenomena by reference to tribal systems located outside the town.

As a working principle for the study of African towns (or urban societies, or urban social systems), this principle of ignoring what goes on "outside" would seem to be unexceptionable. In much the same way, when an anthropologist works in the tribal hinterland, one would expect an analysis of the local social systems—age-sets, clans, lineages, or whatever they might be— without much regard for the turnover of personnel caused by migrant members going away to work in town and without reference to what goes on in that "outside" field.

On the other hand, it seems evident that in regions of labor migrancy a case exists for the study of migrancy itself as a supplement to the study of towns and town-located systems.[2] The fact that the *same* individuals are apt to function as trade union members at one end, and as age-set members at the other, is one which common sense forbids us to ignore. The study of the ongoing structures—at the urban or the rural end or both— therefore seems to require this supplement, if justice is to be done

---

[2] In Southern and Central Africa, sociological aspects of migrancy have been studied at the rural end, notably by Schapera (1947), Gulliver (1957), Watson (1958), and van Velsen (1960).

At the urban end, Wilson's essay on Broken Hill (1941/42) seems to have remained for many years the only major publication focused on migrants as such. My own work on Xhosa migrancy (1961) deals chiefly with the urban end, though based on both rural and urban fieldwork.

to the social realities. Along with its practical implications, the social fact of widespread migrancy must have some implications for theory, and these ought to be worked out. It might well challenge the anthropologist to redefine such concepts as social personality, role, status, or social field—or at least to inquire whether redefinition is necessary—so as to suit a situation where Ego habitually moves back and forth between urban "society" and tribal "society." The concept of migrant, as such, requires sociological scrutiny.

For this purpose it would seem necessary to bring both parts of Ego's total field of activity—the town part plus the hinterland part—into focus together. How is this to be done? It will certainly not be easy to subsume the two parts under the concept of one inclusive "social structure" or "society" in the classic sense. As Nadel (1957) has argued, the diagnostic unity of a social structure, properly so called, lies in the fact that all the roles defined within it bear some logical relation to one another. It would be extraordinarily difficult to discover any logical interlock between all the tribal roles and all the urban roles of all those various people who, as migrants, circulate through the kind of field just described. Especially is this the case since, in so many instances, the town draws migrants from a number of different separate sources. The total migrancy field, in such an instance, consists of the town plus all of those areas from which it draws migrants. In practice nobody bothers to look for the logical interlock of roles which would be necessary to constitute the migrancy field a unitary "structure." It is normally assumed that migrancy, as such, involves an individual in two distinct "structures"; and that more than two distinct structures are involved in the total migrancy field, if more than one tribal (rural) society is sending migrants into the town.

Even the concept of the wider society as defined by modern state boundaries—e.g., South African society or Rhodesian society—would not necessarily enable us to dispense with the plural model and accommodate the role of "migrant" within a unitary model, so long as we insist that the model has got to be one of an organic social structure. Migrancy commonly flows back and forth across state boundaries. For instance, the South African mines draw large numbers of their migrant workers from Portuguese territories, British High Commission territories, and elsewhere.

It seems, then, that the study of a town-plus-hinterland field, with its circulating personnel, cannot well hope to proceed as the analysis of "a social structure," and that the quest for an alternative method of approach would be justified. A reasonable alternative method, it is here suggested, would be to begin at the study of the migrant persons themselves, by mapping out their networks of relations from the personal or egocentric point of view, as well as noting their parts in the various structural systems. In doing this we would not be postulating any structural unity of the migrancy field. We would merely be noting that it is, in fact, a field habitually traversed by migrating persons. The starting-point would be the observed fact that individuals who play roles in town A also play roles in tribal (or rural) societies, B, C or D; the task would be to observe the networks of social relations which arise when this fact is multiplied into a mass social phenomenon, and to analyze their special characteristics.

Probably the easiest and most practical place to begin the study of migrants or migrancy is in town, because of the denser concentration of migrants there as compared with the rural end, and also the availability of different groups (from different rural sectors), which may be useful for comparative analysis. But when choosing a town population as the field of study, we must take particular care not to confuse the objective—the study of migrancy—with that significantly different objective, the study of town-located social systems as such. The "migrancy" objective demands precisely what pursuers of the "town" objective have purposely abjured, namely, a close attention to the extra-town ties of the town-resident migrants.

This phrase, extra-town ties, requires attention. It does not mean just the same as "tribal" ties. Even the study of the town "as a town" may well require reference to "tribal" ties in the sense that "tribal" groups can be significant *within* the town, i.e., as in-groups and categories of social interaction. The Copperbelt studies have amply demonstrated this point. It is another matter to investigate extra-town ties, i.e., those bonds which, during the period of residence in town, continue to bind Ego to specific tribal systems *outside* the town and enable him to resume his place in a specific tribal community (in the hinterland) when the time comes. These are the mechanisms which, as it were, keep open his particular place in some hinterland society— as member of this or that family, lineage, age-set, etc.—and not merely his "tribalism" or persisting tribal "loyalty" (Gluckman, 1960, p. 55) in the vaguer sense of national self-identification. They require that, during his stay in town, he should maintain certain relationships in a latent state and discharge certain roles in absentia.

Irrelevant these extra-town ties may have proved for the study of urban structural systems—trade unions and the like—but if that mode of study throws no light on them, other techniques will have to be sought.

In this article I shall consider some of the practical and theoretical points which arose during a study of migrancy undertaken by me in one South African town, East London, Cape Province, between 1955 and 1959. Results of this study have been published in book form (Mayer, 1961). East London is a major seaport, and an industrial and commercial center, with some 50,000 White inhabitants and nearly 70,000 others. The "others" —who, except for some 10,000 domestic servants, live segregated in the "Locations" or non-White quarters—are predominantly African labor migrants (the Coloured and Asiatic minorities being numerically small here).

MODELS OF ALTERNATION AND OF CHANGE

We may first consider how far some existing models for the study of Africans in towns are appropriate for the specific study of migrancy.

In some urban studies, the double roles of the labor migrant have been theoretically reconciled by a use of the idea of alternation or switching back and forth in time. Thus, Ego, who is now in town, this year plays roles in urban society; next year he will be back in the hinterland playing roles in tribal society; and so forth. Or again: Ego, while in town, is involved in urban sets of relations this morning, at the work-place, but in tribal sets this evening, in his urban domestic life; he plays certain roles according to urban norms each morning, and other roles according to tribal norms each evening.

"Alternation" models have been explicitly contrasted with another kind which we may call models of one-way change. Here the idea was that the migrant, under the influence of town, may gradually abandon his tribal roles and norms altogether. Gluckman (1960, p. 57; 1959, pp. 3–4) has commented on the weaknesses he regards as inherent in an older method of study—the method which postulated "a process of detribalization, which had to be analysed and measured as the tribesman slowly changed." Rejecting this concept of slow change, Gluckman recommended that we "start analysis of town life by saying that the moment an African crossed his tribal boundary he was 'detribalized,' outside the tribe, though not outside the influence of the tribe. Correspondingly, when a man returns from the town into the political area of the tribe he is tribalized again—de-urbanized—though not outside the influence of the town" (1960, p. 58). Gluckman thus postulates alternation as a switching back and forth between two distinct social fields or systems.

Of course, there is a more basic difference involved, too, insofar as one model works with "culture" and the other with "social relations." The earlier model criticized by Gluckman relied largely on the concept of changing *culture;* the "movement" envisaged was from one cultural condition to another, along a one-way track starting from the tribal condition as zero point and ending with complete detribalization. The proposed alternation model, by contrast, postulates an alternation between *social fields*, one whenever the migrant is in town and the other whenever he is in the hinterland. This is one reason why the latter model invites more to synchronic and the former more to diachronic study.

Concurrently, work by Epstein (1958) and Mitchell (1960b) has brought into use a somewhat different alternation model. This might be said to unite more closely the social relations and culture concepts: it postulates involvement (in town) in different sets of relations which in themselves call forth different patterns of behavior. The model brings out the fact that a man even while actually in town can still be alternating. He can switch back and forth between urban and tribal behavior according to the immediate situation. He may be content to follow tribal patterns in his urban domestic life, although he cannot do so at work, and although he would deprecate a tribal system of representation for dealing with the white management of the mines. The operative principle has been termed "situational selection" (Gluckman, 1958, p. 47, citing Evans-Pritchard; Epstein, 1958, pp. 235, 236), i.e., the individual selects behavior patterns appropriate to the sets of relations in which a situation involves him at a given moment.

Here, then, we have, in two forms, a recognition that one man may be alternately urban in some situations and tribal in others. As long as we are concerned with the study of towns (including the study of "tribalism" in towns, in the sense of tribal loyalties), this is a valuable theoretical advance on the older tendency—which perhaps is still the layman's—to contrapose tribal man and urbanized man as distinct entities. Yet, if we are concerned specifically with the study of migrants, the new recognition is not enough. Tending as it does towards a static and schizoid picture of the migrant's social personality, it does not help us much to understand that significant process of social change which can properly be called the "process of urbanization" among migrants. By this I mean a shift in the balance between within-town ties and extra-town ties. A formerly migrant population (I would suggest) has become genuinely urban, or been effectively urbanized, once this shift has become decisive, so that its extra-town ties have collectively shrunk to negligible proportions as compared with its within-town ties. At the fully urbanized stage—to put it more simply—the town-dwelling population is no longer subject to the pull of the hinterland. It has become a purely urban proletariat (and/or bourgeoisie).

That this important and world-wide form of social change also takes place in Africa is well known. Godfrey Wilson had discussed its progress in a Central African setting as early as 1941. In South Africa, where the towns created by Europeans have a longer history than in most parts of the continent, every major city by now takes for granted its fully urbanized African element. These are African townsmen all of whose major social ties are bounded by the city in which they live. Such persons—unlike the migrant Africans who rub shoulders with them in town— have no longer any important personal links with the tribal hinterland, and no "homes" anywhere but in town. They will live, rear their children, and die in town. Historically speaking, this "fully urban" category has developed out of the "migrant" category: its members are ex-migrants, or children or grand-children of migrants. The process is still enough in evidence to constitute a worry for the South African government; influx control, tribal ambassadors, and other measures are employed on purpose to neutralize as far as possible the continuing "redistribution of the Bantu."

In the study of any migrant group in town, then, a critical question would seem to be how far the pull of the hinterland is weakening, if at all. As it weakens, the social personality of the migrant changes in some way. If it weakens sufficiently, his role as migrant comes to an end. The concept of alternation, in either of the forms cited, is not really sufficient for depicting how country-born people can "become townsmen" in the sense of shifting their personal centers of gravity into the town.

Concentration on within-town ties alone, it must be added, cannot enable one to judge, by implication, how far the pull of the hinterland may be weakening. Active involvement in within-town social systems is no index of non-involvement in extra-town systems. The extra-town ties can indeed be simultaneously involved in those very actions which represent participation in an urban system. An "urban" role and a "tribal" role can be discharged *pari passu*. It all depends on how one construes the action. For example, when a man has come to town to earn money for his family in the hinterland, it follows that whenever he discharges his urban role of industrial employee, he is also and ipso facto discharging his extra-town role of a providing father. Thus, his work in factory or mine can be construed as being done "for" his employer in the urban economic system, but equally well as being done "for" his homestead group in the tribal economic system. If we are studying the urban industrial system as such, only the former construction matters. But if we are studying migrancy, both matter. There may be other forms of double participation, less noticeable on the surface. In East London, migrant workers of a certain type choose to spend their off-duty hours incapsulated in a clique of friends—room mates, drinking companions, etc.—who, in fact, are old friends from one "home place" in the hinterland. Since all the men in such a clique have still kin or friends living in the *same* rural home community—people who may call each man to account whenever he goes "home"—the men's actions in town are actually being referred to the moral and social systems of the "home place," quite as much as to those of the town (Mayer, 1961).

TWO LOCAL SITUATIONS COMPARED: EAST LONDON AND COPPERBELT

If one accepts the task of examining the extra-town ties of town dwellers and assessing them in relation to within-town ties, it seems reasonably certain that very different pictures will emerge as between different modern towns in Africa. The pictures will differ not only in the balance between extra-town and within-town ties, but also in the very nature and quality of the ties within each category. (As Mitchell remarks, "the total set of external imperatives is probably unique for each town" [1960b,

p. 171].) It may therefore be useful to compare East London with the type of Copperbelt town explored by Mitchell, Gluckman, and Epstein. In the case of East London, the within-town ties are of a kind that is much less conspicuous and much less massive; the extra-town ties, on the other hand, seem to come into focus more easily than may be the case on the Copperbelt.

(a) **Within-town Ties**

The Copperbelt studies, it will be recalled, have dealt with a phase of development in which the interplay between the workers' common (urban) interests and their sectional sentiments or interests (as members of different tribal groups) is sociologically noteworthy. Hence much emphasis is placed on a theme which might be summarized in the phrase, "trade unions transcend tribes." The analysis demonstrates that in certain interactions in town the workers still attach prime importance to their respective tribal identities, but that industrial work involves them in new sets of relations too, in which they eventually become aware of the irrelevance of tribal categories. It is at work, then, that these town-dwelling Africans can be seen to form "typically urban associations." These are the massive within-town ties referred to.

The growth of the massive associations, it has also been pointed out, seems more favored by the structure of the mining compounds than by that of the municipal locations (Gluckman, 1960, p. 61). It is the monolithic power of the mining company which provokes a similarly monolithic response from the workers' side.

None of this applies to East London. Here there exist neither trade unions nor any other massive associations of or for Africans, except, on a smaller scale, churches and sports clubs. Furthermore, the structure of the East London locations is anything but monolithic. And thirdly, there is no opposition between different tribal groups to enhance the importance of tribal identities or bonds within the town setting. Ninety-six per cent of the whole African population of East London is drawn from a single tribal group; they are Xhosa-speakers, with common Xhosa loyalties.[3] The only group opposition which would make sense in this context, the one between the Xhosa and the Whites, has artificially forbidden any expression on the Xhosa side.

These assertions must be briefly documented. First, the absence of massive urban associations (other than churches and sports clubs) is a direct result of government policy. In South Africa, all associations are repressed or discouraged in which town-dwelling Africans might be able to constitute themselves a pressure-group, whether as town residents, as employees, or as citizens. It is true that rural (Reserve) Africans are allowed or even encouraged to express "their own interests" within the limits of local administrative units, e.g., by complaining to tribal chiefs on internal tribal matters; but no Africans are allowed any lawful means of expression in the modern state machinery or economic system.

This is in clear contrast to the official encouragement (since the 1940's) of African trade unionism in the Copperbelt; and it means that we cannot apply to any South African town the forecast (rightly made by Gluckman in the Rhodesian context) that "as soon as Africans assemble in towns they will try to combine to better their conditions in trade unions and so forth" (1960, p. 57). To be specific, the South African government, which does not recognize African trade unions, also forbids African participation in the recognized White, Asiatic, or Coloured unions. A voluntary African trade union which once played a prominent part in East London has never recovered from the crushing it underwent 30 years ago by the breaking of its attempted general strike. African political parties, notably the African National Congress and its Youth League, have also been unable to function (at least overtly) since they were officially banned

---

[3] Within the Xhosa-speaking group, now some $2\frac{1}{2}$ million strong, oppositions based on internal differentiations (e.g., between "Xhosa proper" and "Mfengu") count for little in face of the common loyalties, which are based on a long history of neighborhood and intermarriage, as well as on common language and cultural similarity.

as illegal organizations. True to the principle of allowing some self-expression in purely local matters, the authorities recognize and encourage Location Advisory Boards (purely consultative) in some urban areas; but in recent years East London Africans have not regarded their Board as serving any real purpose, witness the poll of one or two per cent in the voting for the elected element.

In circumstances like these, obviously, the failure to develop new sets of relations in town, at the political or trade union level, need not signify a corresponding apathy. Fieldwork experience in East London suggested quite the reverse: that there is in fact an immense fund of discontent, ready to be tapped by any "representative" associations, if such were allowed to arise. All we have a right to assert is that no overt expression, no organization or association reflecting common "urban" interests, lies to hand at present for purposes of anthropological study; and that the within-town ties available for study do not add up to massive structural systems like those of a Copperbelt town. (The situation in the Copperbelt in 1935 seems to have been similar; Mitchell [1956] shows how dance groups there became media of political expression accordingly.)

The "atomistic" (Epstein, 1958, p. 154) structure of East London is relevant to this point, too. In a municipal compound (as against a mining compound) there is less pressure for combined action, and less possibility for organizing it (Gluckman, 1960, p. 61). Instead of a single "unitary" structure (the mining company) (Epstein, 1958, p. 123) controlling employment, accommodation, and almost all aspects of the employees' lives, there is a multitude of different employers. The East London locations—entirely municipal—illustrate this atomism in extreme form, for they are largely made up of private, not municipal, housing, i.e., of shanty towns where the houseowners are individual Africans. Four-fifths of East London Africans are crammed into these shanty towns (either as owners or as lodgers) and are therefore not even direct tenants of the only monolithic power on the White side—the municipal corporation.

(b) **Extra-town Ties**

The typical East London worker is a country-bred Xhosa who stays in town, holding down a job, for many years. Those Xhosa who want to make only brief earning sorties from their rural homes usually prefer a nine-month contract in the distant Rand mines or towns: East London is the place for the serious regular earning without which (owing to the poverty of Reserve agriculture) most rural families would not be able to make ends meet. Influx control regulations, nowadays, rather encourage the tendency for men to stay long in town. A migrant who prematurely returns to the country, or gives up his job, is liable to loss of his "permit to remain with the urban area," thus jeopardizing his family's cash income. On the other hand, East London lies so near to the rural hinterland that most migrants can make frequent brief visits "home" *during* their prolonged stay in town. Some can manage "week-ending" and "month-ending" (on off-duty days); others are limited to an annual two weeks at Christmas.

This particular local situation—the combination of easy home-visiting, for those who wish it, with prolonged stay in town—makes it possible to construct a meaningful scale for measuring the strength of the hinterland pull and comparing it as between different migrants, or different stages of a life history. Most migrants when they begin their East London careers are subject to a fairly strong pull, in that they have left their closest kin and dependents (parents, wives, children, etc.) "at home" in the hinterland. These country kin expect to be visited at intervals and to receive regular remittances from the migrant's wages. But the pull need not remain constant. Some migrants crudely deny it; they "vanish" or "melt away" (*nyibilika* in the Xhosa vernacular) in town, entirely dropping all their rural connections and obligations. Others eventually nullify the pull by managing to qualify administratively as "permanent residents of the urban area," moving their families into town, and winding up their interests in the hinterland. The migrants who remain permanently susceptible to the pull are the ones who make the most of their opportunities for home-visiting, and also for associating with fellow "exiles" from the same home place during their stay in town. These twin mechanisms enable them to remain permanently involved not only with kin but also with various structural systems in the hinterland. For instance, they remain acknowledged though largely absentee members of their (rural) men's age-grade "clubs," of the local (rural) council (*Inkundla*), and of their own lineage group. They can eventually return "home" and resume the appropriate roles in full.

MIGRANTS AND "URBAN AFRICANS"

In what has been said above about the process of urbanization and the dropping or rejection of extra-town ties, an antithesis has been implied between two types of people who may live side by side in town: namely the migrant and the "urban African." This, too, is a point where existing models for the study of African urban systems may need some modification for purposes of the study of migrancy.

It will be noticed that the adjective "urban" ought properly to have a different connotation in each of the three models which were touched upon at the beginning of this article. (a) In the "detribalization" model, the urban/tribal antithesis is conceived principally as an antithesis of different human conditions, or ways of life. Urban might then serve as a near-synonym for Westernized, or civilized, or detribalized. It would seem permissible (in this view) to speak of an "urban African," meaning one who has reached the end of the road of cultural change, completely losing his tribal culture and/or status within the tribe. In a given town, some people will be more "urban" than others. (b) The second model represented the urban/tribal antithesis as an antithesis of two social fields, one located in the town and the other in the hinterland. In this view, urban would be a synonym for town-located; any action, interaction, institution, or relation that exists within the "urban" field would appear as "urban." Hence "urban African," if it means anything, will here mean an African who happens to be playing parts in a given town at a given moment, regardless of whether he is going to revert to tribal life later on. No African will be either more or less "urban" than his neighbor in town. (c) The third model represents the antithesis as one of "sets of relations." In contrast to (b), it does not imply that everything located in town is equally urban: on the contrary, the analytic task may be seen precisely as that of sorting out what are termed the truly or "typically" urban sets of relations (in town) from those others which, although town-located, are not "typically" urban. "Typically" urban, in this model, is an epithet for social systems such as trade unions (Gluckman, 1960, p. 58): their urban-ness is not just that they do exist in town, but that they could not well exist anywhere else; they are social phenomena of a type intrinsically associated with urban areas. In this model, the question of what one means by an "urban African" does not arise at all. The adjective is not applicable to persons: it applies only to roles, relations, systems, and the like.

When studying migrancy in East London, there was a clear need for the model to accommodate "urban Africans" as a distinct category of persons. Not only can this category be conceptually distinguished from the migrants (by virtue of its renunciation of extra-town ties), but the East Londoners themselves emphasize the distinction. To them, the urban African (or as they would say, the "real townsman") is a distinct sociocultural category, different from the migrant "who works in town but is of the country," and this distinction is made the basis of some notable social oppositions.

At present about 15 per cent of the adult (i.e., over 15 years old) Africans in East London are townsmen born and bred. These people approximate to the ideal type of the townsman as the man who has all his important social ties bounded by the town and feels no pull from the hinterland. With them must be classed those among the country-born 85 per cent who in due course have dropped or lost their country connections: these also feel no pull from the hinterland. Over against all these "real towns-men" (whether they are such by birth or by adoption) stand all the migrants who still have parents, wives, children, land, cattle, houses, group membership, and tribal status outside the town, and who are thereby subject to the hinterland pull in more or less full force.

Administrative policy does something to underline the difference. The "real townsmen" have more security for themselves and their families in town than the country-oriented migrants have. The latter require special permits—renewable every month—to remain within the urban area (that is, unless or until they qualify as "permanent residents," by achieving the difficult record of 10 or 15 years' continuous employment). To bring in their dependents they require extra permits, which are not easily granted.

To these two bases of differentiation must be added a third: a cultural one. The migrants generally remain adept in their home culture (whether this be Red or School—a distinction to be explained below). Whatever "town ways" they may be called on to practice while in town, they can slip into the ways of the rural culture when they visit home, and when they retire there for good. The "real townsmen" are adept only in "town ways," and they value these positively, whereas many migrants are apt to value them negatively. The "town ways" are those of second or third generation urban proletarians (and a small bourgeoisie); they are different enough from rustic Xhosa ways to constitute a distinct sub-culture.

Naturally, the opposition between urban Africans and migrants is not important in all situations. Broadly speaking, their significance as reference groups is reduced to its lowest level at work and when moving in the White part of town; it reaches its highest level in situations where people are moving entirely among their fellow-Africans, at leisure in the Locations where they sleep and have their social life.

The same applies to another categorization which the Xhosa migrants bring with them into East London from the hinterland.

For generations, the Xhosa countryside has been split by a fundamental opposition between "Red" and "School" people, that is, between tribally minded Xhosa traditionalists on the one hand, and mission and school products on the other. This region of South Africa constitutes one of the oldest areas of White settlement south of the Sahara—White and Black having both claimed it as home since the 1820's—but the Xhosa did not quickly or easily submit to White rule. Throughout the nineteenth century those of them who had not been won over by the missionaries continued to harass the Whites in a series of fierce wars (the "Kaffir Wars"). The Red Xhosa are the descendants and cultural heirs of these nationalist resisters: theirs is the section which has been looking askance at White men, and White men's ways, since the days of George IV. Even today they are typically, and proudly, pagan and illiterate; it is their stereotyped comment that "White men's ways are for White men, not for us Xhosa." The School section, on the other hand, who have received mission and school teaching over the same period of five generations, are a Christianized peasant folk who internalize many of the values of civilization. Their aspiration is to move closer to equality with White people, and they tend to look down on the "raw" or "out-of-date" traditions of the "Red blanket wearers," who would rather prefer to withdraw out of White people's reach.

This opposition of conservatives and progressives—outwardly symbolized, in the country, by markedly different dress and appearance—does not only serve to demarcate two further sub-cultures: it has also long functioned as a group opposition. Within each rural neighborhood, the Red and School elements keep each to themselves, voluntarily abstaining from avoidable association, organizing activities as far as possible strictly within their own section. Intermarriage is rare. Worship, recreation, entertainment are separate. The cleavage has been elevated onto a moral plane; not mixing with the "other" kind of person is made a moral issue, from childhood onwards (Mayer, 1961, ch. 2).

In the East London Locations—as fieldwork revealed—three reference groups, viz., real townsmen, School migrants, and Red migrants, remain clearly distinguishable. The habits of mutual aloofness which serve to keep Red and School separate in the country are also carried on in town. The Red element stay conspicuously out of School and town people's activities. The barrier between School migrant and "real townsman," though less emphasized, is there too. In it are comprised those oppositions of sentiment and interest which divide yokels, at home in peasant Africa, from cockneys, reared in the slums of a Western-type industrial city.

THE STUDY OF CATEGORICAL RELATIONS: CHANGE AND MOBILITY

It was stated that the three reference groups just enumerated— "real townsman," Red migrant, and School migrant—have little or no significance at work. How they might be submerged in contexts involving workers' common interests is not the question that arises in trade-unionless East London, but it is observable that behavior patterns at work do not reflect them to any extent. White employers expect all types of Xhosa to play, and the Xhosa do play, similar parts in the urban economy. Although these are urban, not rural parts, the job ceiling is so low that different degrees of "Westernization" can be only slightly (if at all) reflected. The vast majority, migrant or townsmen, Red or School, are concentrated in unskilled and semi-skilled occupations. (As an illiterate factory hand remarked, "Provided you can move fast, education doesn't count here.")

In terms of "cultural patterns" or "behavior," then, we have three sub-cultures which can only be clearly perceived in spheres of life other than work. In the working context, all behavior is brought to a common pattern; and this pattern is necessarily "urbanized," that is, adapted to the demands of its industrial context. If a Copperbelt miner is a miner, so is a Xhosa factory hand a factory hand—though practically without the possibility of rising to a skilled position or joining a trade union. The ability of otherwise "tribal"-seeming people to produce "urban" behavior while actually engaged in work, no longer excites comment or interest in this centenarian town. It is a form of situational selection that can be taken for granted. But to say this leaves another question unanswered, namely, what kind of behavior will be preferred when Ego is away from the working situation. For we are not dealing with a homogeneously "tribal" (i.e., un-Westernized) population, all of whom could be expected to follow "tribal" custom or behavior whenever they are free to do so. On the contrary, we have three sub-cultures, two of which expressly repudiate "tribal" habits and norms to a greater or less degree. It is therefore necessary to go into the question of away-from-work behavior with special care.

The spheres in which the three sub-cultures appear distinctly are (in particular) domestic, family, sociable, and religious life—i.e., all those not directly regulated by the demands of work. Correspondingly, if we turn from "culture" to "social relations," we find social oppositions which can only be observed in other-than-work contexts,—in kinship, marriage, domestic, friendly, religious, and sociable relations, and in voluntary associations (including those for religion). It is in these spheres that one notices the strong tendency for East London Africans of each category to keep to "their own kind." Despite the common involvement in urban work, clearly the town does not function as a melting pot, nor yet a transmuting pot. Red men, in particular, express a strong distaste for "getting mixed up with" other categories in town. They choose their friends and domestic partners almost exclusively from among other Red migrants.

Hence, part of the study of migrancy in East London is the study of "categorical" relations, as defined by Mitchell (1956, 1959): the relation between the urban category and each of the two migrant categories, and likewise of relations between these two migrant categories (Red and School).

There is, however, one critical difference between the type of category described for the Copperbelt and the type encountered in East London. The difference is mobility. The Copperbelt categories (except the cross-cutting one of social class) are ethnic, birth-determined; from Ego's point of view they are ascribed. The East London ones are determined ultimately by personal choice, whether in the sphere of cultural practice or of voluntary (associational) ties. Thus they are achieved rather than ascribed. If an individual in the East London situation wishes to do so, and will take pains to acquire the necessary social skills, he can move from one category into another, much as a person in a class-differentiated society can move from one class into another. Just as with class, it is a question of social relations and cultural practices taken in conjunction—the person who moves must select new habits and also new associates. And just as with class, the voluntary moving is mainly in one direction. It is far commoner to move out of, than into, the Red category, almost the only exceptions being a few non-Red women who marry Red men (contrary to usual practice).

There is always a certain amount of movement going on, as fieldwork showed. In the country, it is not easy for a Red person to "become School," because conservative kin and seniors oppose this on moral grounds. The change of reference group becomes notably easier in the crowded town setting, where the migrant— if he wishes—can take steps to evade the watchful eyes of conservative aquaintances. A minority of Red migrants, accordingly, do "become School in town," and a minority of all migrants (both Red and School) "become townsmen" who will never willingly acknowledge the pull of the hinterland again.

The Xhosa vernacular has several pointers to this process of mobility. It is significant that the terms for people who change, or people in transition, are derogatory. There is *irumsha*, the "speaker of another language" (especially English), the cultural turncoat who adopts and values town ways. The neutral term *igoduka*, the "home visitor," who remains a faithful visitor to the hinterland while staying in town, contrasts with the derogatory term *itshipha*, the "absconder," who gets swallowed up in town and abandons his hinterland dependents. Derogatory, too, is *igqoboka*, the man "with a hole" caused by his conversion to Christianity (as distinct from the "born" or established Christian).

Obviously, these terms and the concepts they stand for have nothing to do with urban *work*. No man is irumsha by virtue of speaking English to his employer. Nor will a "home visitor" be at all distinguishable from an "absconder" in the working situation. The contrast can only be seen by reference to those other situations, already enumerated, where Africans are together among themselves, in the urban Locations, and are relatively free to organize their own activities and relationships.

We may say that the Xhosa are correctly postulating a distinction between the *necessarily* urban behavior of a migrant while at work, and the *voluntarily* urban behavior which he may or may not adopt in other town-located situations. While the behavior selected within the working sphere is necessarily "urban," the migrant's behavior in other spheres lies somewhere along a scale from Red ("tribal" or "least urban") to "really urban"; furthermore, it may move along that scale in the course of time. Here, in the Locations, three sub-cultures or sets of patterns— Red, School, and "really urban"—are available as alternatives. And here a man's own choices and decisions have a particular significance in that they indicate whether he wishes to remain within his original social category or to adopt a different one (e.g., whether he will "remain Red" or will "become School" or "really a townsman").

A simple two-valued model of situational selection, therefore, is not appropriate for the study of migrants in East London. While we can take it for granted that "urban" behavior will be selected in working situations, we also have to reckon with this further process of selection which is demanded in nonworking situations (i.e., between Red, School, and "townsmen's" patterns), and whose outcome cannot be predicted on *a priori* grounds.

THEMES FOR STUDY: SOCIAL NETWORK AND PERSONAL CHOICE

In this way, it can be said, an effort has been made to combine certain features of the "alternation" and the "change" type of model. The valid objection to detribalization as a working concept, after all, is not that it implies change, but that it tends to imply synchronized change of the whole man. Provided we recognize that a man need not move (or stand still) as a whole, provided we allow for his perhaps remaining "tribal" in some situations while becoming "urban" in others (however we define those adjectives), there is no *a priori* objection to using the idea of change. Indeed, the difficulty of accommodating movement, or process, has already been noticed as a main limitation of any model that works solely in terms of situational selection.

In practical terms, the study of migrants in East London had two related aspects. One was investigation of individual migrants' networks of personal relations, i.e., their total networks, town-located plus country-located, so as to determine the balance of within-town and extra-town ties, and the likelihood of a shift. The other was investigation of behavior patterns, attitudes, and values with special reference to aspiration or the desire for change. Details are given in the volume mentioned above (Mayer, 1961). Here it will suffice to say that two polar types emerged. In one type (it appeared) the town-located part of the network came to take clear precedence over the country-located part, until it could be said that all of the migrant's most important personal ties were now contained within the town, much as they are with town-born people. There would also be a shift towards "urban" behavior and values—a desire to adopt "real townsmen" as one's reference group. Connections with the country home might be kept up for security reasons, but while in town the migrant would prefer the company of new friends found in town. In the opposite type, ties with non-townsmen remained paramount. Besides attaching importance to friends and groups "at home" in the country, the migrant while in town would restrict himself as far as possible to the company of "home friends" (*amakhaya*)— fellow-exiles coming from his own place. "New" friendships, i.e., with people not known at home, would be eschewed. Emphasis would be laid on resisting the lures of town, remaining faithful to "home" cultural values, and returning "home" as often or as soon as possible. Voluntary activities in town would be imitations of, or near substitutes for, Red rural prototypes (beer drinks, ancestor sacrifices, Red dances etc.). On returning "home," the exiled amakhaya could fit in almost as if they had not been away.

It can be said that in East London a migrant's propensity to change culturally (or to resist change) is ultimately bound up with the fate of his extra-town ties. More than anything else, what keeps the conservative Red type of man faithfully Red during all his years in town is his continuing to be bound to one specific Red family, lineage, and community "at home" in the country. It is from here that the critical moral pressures emanate: the wish to go on fitting in here can be called the underlying drive. Two mechanisms keep up the force of these extra-town ties (and thus the continued acceptance of the original home culture). These mechanisms (as I have described in *Townsmen or Tribesmen*) are (a) home-visiting, and (b) organization of relations between amakhaya while in town. I have referred to their total effect as "incapsulation."

The contrast offered by the School migrant (and also the "deviant" Red migrant who breaks out of incapsulation) shows that (a) is not effective without (b). If a migrant while in town turns his back on his amakhaya and plunges into "mixed" society, visits home do not serve to keep up extra-town ties to the same extent. Much of the content is lost. The way is open for cultural change, quite apart from the obligatory kind of urbanization demanded in the working sphere.

A point to be stressed once again is that these polar types, and other types intermediate between them, result from the migrants' *voluntary* organization of their private and domestic lives. Much as we see a distinction between *necessarily* "urban" behavior, at work, and *voluntarily* "urban" behavior, outside work, so we can say that certain relations—at work—are thrust upon the migrant, but that outside working hours he *voluntarily* chooses his associates. Even his domestic circle in town (room-mates, landlord) is a matter for his personal decision. Town, in any case, offers opportunity for more numerous and more varied kinds of social relations than are possible in a "tribal" rural community. It is the migrant, coming in from outside—starting with a clean sheet as it were—who can make fullest use of the opportunities. Also dependent on his own choice is the matter of keeping up his ties with old friends "at home" in the country, or letting them drop.

It seems sometimes to have been implied that prolonged residence in the "atmosphere" of town will automatically tend to "change" people and make them "urbanized." East London does not bear this out. There, while some are born "urban," and others achieve urbanization, none can be said to have urbanization thrust upon them. There is a power of choice; some of the migrants begin to change; but others voluntarily incapsulate themselves in something as nearly as possible like the tribal relations from which their migration could have liberated them. The study of urbanization of migrants, in the particular form I have outlined here, is a study of such choices and of the determinants that lie behind the choices.

REFERENCES

EPSTEIN, A. L. (1958) *Politics in an Urban African Community*. Manchester, Manchester University Press.

GLUCKMAN, M. (1958) Analysis of a social situation in modern Zululand. *Rhodes–Livingstone Paper* No. 28.

GLUCKMAN, M. (1960) Tribalism in modern British Central Africa. *Cahiers d'études africaines* no. 1, 55 ff. Paris.

GLUCKMAN, M. (1961) Anthropological problems arising from the African industrial revolution. In *Social Change in Modern Africa*, A. Southall, ed. Oxford University Press.

GULLIVER, P. H. (1957) Labour migration in a rural economy. Kampala. *East African Studies* No. 6. East African Institute of Social Research.

MAYER, P. (1961) *Townsmen or Tribesmen*. Cape Town, Oxford University Press, for Rhodes University Institute of Social and Economic Research.

MITCHELL, J. C. (1956) The Kalela dance. *Rhodes–Livingstone Paper* No. 27. Manchester, Manchester University Press.

MITCHELL, J. C. (1959a) The causes of labour migration. *Bulletin of the Inter-African Labour Institute*, vol. VI, no. 1.

MITCHELL, J. C. (1959b) The study of African urban social structure. Unpublished paper for CCTA Conference on Housing and Urbanisation, Nairobi.

MITCHELL, J. C. (1959c) Social change and the new towns of Bantu Africa. Unpublished paper for Round Table Conference on Social Implications of Technological change. Paris, Social Science Council.

MITCHELL, J. C. (1960a) Tribalism and the plural society. Inaugural lecture, University College of Rhodesia and Nyasaland. London, Oxford University Press.

MITCHELL, J. C. (1960b) The anthropological study of urban communities. *Johannesburg, African Studies*, **19**, 3, 169–72.

NADEL, S. F. (1957) *The Theory of Social Structure*. London, Cohen & West.

SCHAPERA, I. (1947) *Migrant Labour and Tribal Life*. Oxford University Press.

SOUTHALL, A. W. and P. C. W. GUTKIND (1957) Townsmen in the making. Kampala, *East African Studies* No. 9. East African Institute of Social Research.

VAN VELSEN, J. (1960) Labour migration as a positive factor in the continuity of Tonga tribal society. In *Social Change in Modern Africa*, A. Southall, ed. Oxford University Press.

WATSON, W. (1958) *Tribal Cohesion in a Money Economy*. Manchester, Manchester University Press.

WILSON, G. (1941) Economics of detribalisation in Northern Rhodesia: Part I. *Rhodes–Livingstone Paper* No. 5. Livingstone, The Rhodes–Livingstone Institute.

(1942) *Idem*, Part II. *Rhodes–Livingstone Paper* No. 6.

Biographical Notes

BERGER, Bennet M. Professor of Sociology and Chairman of the Department of Sociology, University of California at Davis.

Major publications include:

Working Class Suburb: A Study of Auto Workers in Suburbia, Berkeley and Los Angeles, 1960; On Talcott Parsons, *Commentary*, 1962; Suburbia and the American Dream, *The Public Interest*, 1966; Self Hatred and the Politics of Kicks, *Dissent*, 1966. Black Culture and the Planning of a Pluralist Environment, forthcoming in Symposium of the School of Environmental Design at the University of California at Berkeley.

DENNIS, Norman. Lecturer in Sociology at the University of Newcastle upon Tyne.

Major publications include:

Coal is Our Life (with Cliff Slaughter and Fernando Henriques), Eyre & Spottiswoode, 1956; Stress and Release in an Urban Estate (with John Spencer and Joy Tuxford), Tavistock Publications, 1964.

DURANT, Ruth. see *GLASS*.

GANS, Herbert J. Senior Research Sociologist, Center for Urban Education and Adjunct Professor of Sociology and Education, Teachers College, Columbia University.

Major publications include:

The Urban Villagers: Group and Class in the Life of Italian-American, New York, Free Press of Glencoe, 1962; The Levittowners: Ways of Life and Politics in a New Suburban Community, New York, Pantheon Books, 1967; People and Plans: Essays on Community and the Planning Process, to be published by Basic Books in 1968.

GLASS (née Durant), Ruth. Director of Research, Centre for Urban Studies, University College, London.

Major publications include:

Watling, A Social Survey, P. S. King and Son, 1939; Middlesbrough: The Social Background of a Plan, 1947; Urban Sociology in Britain, a Trend Report, 1955; Newcomers, The West Indians in London, 1960; London, Aspects of Change (ed.), 1964; London's Housing Needs (with John Westergaard), 1965.

MAYER, Philip.   Head of Department of Anthropology, Durham University.

Major publications include:

Townsmen or Tribesmen, O.U.P., 1961; Gusii Bridewealth, Law and Custom, O.U.P., 1954; The Lineage Principle in Gusii Society, O.U.P., 1950; Two Studies in Applied Anthropology in Kenya, H.M.S.O., 1949; Editor of Triology, Xhosa in Town, O.U.P., 1961–63.

MUSIL, Jiři.   Head of the Sociological Department of the Research Institute for Building and Architecture, and Lecturer in Sociology at the University of Brno.

Major publications include:

Social Problems of New Cities, 1960; Sociological Aspects in House Planning, 1965; Housing in Multi-Storey Flats, 1965; Housing Needs and Policy in Great Britain and Czechoslovakia, Glasgow University, 1966; Sociology of of Redevelopment Areas in Cities, 1967; Urban Sociology; Contemporary Cities, 1967.

NAKAMURA, Hachiro.   Associate Professor, Faculty of Humanities, Kanto Gakuin University, Japan.

Major publications include:

Urban Development and Ward Associations in Hino, *Local Community and Urbanization*, 1962, International Christian University publication; Some Types of *Chonaikai* in the Process of Urban Development, *Local Community and Urbanization*, 1963; A Framework for the Classification of Urban People: Analysis based on Shonan Area Study, *Toshi Mondai*, 57, (6), 1967.

PAHL, R. E.   Senior Lecturer in Sociology at the University of Kent at Canterbury. Currently engaged in research on the life styles and career patterns of middle managers.

Major publications include:

Urbs in Rure, L.S.E. and Weidenfeld and Nicolson, 1965; Patterns of Urban Life, Longmans, 1969; A Collection of Essays in Sociology and Planning, to appear in 1970 published by Longmans.

PFEIL, Elisabeth.   Professor at the Academy of Economics and Politics, Hamburg, and Lecturer in Empirical Sociology and Urban Sociology at the University of Hamburg.

Major publications include:

Grosstadtforschung, Bremen-Horn, 1950; Wohnwünsche der Bergarbeiter, Tübingen, 1954; Die Berufstätigkeit von Müttern, Tübingen, 1961; Die Familie im Gerfüge der Grosstadt, Hamburg, 1966; Die 23-jahrigen. 1. Stufe einer Generationenuntersuchung, Tübingen, 1968.

REX, John.   Professor of Social Theory and Institutions, University of Durham.

Major publications include:

Key Problems of Sociological Theory, Routledge & Kegan Paul Ltd., 1961; Race, Community and Conflict (with Robert Moore), O.U.P., 1967.